STRUMMING
FOR LIFE

RIFFS OF RESILIENCE, A STROKE WARRIOR'S
FIGHT BACK THROUGH MUSIC!

CHARLIE WEBBER

Published by: American Real Publishing
americanrealpublishing.com

TABLE OF CONTENTS

My Heroes

"I have come to know Charlie through our email exchanges over the past couple of years. I run a guitar instructional website called ActiveMelody in which I write guitar material each week and teach how to play it and why it works. Charlie started sending me the occasional video of him playing these compositions a few years ago (shortly after his stroke) and it has been incredible to watch the growth and gain in his abilities as a player through the videos he sends. He has become far better than an average player, and just watching and listening to him, you would never know that he had endured a stroke at all. What a cool way to strengthen your motor skills! Congratulations, Charlie. You have done an incredible job!"

—**Brian Sherrill,** ActiveMelody.com

"GOD is utterly amazing, and I am so blessed that you are recovering well. I have never stopped praying for you. I have had a tragedy myself, but I am so thankful that GOD granted me more time on earth. Air Force Strong!"

—**Marci Robinson, HR Specialist at United States Army**

"I have known Charlie since 2012, when we played together in praise & worship bands. He has always been a positive influence in my life in thoughtfulness, words, and deeds. His dedication to excellence in all that he does is an inspiration to those whose life he touches. His amazing recovery that defies medical science is a testament to his faith and the healing power of music! God has blessed him in a distinct way to be a light to others through the difficult trials of this world, demonstrating that with God nothing is impossible! God bless you, Charlie, and keep on strumming."

—Shawn Donahoo, Orchestral Composer/Digital Artist

"I have had the privilege of calling Charlie Webber my friend for 15 years, and his journey of recovery and relearning to play the guitar after a life-threatening stroke has deeply impacted me. In *Strumming for Life*, he invites us into the raw, real, and remarkable story of how he fought to reconnect with something that had always been a part of him. But this story goes far beyond music—it is about grit, grace, and the quiet courage to keep going when life knocks you down. And woven through every page, you see the hand of God at work—restoring, strengthening, and guiding him each step of the way. Ultimately, this book is a beautiful reminder that with faith in God and a heart willing to persevere, nothing is impossible. Charlie's story will encourage anyone who has ever had to start over."

—John Bentley, Motivational Speaker, Pastor,
Owner of Power to Transform,
Founder of You Are A Gift Foundation

"Mr. Charles Webber is a special person who has used an incredibly challenging time as a powerful testimony of faith, persistence, and passion. He is an amazing storyteller, has a special ability to make connections with people, and drives to achieve goals that are so admirable. I know this book truly reflects this. I had the honor of working with Mr. Webber early in his recovery from his stroke and continued on for a couple of years. We developed a sweet friendship through his occupational therapy journey. He demonstrated resilience and an ability to push through fear that is hard to come by. One of the proudest moments in my career was when Mr. Webber came in and told me he had picked up his guitar again after working so incredibly hard in his rehabilitation. It still brings tears to my eyes. We continued to work on the function of his arm and hand along with many other related skills, and his drive and determination never wavered. While I was hopefully helping him learn and recover skills, the impact he had on me was even greater. I passionately believe Mr. Webber has turned what he has gone through into a powerful tool to encourage, shine light on our Lord, and make connections that help others push through tough times and find beauty on the other side. I am so grateful to know Mr. Webber and his precious wife and look forward to watching him continue making breakthroughs and encouraging people with this new book. He always said he was a stroke warrior, and the term *warrior* truly embodies who he is and his story."

—Lauren Lindquist, Occupational Therapist

"Mr. Webber was my very first stroke patient to ever work with! As a new graduate straight out of PTA school, I was incredibly nervous to work with him, but he helped shape me into a confident therapist who could take on anything. He was in a wheelchair the first day we met, and I will never forget it. I said to him, 'You are the first stroke patient I have ever worked with,' and he jokingly replied, 'Well, this is also my first stroke.' We became the best of friends after that! "As he taught me how to speak Portuguese, we worked together to improve his strength, balance, and coordination. I would constantly think of new exercises and activities for Mr. Webber to perform, as he would look at me and say, 'I do not know about this, Ashley,' but every time we would accomplish it together! From a wheelchair, quickly to a walker, then to no assisted device at all, I would remember the goal he told me he desired to accomplish, and I would be his biggest cheerleader. Together with his wonderful wife, Miss Lisa, and our incredibly special therapy team, we would all celebrate in his success. Mr. Webber also spoke of wanting to play his guitar again one day, and as the motivated person he was, I knew it would happen. I remember the day he came in and told me about strumming his guitar for the first time. Then soon after he had videos of him playing again with his church family. I was so excited for him to have been able to reach his goal and do one of the things that made him so happy again.

"With arduous work and God's grace, Mr. Webber is a testimony of not giving up. He was and has always been the most motivated stroke patient with whom I have ever worked. I will forever be thankful for all the things he taught me and how he trusted me to be his therapist and do all the things I would throw his way! I am the therapist I am today thanks to all my wonderful patients. Mr. Webber was not only my patient but him and Miss Lisa became my friends whom I love. I will always be proud of all his accomplishments!"

—Ashley Silva, Physical Therapist

"Charles 'Real Deal' Webber, peace and blessings to you and Miss Lisa! My brother from another mother, it has been an hour and privilege to serve in our great Air Force with you. It is also incredibly special to serve in the Chapel ministry with you, my brother. Man, when I first heard you play, I said, 'Who is this cool man strumming those chords?' God has truly blessed you, Charles, to play and write music! Your unique style and smoothness allow you to connect immediately with people. You are a strong community advocate, teaching out to those who need encouragement. I appreciate the fact of how you always made time for our personal conversations. Continue to let your light shine for Jesus Christ. You are indeed an AWESOME hubby and the example and love you have for Miss Lisa is contagious. The most important thing for me, brother, has been your resilient spirit and tenacity. You did not quit, you did not give up, and just did not throw in the towel. You told the impact of the stroke, 'Not today, Jose!' You went to work with a made-up mind, and you are doing just fine. Thank you, brother, for your godly examples…your leadership, the way you honor God with your gifts and talents, and how you love your wife and family. I dedicate the following poem to you:

> If a task once begun
> Never leave it until it's done
> Be the labor great or small
> Do it well or not at all.

"This poem epitomizes your love for life and service into the Lord. Love and appreciate you my brother!!!"

—Nathan Turner Sr., Pastor, Retired Chief Master Sergeant USAF

"Hi, Charles. Your Faith in believing in this recovery journey has helped give me hope. You're an inspiration to this community. The love you give to this stroke community is really incredible, let alone the recovery you've shown us is everything, just like the love you give."

—Musong Kim, Olympia, WA Stroke Buddies Group

INTRODUCTION

In 2021, Charles Webber, an average guy from Rhode Island, experienced a life-altering stroke that turned his world upside down in an instant. Despite this devastating event, he found solace in his family, friends, and the memories of his childhood on the beautiful island of Aquidneck, Rhode Island. Charles's resilience and determination led him on a remarkable journey of self-discovery and musical exploration, ultimately bringing him back to his passion for playing the guitar.

A Childhood on Aquidneck Island

Charles fondly recalls his childhood on Aquidneck Island, where he enjoyed countless family gatherings, sunny days at the beach, and sailing adventures. Growing up on this picturesque island, surrounded by the towns of Portsmouth, Middletown, and Newport, he developed a deep appreciation for nature and the simple joys of life. His experiences on Aquidneck Island shaped his love for the ocean and laid the foundation for his adventurous spirit.

Joining the Air Force and Finding Love

In the early 1980s, Charles made a pivotal decision to join the Air Force, expecting to serve for only four years. Little did he know that this decision would lead to a distinguished thirty-year career, culminating in the achievement of the highest enlisted rank as a Chief Master Sergeant. During his time in the Air Force, Charles met and married his wife, Lisa, and together they welcomed their son, Chad, into the world. The family's military adventures took them to various locations, including a memorable stint in England where Charles played guitar in a local band and experienced the thrill of performing at English clubs.

Facing Adversity with Resilience

After a stroke, he initially found himself consumed by blame and frustration. However, through introspection and self-discovery, he realized that blaming external factors only hindered his ability to take control of his recovery journey. By accepting responsibility and focusing on solutions rather than excuses, Charles embarked on a path of healing and transformation. As he navigated the challenges of regaining his musical abilities post-stroke, he found solace in the power of minor chords and the magic of creating beautiful sounds with his guitar.

Lessons Learned and Gratitude Expressed

Through his journey of recovery and self-discovery, Charles learned valuable lessons about accountability, resilience, and the importance of embracing challenges with a positive mindset. His unwavering faith and gratitude for the support of his family, friends, and the divine presence of God guided him through the darkest moments of his stroke recovery. As he continues to progress on his musical journey, Charles remains grateful for every small victory and the opportunity to share his story of hope and resilience with others.

What to Expect From Reading This Book

Charles Webber's guitar stroke recovery journey is a testament to the power of resilience, faith, and the human spirit. Through his steadfast determination and belief in himself, he has overcome adversity, embraced challenges, and found joy in the healing power of music. As he continues to strum his guitar and share his story with the world, Charles serves as an inspiration to all who face challenges and setbacks in life. As each chord strums and every note echoes through the air, he paints a musical masterpiece that resonates with the power of resilience, the melody of courage, and the harmony of unwavering faith. Just like a thrilling adventure waiting to unfold, the upcoming chapters promise to dive deeper into the transformative journey of recovery, unraveling tales of strength, courage, and the indomitable spirit that intertwines to create a symphony of hope and perseverance. Get ready to embark on an exhilarating voyage through the chapters ahead, where each page unfolds a new melody of inspiration and triumph.

CHAPTER 1
My Serious Injury and Renewed Faith

When I suffered my dangerous stroke, it felt like the first chapter of life as "shattered mirrors." I still do not understand why I felt this way.

Before my stroke, I felt optimistic as dreams danced in the streets of my mind and my ambitions soared high. I was known for having a sharp wit, kind heart, and insatiable curiosity. Through the years of my musical guitar journey, I was confident of being a talented artist, specializing in creating intricate musical mosaics, especially when I played guitar for the United States Air Force.

One fateful day, as I finished a home studio recording, tragedy struck. I suffered an extremely dangerous stroke leaving me with severe hidden injuries, including a serious brain injury. My world turned upside down as I laid in the emergency ICU holding room, trying to figure out what was up or down, left to right, and going in and out of consciousness. I would have sworn as the medical rescue technicians were moving me from the ambulance to the emergency room entrance, the security guard asked me for identification, what the cat hair!

When I finally gained some sort of awareness, the world appeared fragmented, again like shattered mirrors reflecting distorted images. My once-vibrant colors now muted, and my thoughts tangled like a ball of yarn. Doctors informed me that the stroke had left me with some possible lasting damage to my brain that is affecting the entire right side of my body, and the road to recovery would be long and arduous.

While the days were moving slowly in my new ICU accommodation, I was praying to God to have mercy on me, hopefully beginning to build my determination to reclaim my life. I thought of myself as a strong Christian, I believe in God, Jesus Christ, and the Holy Spirit, but I was too complacent in my faith. I have to share another obstacle during that time my family and friends could not visit me because of COVID restrictions. When I think back to that time, it was tremendously difficult and lonely; I needed my family so badly! Finally on day five, my wife got the okay to visit me after passing a COVID test. When she came around the corner and I saw her face, in a snap my darkness turned into light, my hope came rushing in like a tidal wave. We cried and hugged for what seemed like an eternity. God answered my prayers, Amen!

After four weeks or so, my care physicians transferred me to an inpatient rehabilitation center, again no visitors because of COVID constraints, so I embarked on my journey of rehabilitation, self-discovery, and a deeper relationship with God. Now my days were filled with therapy sessions, exercises to retrain my brain, and moments of frustration as I struggled to piece together my shattered memories and thoughts.

Despite the challenges, I found solace through my faith. With trembling hands and a heart full of hope, I began creating a new mosaic of life, one that reflected a journey from darkness to light, from brokenness to resilience. Each piece carefully placed represented a step forward, a triumph over adversity, and a new and robust relationship with God. Amen!

During the next six weeks of inpatient rehabilitation, I grew mentally stronger as well as achieving some physical breakthroughs, mirroring the depths of my soul, the strength of my spirit, and faith in our Savior Jesus Christ. However, an inner voice was whispering that there was a lot more to come, especially with my renewed faith in God.

CHAPTER 2
Melodies of Resilience

Before my stroke, music flowed in my veins, and my fingers danced effortlessly along the fretboard of my cherished guitar. Even at an early age, my passion for music had been a guiding light with a tremendous amount of never-ending curiosity and solace in times of joy and sorrow.

What in the cat hair was the initial spark to learn to play guitar? The seed was planted when I was ten years old. My next-door neighbor was a full-time musician; he and his bandmates were very well known in Rhode Island and Massachusetts. Picture this: my neighbor, let us dub him Big G, unraveling the secrets of guitar playing right in his front yard, or should I say his dooryard. The adventure began when Big G unknowingly planted the seed of curiosity for music and the beauty of the guitar in my own soul. With unwavering determination, I embarked on a musical quest, with an ardent desire to learn how to strum the strings of a guitar and an insatiable thirst for knowledge. As the chords resonated through the neighborhood, Big G painted the air with melodies that defied earthly boundaries. Each note he played carried a sense of mystery and wonder, as though he had tapped into a magical realm of music that was his and his alone. Watching him practice under the open sky filled with a sense of exploration and awe, as if by simply sitting within earshot, you were invited into a world of fantastic possibilities where dreams turned into reality at the strum of a guitar string. Big G's magical tunes enchanted all who listened, igniting a spirit of adventure that inspired even the most hesitant of souls to dance to the beat of their own musical journey. In those life changing transactions, I wanted to play guitar like him. From that moment on, I had always been drawn to music. But it was during a concert I attended as a teenager that I experienced a moment of pure magic; the band was called Yes. As the guitarist strummed the strings, filling the air with enchanting melodies, I found myself captivated and deeply moved. The emotions that the music evoked within me were unlike anything I had ever experienced before. In that moment, I knew I had to learn to play the guitar, and this is when I hijacked my first guitar—this is a whole different story in itself.

When I think back to those early days, I remember experiencing discoveries of self-expression and creativity, the adventure with the journey of learning, and enjoying the community and camaraderie with the friends I met. Through the guitar strings, I discovered a means to convey my emotions, thoughts, and experiences in a way that words alone could not. The guitar became my outlet, allowing me to share my innermost feelings with the world, even when words failed me. Learning to play the guitar was not always an easy journey. It required dedication, patience, and countless hours of practice. Yet, despite the challenges, the sense of accomplishment I felt with each note I mastered was unparalleled. The guitar became a teacher, shaping my discipline and persistence, while also rewarding me with the joy of progress. One of the most surprising and delightful aspects of my guitar journey was discovering the vibrant community that exists around this instrument. Guitarists from all walks of life come together to share their passion, exchange tips, and inspire one another. Whether it's playing in a band, attending workshops, or open stage jam nights, the camaraderie among guitarists is truly special. Overall, I learned guitar has the unique ability to transcend language barriers and connect people from diverse cultures and backgrounds. It serves as a universal language that can be understood and appreciated by all. Whether I am strumming my guitar in my bedroom or performing on a stage, I am able to communicate with others through the language of music, forging connections that go beyond words.

***

As you know now, tragedy struck when I experienced a stroke that left me with a critical injury to the right side of my body, especially my right hand, the hand that had strummed melodies of hope and despair for years. The doctors informed me that the damage is serious, rendering my right hand unable to play the guitar as I once did. Devastation engulfed me as I grappled with the loss of my ability to play the guitar, a loss that felt like a piece of my soul had been ripped away. The world around me seemed muted, devoid of the harmonious notes that had once woven the fabric of my existence.

So, with determination and faith, I embarked on a journey of musical exploration, and I found myself faced with the challenge of transforming and crafting melodies of resilience. With a memory like yesterday of Big G playing his guitar on his dooryard, watching the band Yes at the Providence Civic Center, faith in God, and a spirit as inspired and daring as a fearless explorer discovering new lands, I delved into the world of composition, weaving together notes and rhythms to create a tapestry of strength and grit. Each chord and melody became a steppingstone on my adventurous path, guiding me through harmonies that echoed the resilience within my soul. Hand in hand with my creativity, I orchestrated a symphony of determination and unwavering spirit, embracing the unknown with a melody that resonated with courage and fortitude.

CHAPTER 3
After My Brain Injury

Experiencing a brain attack, commonly known as a stroke, can have a significant impact on both physical and emotional well-being. When something blocks the blood supply to part of the brain that controls fine motor skills and emotions, the consequences can be life-altering. I am open and willing to share the details of my personal experience with a brain injury caused by a stroke, including the initial doubts and fears I had about recovery.

Throughout my journey of recovery, my faith and trust in God has been a source of strength and comfort. Believing in the higher power of God has helped me find peace and resilience during the most challenging moments of my recovery and this continues today. While the road to recovery may be long and difficult, having faith in our God and our Savior Jesus Christ has given me the courage to push through obstacles and remain hopeful for the future. This made me think of a great song lyric, "We can bury the pain of our past, but it doesn't mean it's dead." And what does the Bible remind us? "Come to me, all you who are weary and are carrying heavy burdens, and I will give you rest. Take my yoke upon you, and learn from me, for I am gentle and humble in heart, and you will find rest for your souls. For my yoke is easy, and my burden is light." (Matthew 11:28-30)

Physical Impact
The physical impact of my brain injury was immediately apparent following the stroke. I struggled with fine motor skills, such as writing and grasping objects, which made simple daily tasks daunting. The loss of control over my physical abilities was frustrating and overwhelming, leading to feelings of helplessness and vulnerability. Physical therapy and rehabilitation played a crucial role in helping me regain strength and mobility in the affected areas, but the journey is filled with setbacks and

challenges. This continues today even more intensely as I am trying to learn to play guitar again from the ground up. I waited over a year to pick up guitar again for many physical and emotional reasons, but I missed my friend and strumming for life. When I finally mustered up the courage to pick it up, it was not pretty, and tears fell from my eyes trying to strum a G major chord in the first position. But I had finally broken the ice, and I was determined through God's help to play again. I am so grateful for our God, my family, my friends, and all the Stroke Warriors I have had the honor to meet through social media for their encouragement and support. Our Godly Bible has so much wisdom, "A friend loves at all times, and a brother is born for a time of adversity." (Proverbs 17:17)

Emotional Impact

In addition to the physical challenges, the emotional impact of my brain injury was equally significant. The part of my brain that controlled emotions was affected by the stroke, causing mood swings, anxiety, and depression. Coping with these emotional changes was a daunting task, as they often felt out of my control. Therapy and support from loved ones helped me navigate the emotional rollercoaster that followed the brain attack, but the road to emotional healing has been long, arduous, and continues today as you read this. "And the God of all grace, who called you to his eternal glory in Christ, after you have suffered a little while, will himself restore you and make you strong, firm, and steadfast." As 1 Peter 5:10 says, God has a plan to heal our hearts and lives after tough times.

Initial Doubts and Fears About Recovery

In the initial stages of my recovery, doubts and fears loomed large in my mind. Would I ever fully regain my physical abilities? Could I learn to manage my emotions and regain control over my thoughts? The fear of the unknown is paralyzing, leading to moments of despair and hopelessness. However, I discovered through time, patience, and perseverance, I am beginning to see small improvements in both my physical and emotional well-being. Each small victory gives me the courage to continue pushing forward, despite the challenges that lay ahead. Sing (praise) in expectation; sing when you are barren and empty (Isaiah 54:1), knowing

God can do what man has called impossible.

Where I Am Going from Here

Experiencing a brain injury due to a stroke has been a life-changing event that tested my physical and emotional resilience. Through faith, therapy, and support from loved ones, I have been able to make significant strides in my recovery journey. While the road ahead may still be full of uncertainties, I remain hopeful and determined to continue moving forward, one step at a time. I am also discovering and experiencing the physical and emotional impact of my brain injury caused by this stroke, along with the initial doubts and fears about recovery. I cannot stress enough that faith, therapy, and support played crucial roles in my journey of continuing healing. By sharing my firsthand experiences with my brain injury that caused a dramatic change in my life, I hope to provide insight and inspiration to others facing similar challenges. Through faith, perseverance, and a dedicated support system, the road to recovery may be long and difficult, but it is possible. Trust in the process, believe in your inner strength, trust in God, and never lose hope for a brighter tomorrow.

CHAPTER 4
A Journey of Renewed Faith in God

In life, challenges and unexpected events can sometimes lead us to dark and uncertain places. Such was the case for me when a sudden stroke caused a traumatic brain injury that forever changed my life. In the aftermath of this life-altering event, I found myself grappling with physical limitations, cognitive challenges, and a sense of uncertainty about the future. However, in the midst of the darkness, a glimmer of light shone through as I discovered a renewed faith in God that brought me solace, strength, and hope.

Seeking Solace and Strength in Prayer
During the long and arduous journey of recovery, I turned to prayer as a source of comfort and guidance. In the quiet moments of reflection and solitude, I found solace in the act of prayer, pouring out my fears, doubts, and hopes to a higher power. Through prayer, I found the strength to carry on, even when the road ahead seemed daunting and filled with obstacles. I learned to trust in God's plan for me, knowing that He would never give me a burden too heavy to bear.

Recognizing Blessings and Moments of Grace
As I navigated the ups and downs of recovery, I began to recognize the blessings and moments of grace that were scattered along the way. Whether it was a kind word from a stranger, a breakthrough in therapy, or a small sign of progress in my healing journey, I saw God's hand at work in the midst of adversity. These moments of grace served as reminders that I was not alone, that God was walking beside me every step of the way, guiding me and lifting me up when I stumbled.

Deepening Spiritual Connection and Gratitude

Through the process of recovery, my spiritual connection deepened, and my gratitude grew stronger. I learned to appreciate the simple joys of life, the beauty of a sunrise, the laughter of loved ones, and the gift of each new day. I began to see my struggles not as obstacles to overcome but as opportunities for growth and transformation. My faith in God became the rock upon which I anchored my soul, providing me with the strength and courage to face each new day with hope and resilience.

Learning to Play Guitar Again, Strumming for Life

One of the most significant milestones in my recovery journey was the day I picked up my guitar again. Music had always been a source of joy and solace for me, and the thought of never being able to play again had weighed heavily on my heart. But through determination, perseverance, and the grace of God, I slowly regained my ability to strum the chords and create melodies once more. Playing the guitar became a form of therapy for me, a way to express my emotions, release my fears, and celebrate the triumph of the human spirit over adversity.

In conclusion, the journey of recovery after a brain injury caused by a stroke is a challenging and often taxing one. However, through faith, prayer, and gratitude, it is possible to find solace, strength, and hope in the midst of adversity. By recognizing the blessings and moments of grace that are scattered along the way, deepening our spiritual connection, and embracing life's challenges with courage and resilience, we can emerge from the darkness with a renewed sense of purpose and a deeper faith in God's plan for our lives.

CHAPTER 5
My Road to Recovery

As I sat in the hospital bed feeling overwhelmed and uncertain about what the future held, I knew the road to recovery after my stroke would not be easy. The medical team assured me that with the right treatment and rehabilitation, I could regain some of what I had lost. Nonetheless, I knew I would face many challenges along the way.

Medical Treatment and Rehabilitation
The journey of recovery began with intensive medical treatment and re-habilitation. I underwent various tests, scans, and procedures to assess the damage caused by the stroke. The medical team prescribed medications to manage my symptoms and prevent further complications. Physical therapists worked with me to regain strength and mobility in my affected limbs, regain my speech to communicate again, and deal with symptoms of executive dysfunction.

Challenges Faced During the Recovery Process
Recovering from a stroke is not a linear process. I faced many challenges along the way, both physically and emotionally. There were days when I felt frustrated and discouraged by the slow progress. The fear of another stroke loomed over me, causing anxiety and uncertainty about the future.

Discovering New Ways to Cope with the Situation
Despite the challenges, I was determined to find new ways to cope with the situation. I sought support from family and friends, who provided encouragement and guidance throughout the recovery process. I also turned to music, my lifelong passion, as a source of comfort and motivation.

Relearning to Play Guitar

One of the biggest challenges I faced during my recovery was relearning how to play the guitar. As a musician, the thought of not being able to express myself through music was devastating. However, with determination and perseverance, I slowly began to regain my skills.

Frustrations and Setbacks in Relearning

Relearning to play the guitar was not without its frustrations and setbacks. There were days when my fingers refused to cooperate, and the music sounded discordant and out of tune. I felt a sense of loss and longing for the effortless joy I used to feel when playing.

Small Victories and Moments of Progress

Despite the challenges, there were small victories and moments of progress that kept me motivated. I celebrated every chord change mastered and every melody played without error. These small wins reminded me that progress, no matter how slow, was still progress.

Finding Joy and Purpose in Music Again

As I continued on the road to recovery, I found joy and purpose in music once again. Playing the guitar became not just a form of therapy but a way to express my emotions and inspire hope in others facing similar challenges. Music became my companion and confidante, guiding me through the darkest moments of recovery.

The road to recovery after a stroke is never easy, but with determination, support, and a passion for life, it is possible to find joy and purpose once again. By facing challenges head-on, seeking new ways to cope, and celebrating small victories along the way, we can overcome the obstacles in our path and emerge stronger than ever. Most of all—trust in God!

CHAPTER 6
Embracing the New Normal

Embracing the new normal after experiencing a life-altering event can be challenging. However, through the process of acceptance of limitations and embracing resilience, I was able to find a new sense of purpose and meaning in my life. In this chapter, I will share my story in the hopes of inspiring and encouraging those who may be facing similar challenges. Together, we can look toward the future with hope and optimism.

Trusting in our Savior Jesus Christ has been a cornerstone of my journey toward acceptance and resilience. Through prayer and faith, I was able to find the strength to face the challenges that came my way after my stroke. I leaned on the teachings of Jesus to help me navigate the uncertainties and fears that accompanied my new normal. By placing my trust in Him, I found peace and relief in knowing that I was never alone in my struggles.

Figuring Out the New Normal

After my stroke, I was faced with a new reality that required me to make significant adjustments to my daily life. Simple tasks that once came easily to me now posed a challenge, and I had to learn to adapt to my limitations. Embracing the new normal meant accepting that some things would never be the same again, but that didn't mean life was over. I found ways to work around my limitations and discovered new strengths and abilities within myself.

Acceptance of Limitations and Embracing Resilience

One of the most important lessons I learned on my journey was the importance of accepting my limitations while also embracing resilience. It's okay to acknowledge when something is difficult or impossible, but it's how we respond to those challenges that truly matters. By cultivating a spirit of resilience, I was able to push through the tough times and come out stronger on the other side. Embracing resilience meant not giving up when things got tough and finding creative solutions to overcome obstacles.

Sharing My Story with Others
As I navigated the ups and downs of life after my stroke, I felt compelled to share my story with others. By opening up about my struggles and triumphs, I hoped to inspire and encourage those who may be facing similar challenges. Sharing my story allowed me to connect with others who understood what I was going through and provided a sense of community and support. Together, we found solace in knowing that we were not alone in our struggles and that there was always hope for a brighter tomorrow.

Looking Toward the Future with Hope and Optimism
Despite the challenges I faced, I always held onto a sense of hope and optimism for the future. By focusing on the positives and looking toward the possibilities that lay ahead, I was able to see beyond my limitations and envision a life full of promise and potential. Trusting in our Savior Jesus Christ gave me the courage to face tomorrow with confidence and faith, knowing He had a plan for me that was greater than anything I could imagine.

Embracing the new normal after my stroke was a journey filled with ups and downs, but through acceptance of limitations and embracing resilience, I was able to find strength and purpose in my struggles. By sharing my story with others and looking toward the future with hope and optimism, I found a renewed sense of joy and fulfillment in life. Trusting in our Savior Jesus Christ was the key to navigating the challenges that came my way, and I am forever grateful for His guidance and grace. May my story serve as a reminder that no matter what stumbling blocks we face, there is always hope for a cheerful future.

After a year of battling the physical and emotional aftermath of a stroke, I decided it was time to conquer one of my biggest fears—playing the guitar again. The instrument that once brought me joy had become a daunting reminder of my limitations, but I gathered my courage and dusted off my beloved guitar. With trembling hands, I strummed the strings, producing a few off-key notes. Despite the initial struggle, a sense of determination washed over me. I was not going to let my stroke define me or hold me back any longer.

Inspired by this moment of bravery, I made a bold decision to start a video vlog journal to document my journey of relearning to play the guitar. Each day would mark a new chapter in my recovery story, a testament to resilience and passion. As the camera rolled, I played my first song—a simple melody that echoed the strength and vulnerability within me. The strings vibrated with emotion, serving as a reminder that healing comes in many forms, including music.

With each video entry, I shared not only my progress but also my setbacks and triumphs. My audience grew, filled with individuals who found hope and inspiration in my journey. The guitar became a symbol of resilience, a tool for self-expression, and a beacon of light in the darkness. One year after my stroke, I realized that the courage to face my fears was within me all along. And so, my video vlog journal, became a testament to the power of perseverance, the beauty of self-discovery, and the magic of music to heal even the deepest wounds.

Recovery Week 1
Picking Up My Guitar Again

Forget the former things; do not dwell on the past. See, I am doing a new thing! Now it springs up; do you not perceive it? I am making a way in the wilderness and streams in the wasteland.

—Isaiah 43:18-19

https://www.youtube.com/watch?v=YzvGOZ726mI

This week marks the beginning of my musical comeback, and I am excited to share my progress, setbacks, and emotions with you all. With little movement on my right side, strumming is very difficult, as you see in the video. Despite the physical challenges I face, I refuse to let a stroke hold me back from pursuing my passion for music. With pure resolve, I am determined to slowly relearn how to play the guitar and regain control over my right hand. Each strum may be a struggle, but every note played is a victory that fuels my motivation to keep pushing forward.

I believe playing the guitar can be an essential part of my rehabilitation journey. I hope this new journey will help me improve my motor skills and coordination, but it also serves as a form of emotional therapy. Music has a way of touching our souls and expressing what words cannot, providing comfort during challenging times. Through my vlog, I hope to showcase the healing power of music and inspire others to pursue their passions, no matter the obstacles they may face.

In Week 1, I focused on practicing very basic strumming by only using my thumb; it was a little painful. While it was challenging at times, I noticed a slight improvement. I have researched that music therapy has been proven to be beneficial for stroke survivors in their rehabilitation process. By engaging in musical activities, I believe individuals can improve their physical, emotional, and cognitive functions. I am hoping music therapy can strengthen my motor skills, enhance my mood and motivation, and stimulate brain activity to aid in my recovery. Playing guitar has always been a creative outlet for me. I want this back again, I pray, Amen.

I know this musical journey will be both challenging and rewarding for me. Through this vlog, I hope to inspire others to overcome their obstacles and pursue their passions fearlessly. While the road to recovery may be long and arduous, I know in my heart the power of music can uplift and heal us in ways we never thought possible. Stay tuned for more updates on my progress and musical adventures as I continue to relearn to play my guitar one year after my stroke. Remember, it's never too late to follow your dreams and passions, regardless of the obstacles that stand in our way. My goal is to stay persistent, motivated, and true to myself as I navigate through life's challenges.

Recovery Week 2
Finding Strength in Faith

*Heal me, O Lord, and I shall be healed; save me, and I shall
be saved: for thou art my praise.*

—Jeremiah 17:14

https://youtu.be/TtM9D-raB_4

Experiencing a stroke can be a life-altering event, especially for musicians
who rely on their dexterity and motor skills to play an instrument. As I
embarked on this challenging journey, Week 2 presented a new obstacle
in the form of swelling in my right hand due to compromised blood flow.
Despite the discomfort, a glimmer of hope flickered within me as I noticed a slight improvement in wrist movement, fueling my determination
to press on.

A Journey of Faith and Determination. Navigating the highs and lows
of stroke recovery, I found solace in turning to my Christian faith for
strength and inspiration. With each strum of the guitar strings, I poured

my heart and soul into the music.

Do you ever feel a deep connection to music? Have you experienced the healing power of a song that resonates with your soul?

Music has a way of touching us in ways that words alone cannot. For me, playing the guitar has been a form of therapy, a way to express my emotions and connect with something greater than myself. Embracing the healing power of music as a unique ability to speak to our hearts and souls. It can lift us up when we are feeling down, inspire us to keep going when the going gets tough, and provide us with a sense of peace and comfort in times of need. For me, playing the guitar has been a powerful form of self-expression and healing. Each chord progression, each melody, serves as a reminder of the progress I have made and the challenges I have overcome. Through the melodies of my favorite Christian songs, I have found a sense of peace and purpose. I know that I am not alone in my journey toward recovery. I feel a renewed sense of hope and determination. I am fueled by the knowledge that I am strumming for life, for faith, and for the glory of God.

In the face of adversity, I made a promise to myself to keep pushing forward with unwavering determination and trust in our God. Despite the setbacks and obstacles that lay ahead, I remained steadfast in my belief that through God's grace I would emerge stronger and more resilient than ever before.

As Week 2 came to a close, I reflected on the progress I had made and the challenges I had faced. I felt a sense of peace and clarity wash over me. I knew I was on the right path toward recovery. Armed with faith, determination, and a renewed sense of purpose, I continued to strum on, knowing that with each note played, I was one step closer to healing, one strum closer to victory. The journey of healing and recovery is not always easy, but with faith, trust, and perseverance, anything is possible. Music has been my saving grace, my outlet for emotions, and my source of strength. I am reminded of the power of music to heal, uplift, and inspire. So, the next time you are facing a challenge, consider picking up an instrument or listening to your favorite song. You may just find the strength and courage you need to keep going.

RECOVERY WEEK 3
The Journey of Musical Healing

Psalm 103, attributed to David, is a hymn praising God, highlighting His goodness, mercy, and faithfulness. It starts with the exhortation to "Bless the Lord, O my soul; and all that is within me, bless his holy name."

https://youtu.be/wzCduY75EFY

In Week 3, I found solace in the powerful words of Luke 6:19, "…and the people all tried to touch him, because power was coming from him and healing them all." With this verse as my guiding light, I embarked on another week of relearning my beloved instrument, determined to overcome any obstacles in my path.

Rekindling the Musical Flame. As I delved deeper into my practice sessions, I bravely tackled new challenges and pushed myself to explore unfamiliar territories on the fretboard. Despite the lingering effects of my stroke, such as a swollen right hand and limited wrist movement, I refused to be deterred. With each note I struck and chord I played, I felt a renewed sense of purpose and bliss wash over me.

Embracing the Learning Curve. While my right-hand movements may not be as fluid as they once were, I found comfort in the familiar melodies that emanated from my guitar. The journey of relearning was not without its struggles, but with each imperfect strum and missed note, I grew stronger and more determined. As I navigated through chord progressions and experimented with different strumming patterns, I felt a sense of freedom and empowerment that only music can provide.

Trusting in Divine Guidance. Throughout this journey, my faith in God has been my anchor. I firmly believe that with His guidance and grace, I can conquer any obstacles that come my way. Each practice session became a prayer, a testimony to my deep trust in His plan for me. While the road to recovery may be long and arduous, I know that with faith and perseverance, I will continue to improve.

Celebrating Small Victories. As I reflect on the past week, I am reminded of the importance of celebrating even the smallest victories along the way. Every chord I successfully played, every riff I mastered, demonstrated my strength and resilience. With each step forward, I grew more confident in my ability to reclaim my passion for music and overcome any challenges that may arise.

In conclusion, Week 3 has been a testament to the power of perseverance, faith, and the healing nature of music. As I continue to push forward, I am filled with a renewed sense of hope and determination. I refuse to let setbacks define me, and I will boldly march forward, strumming my way to a brighter future. With each chord I play, and each note I strike, I am one step closer to reclaiming my musical legacy, and nothing will stand in my way.

RECOVERY WEEK 4
Pushing Myself to New Limits

Jesus traveled through all the towns and villages, teaching in their synagogues, preaching the Good News about the kingdom, and healing all kinds of diseases and sicknesses.

—Matthew 9:35

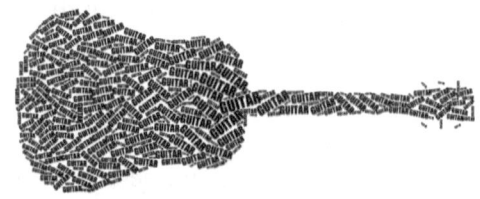

https://youtu.be/QexsBQlNLlk

Thank you, God, for allowing me to feel a little more flexibility in my wrist during Week 4. It has been a challenging but rewarding week as I continue to navigate through the ups and downs of regaining my musical abilities after experiencing a setback. Let me continue to take you through my journey and the progress I have made, strumming for life!

One of the main challenges I faced was swelling in my right hand. To help reduce the swelling and promote healing, I started wearing compression gloves regularly. This not only provided support to my hand but also helped to alleviate some of the discomfort I was experiencing. It was a small step, but one that I found to be essential in my recovery process.

As I continued my daily practice sessions, I decided to explore different playing styles to test the strength and dexterity of my hand. I started off with practicing an arpeggio style rhythm, focusing on playing each note clearly and crisply. It was a great exercise in control and precision, helping me to refine my technique.

On the second tune I practiced, I tried my hand at a rock tune in the key of A major. This was a bit more challenging, as it required faster movements and coordination between my fingers. Despite the difficulty, I persisted and eventually managed to play the tune with a sense of accomplishment. I attempted to play a little lead guitar, incorporating bends and slides into my playing. It was a new territory for me, but one that I approached with determination and a willingness to push my limits. The feeling of playing lead guitar again was invigorating and gave me a newfound sense of motivation.

Finally, I decided to challenge myself with a blues boogie rhythm, trying to strum a few strings at a time and maintain a steady groove. This proved to be one of the most physically demanding exercises, requiring strength and endurance in my hand. Despite the initial struggles, I persisted and gradually improved my ability to play the rhythm with more ease.

Looking back on Week 4 of my recovery journey, I can say that it was a good practice week. I faced challenges head-on, pushed myself out of my comfort zone, and made significant progress in regaining my guitar skills. The feeling of improvement and growth was immensely rewarding and encouraged me to continue on my path to full recovery.

As I move forward, I am grateful for the support and encouragement I have received from my loved ones and the strength I have found within myself. While the road to recovery may be long and difficult at times, I am determined to keep pushing forward and reclaiming my passion for music. Thank you for joining me on this journey, and here's to many more successful weeks ahead.

RECOVERY WEEK 5
Thank You, God, For Endurance

He sent His word and healed them and delivered them from their destructions.

—Psalm 107:20

https://youtu.be/1AayVoOdxk0

As I have been experiencing these past weeks, recovering from a stroke and learning to play guitar again is a challenge that requires willpower and patience. I am continuing to share how I am navigating through the recovery process, facing obstacles and celebrating victories along the way. Thank you for joining me on this journey of resilience and musical passion, strumming for life.

Thank you, God, for giving me the endurance to play the entire song "Wonderful Tonight" by Eric Clapton. This week was particularly bold and challenging, as I attempted to master both the rhythm chords and guitar leads. Despite the swelling in my right hand after removing my compression glove, I pushed through with sheer grit. Will this swelling ever go away? My doctor reassures me that it's just a matter of time, as blood flow in my arm slowly improves.

I noticed a new habit forming, I am constantly looking at my rhythm hand while playing. I remember a time when my two hands were in perfect sync without the need for constant visual reassurance. How can I break this habit and return to the effortless coordination I once had?

I am discovering how endurance is a crucial factor in my recovery process. It allows me to push past physical limitations and mental barriers, enabling me to achieve milestones once thought unattainable. With each practice session, my endurance grows, helping me to break through plateaus and reach new heights in my musical journey.

Throughout the recovery journey, there are hurdles to overcome and victories to savor. Every small step forward is a triumph in itself, reminding me of the progress I've made and the strength I possess. From mastering challenging riffs to regaining dexterity in my fingers, each accomplishment is a testament to the resilience and determination we all have.

I am learning that recovering from a stroke and relearning to play guitar is a daunting task, but it's important to remember that we don't have to go through it alone. Seeking support from loved ones, fellow musicians, and medical professionals can provide the encouragement and guidance needed to navigate through the ups and downs of the recovery process. Remember, it's okay to ask for help when you need it.

Music has a unique ability to heal, inspire, and uplift. As I journey through my guitar stroke recovery, I am letting the music be my refuge and my strength. So, fellow Stroke Warrior musicians, whether you are attempting to strum a familiar chord progression or improvising a soulful melody, let the music guide us through the challenges and celebrate the victories along the way.

My guitar stroke recovery journey is a test of resilience, endurance, and passion. By embracing the challenges, seeking support, and letting the power of music be our guide, we can overcome obstacles and reach new heights in our musical journey. Remember, every small step forward is a victory, bringing us closer to our goal of playing with confidence and joy once again.

Recovery Week 6
Exciting Breakthroughs and Progress

You shall serve the Lord your God, and He will bless your bread and your water, and I will take sickness away from among you.

—Exodus 23:25

https://youtu.be/iCsuRbwQY5g

After weeks of dedicated practice, I am starting to see some exciting progress in my playing. In Week 6, I experienced some significant breakthroughs that gave me hope for the future.

First and foremost, I want to thank our God for showing me that my guitar stroke recovery playing is moving in a positive direction. It has been a difficult road, but I am grateful for the progress I am making.

During Week 6, I felt I had some significant breakthroughs. One of the most exciting moments was when I played an original musical idea for the first time in over a year. It was a moment of creative inspiration that reminded me of why I love playing the guitar.

During my practice sessions, I also attempted more scales and experimented with more interesting chord voicings. By exploring new techniques, I was able to push myself out of my comfort zone and challenge myself to try new things. This experiment led to some exciting and unexpected results.

One of the highlights of my Week 6 practice was the discovery that I could hopefully create some interesting harmony and melody lines on my guitar. By combining different chord voicings and scales, I was able to create rich and layered sounds that I had never explored before. It was a thrilling experience that reignited my passion for music.

Finally, I was thrilled to discover I had the endurance to play and record two separate guitar parts. This was a significant milestone for me, as it showed me that my strength and stamina were improving. It was a reminder that hard work and dedication can lead to tangible results.

For me, Week 6 was filled with exciting breakthroughs and moments of creative inspiration. Through dedicated practice and a willingness to explore new techniques, I was able to push myself beyond my limits and discover new possibilities in my playing. I am excited to see where this journey will take me next and grateful for the progress I have made so far.

Remember that progress is not always linear, but if you stay on the course, you can achieve your musical goals. Keep pushing yourself out of your comfort zone and exploring new techniques, and you will continue to see growth and improvement in your playing. Is it challenging at times? Absolutely. But the rewards of making music and expressing yourself are always worth it in the end. So keep strumming, keep practicing, and never give up on your musical dreams.

RECOVERY WEEK 7
A Journey of Discovery

For neither herb nor poultice cured them, but it was your word, O Lord, that heals all people.

—Wisdom of Solomon 16:12

https://youtu.be/6J1QYT-jzBA

Thank you to our Savior Jesus Christ for allowing me to strum for life. Week 7 filled with interesting practices and exciting discoveries. Despite still experiencing swelling in my right hand, I continued to focus on refining my skills and exploring new musical ideas. In this week's vlog post, I will share my experiences, challenges, and breakthroughs as I worked on two musical ideas, experimented with fun chord progressions, and even attempted to play some lead guitar work.

During Week 7, I dedicated my practice sessions to developing two musical ideas that had been lingering in my mind for some time. I spent hours experimenting with different chord progressions, melodies, and rhythms, pushing myself to think outside the box and break away from traditional song structures. Despite the limitations imposed by my recovery process, I found immense joy in the creative process of shaping these musical ideas into tangible pieces of music.

One of the most rewarding aspects of my practice sessions was the opportunity to delve into lead guitar work. While my right hand still struggled with swelling and stiffness, I challenged myself to explore the intricacies of playing lead guitar. Though the journey was filled with frustrations and setbacks, I embraced these challenges as valuable learning opportunities, pushing myself to overcome physical limitations and expand my musical horizons.

Throughout this week, I remained steadfast in my focus on refining my right-hand technique. Despite the persistent swelling and discomfort, I approached each practice session with a positive attitude, determined to strengthen my right hand and improve my overall guitar playing skills. By dedicating time to specific exercises and drills designed to enhance my right-hand dexterity, I began to notice gradual improvements in my playing technique and control.

As I navigated the challenges of my recovery process, I learned the importance of patience, resilience, and self-compassion. While the road to full recovery may be long and arduous, I remained committed to my passion for music and my desire to overcome obstacles with grace and determination. Through the ups and downs, I found inspiration in the power of music to heal, uplift, and transform.

Again, this hebdomad my guitar stroke recovery video vlog was a journey of exploration and growth. Despite the challenges posed by my recovery process, I embraced each practice session with gratitude, passion, and dedication. By working on two musical ideas, experimenting with fun chord progressions, and attempting to play lead guitar work, I deepened my connection to music and reaffirmed my commitment to the healing power of creativity. As I look ahead to the coming weeks, I remain hopeful, optimistic, and determined to continue my musical journey with courage and joy.

RECOVERY WEEK 8
Playing "God I Look to You" by Francesca Battistelli of Starlight

A cheerful heart is good medicine, but a crushed spirit dries up the bones.

—Proverbs 17:22

https://youtu.be/fkts7mGg-y4

As a devout Christian and musician, I constantly find solace and inspiration in playing Christian songs. This week, I decided to challenge myself by learning and playing one of my favorite Christian songs, "God I Look to You" by Francesca Battistelli of Starlight. What made this experience particularly interesting was the fact that I attempted to play several guitar parts. Creating harmonies, I hope to add depth and beauty to the song.

This musical endeavor not only allowed me to connect with the powerful lyrics of the song but also served as a form of therapy and healing for me. As I strummed the chords and added layers of harmony fills, I felt a sense of peace and gratitude wash over me. I couldn't help but thank God for guiding me through a challenging time in my life and providing me with a light to lead me toward recovery.

Playing "God I Look to You" on the guitar was a cathartic experience for me, as it allowed me to pour out my emotions and express my deepest feelings through music. The progress I made with my guitar playing during this session surprised me, and I couldn't help but feel overwhelmed with gratitude. Thank you, God, for blessing me with the ability to create beautiful harmonies and melodies through my music.

One of the most rewarding aspects of playing multiple guitar parts for "God I Look to You" was the opportunity to explore different harmonies and textures within the song. By layering various guitar lines, I was able to create a rich and intricate sound that I hope added a new dimension to the music. The process of experimenting with different arrangements and melodies was both challenging and exhilarating, pushing me to expand my musical abilities and creativity.

I found that playing multiple guitar parts not only enhanced the overall sound of the song but also allowed me to deepen my connection to the music on a personal level. As I navigated through the intricate chords and melodies, I felt a profound sense of communion with God and the message of the song. Each strum of the guitar strings served as prayer, a form of worship, and a way to express my faith in a tangible and heartfelt manner.

Grateful for the Healing Power of Music. This week's experience of playing "God I Look to You" by Francesca Battistelli of Starlight was truly transformative. Through music, I was able to find relief, rebuilding, and revelation, connecting with God in a meaningful and profound way. The act of creating harmonies and melodies on the guitar served as a form of therapy and worship, allowing me to express my gratitude and faith through music.

As I continue on my musical journey, I am grateful for the guidance and light that God provides me every step of the way. Playing "God I Look to You" was a reminder of the healing power of music and the importance of faith in overcoming challenges. I am thankful for the opportunity to create beauty through my music and to share my faith with others through the songs I play. Thank you, God, for the gift of music and for the continuous blessings that you bestow upon me.

RECOVERY WEEK 9
I Enjoyed This Week's Practice!

*This is the confidence we have in approaching God: that if
we ask anything according to his will, he hears us.*

—1 John 5:14

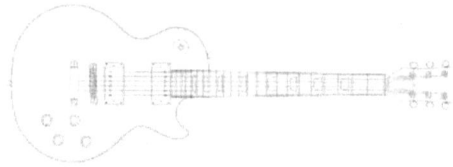

https://youtu.be/aFwOOf1L64I

I am so blessed for the opportunity to practice this week. I felt a sense of accomplishment and growth as I ventured out a little further in my playing. I decided to challenge myself by delving into chord progressions and voicings that were inspired by the legendary band Led Zeppelin.

As I immersed myself in the music, I added a touch of 50s-style guitar lead to elevate the soundscape. During the recording of my practice session, I noticed I was not focusing intensely on my right hand, trusting every note was played with precision and passion. It was a moment of pure joy and fulfillment to see how far I had come on my musical journey.

In the midst of my practice session, I decided to push the boundaries of creativity and artistry. I challenged myself to play an original composition, blending and shaping music concepts in unique ways. It was a thrilling experience to take advantage of layering songs with intricate guitar parts, creating a multi-dimensional sound that truly resonated with me.

The process of composing and playing the new tune allowed me to tap into my inner artist and express myself in ways I hadn't thought possible. It was a liberating feeling to break free from traditional norms and explore the vast possibilities that music offers.

As I wrapped up this week's practice session, I couldn't help but feel immense gratitude for the gift of music in my life. I am thankful for the opportunity to grow and evolve as a musician, constantly pushing myself to new heights and exploring uncharted territories.

I want to take a moment to thank everyone who has supported me on this journey, especially the one above, our God on high. It is through His grace and guidance that I am able to find joy and fulfillment in my music. I look forward to the adventures that lie ahead and the discoveries waiting to be made through the power of music.

My Guitar Stroke Recovery has been a transformative experience for me, allowing me to expand my horizons and explore new possibilities in my music. I am excited to continue this journey of growth and creativity, always striving to reach new heights in my musical endeavors. Thank you for joining me on this incredible ride strumming for life.

RECOVERY WEEK 10
Faith and Dedication

Bless the LORD, O my soul: and all that is within me, bless his holy name.

—Psalm 103:1

https://youtu.be/O1BvNKAkZnM

Every week I am making progress with dedication and patience. God has truly blessed me this week as I continue on my journey of relearning to play the guitar. Week 10 has been filled with challenges, breakthroughs, and moments of pure joy. I have pushed myself to the limits, experimenting with new techniques and chord expressions, all in an effort to regain my musical abilities.

This week, I really pushed the limits, I decided to focus on using both the pick and my finger in concert to create octave chord voicings. Before my stroke, I could play these voicings in my sleep. It has been a struggle to relearn this technique, but with each practice session, I can feel myself getting closer to my goal. The famous jazz guitarist George Benson is famous for using this technique, and I am determined to master it once again.

Once again, this week, I challenged myself to record an original musical idea for guitar. I recorded two guitars, with the rhythm section featuring very interesting chord voicings that are not commonly used by most guitar players. I wanted to add a very nice but slow melodic guitar solo to the piece, but I am still struggling with my right-hand speed. However, I have faith that with practice, my strumming skills will improve.

Again, God has truly blessed me with the progress I have made. Despite the challenges, setbacks, and frustrations, I am eternally grateful for the opportunity to relearn and rediscover my love for playing the guitar. Each small victory brings me one step closer to where I want to be, and I am determined to keep pushing forward.

As an experienced guitar player, I understand the importance of patience, dedication, and perseverance when it comes to recovering from a stroke and relearning to play. I have full confidence in my abilities and trust that with time and practice, I will once again become the musician I once was. I have trust in God, Amen!

To put this all together, Week 10 has been filled with challenges and triumphs. I have pushed myself to the limits, experimented with new techniques, and recorded an original musical idea for guitar. I am filled with gratitude for the progress I have made and the blessings I have received along the way. While the road ahead may be long, I am committed to continuing my journey of relearning to play the guitar with faith and determination and most importantly—strumming for life!

Overall, my journey has been filled with obstacles, triumphs, and moments of pure joy. With each practice session, I am getting closer to regaining my musical abilities and rediscovering my love for playing the guitar. God has blessed me with the strength, determination, and faith to keep pushing forward, and I am grateful for the progress I have made so far. My recovery journey may be long, but I am confident that with dedication and perseverance, I will become the musician I once was.

Recovery Week 11
Picking with Cm7 Arpeggios, Grateful for the Journey

Jesus looked at them and said, "For human beings it is impossible, but not for God. All things are possible for God."

—Mark 10:27

https://youtu.be/amH60JrBXUw

I felt so blessed this week. Thank you, God, for showing me a path to recovery! The great healer indeed, as my progress with the guitar stroke recovery has been steady and full of small victories. Week 11 has primarily focused on the idea of picking with Cm7 arpeggios, aiming to gain better control of my right hand and enhance my overall technique.

This week, I decided to challenge myself further by recording another original musical idea. I recorded two guitar parts on the rhythm recording, attempting to incorporate more intricate strumming patterns with an up-down motion. It was quite challenging, but the end result was truly rewarding.

In addition to the rhythm recording, I also attempted to play my original solo with a bit more speed. This required a lot of focus and precision, as I tried to maintain the flow and expressiveness of the solo. I chose to use very interesting scales, staying within the parameters of Cm7 arpeggios, which added a unique flair to the tune.

While the tune was not perfect, the experience of playing it was pure joy. The journey of recovery and improvement is all about progress, not perfection. Each challenge and obstacle overcome is a step closer to achieving mastery and fulfillment in music.

As I reflect on this week of my guitar stroke recovery, I am filled with gratitude for the progress made and the lessons learned. Each practice session is an opportunity for growth and self-discovery, and I am thankful for the chance to pursue my passion for music.

Navigating the challenges of my recovery and musical improvement has been a rewarding experience filled with ups and downs. Embracing the imperfections and celebrating the small victories along the way has allowed me to grow both as a musician and as a person. This amazing week was a reminder of the power of dedication, perseverance, and gratitude in the pursuit of musical excellence. Thank you, God, for guiding me on this path to recovery and inspiring me to keep pushing forward in my musical journey.

RECOVERY WEEK 12
Really Enjoyed My Practice

Oh, my God, He will not delay, my refuge and strength always. I will not fear, His promise is true. My God will come through always, always.

—"Always," by Kristian Stanfill of Passion

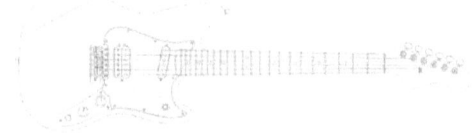

https://youtu.be/N1bLuNvymPw

Another great week of blessings from our God! As I sat down to practice this week, I was filled with a sense of gratitude and gladness. I knew that with His guidance, would be able to improve my skills and grow as a musician. This week, I decided to challenge myself by learning and recording the beautiful song "Always" by Kristian Stanfill.

I must admit, I was not flawless in my rendition of the song. There were definitely mistakes here and there, and I know I still have a lot to learn. However, I also know that every mistake is a learning opportunity, and I am determined to improve. One area I need to work on is my recording mix techniques. I want to create a more polished and professional sound, and that will require some experimentation and practice.

During my practice sessions this week, I focused a lot on my pick hand. I know that control, strength, and timing are key factors in becoming a proficient guitarist, and I am dedicated to honing these skills. I noticed when I concentrated on my pick hand, I was able to produce cleaner and more precise notes. But I still have a lot of work to do in this area, and I am committed to putting in the time and effort to improve.

One thing I realized is that I need to smile more when I am recording my videos. I tend to get so focused on playing the right notes that I forget to enjoy the music. I need to remember that music is meant to be fun and expressive, and I want my videos to reflect that joy. So, moving forward, I will make a conscious effort to smile and let my passion shine through in my recordings.

In my practice, I challenged myself by playing three separate guitar parts for the song "Always." This was a difficult but rewarding experience, as it forced me to really listen to the music and concentrate on each part individually. I found that by breaking the song into separate components, I was able to better understand the overall structure and nuances of the piece.

As I played through the song this week, I noticed a subtle but important change in my right wrist movement. I felt just a bit more freedom and fluidity in my playing, which allowed me to produce a smoother and more dynamic sound. This small improvement may seem insignificant to some, but to me, it represents progress and growth. I am thankful for the guidance of the Lord in helping me develop as a musician.

Overall, I really enjoyed my practice for Week 12. I faced challenges, made mistakes, and learned valuable lessons along the way. I know I still have a long journey ahead of me, but I am excited to continue growing and improving as a guitarist. With the Lord's help and a lot of hard work, I am confident I can reach my musical goals. Thank you, Lord, for this opportunity to learn and create beautiful music.

Recovery Week 13
A Journey of Musical Growth and Gratitude

Thank You, Jesus, You set me free. Christ my Saviour, You rescued me.

—Song by Hannah Hobbs and Hillsong Worship

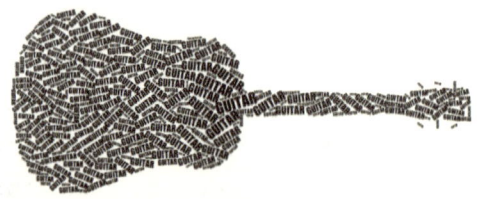

https://youtu.be/lFkRbd3sDNA

I am filled with a sense of musical growth and gratitude. This week was pivotal in my journey. I focused on refining my skills, exploring new techniques, and pushing myself creatively. Through dedication and passion, I was able to make significant progress and reach new milestones in my musical journey.

I am truly grateful for the progress I have made this week. It felt like I had a major breakthrough, where I gained more confidence and control over my picking hand. I attribute this success to my commitment and faith. With each practice session, I was able to see tangible improvements in my playing technique and musical expression. Thank you, God, for guiding me through this journey and blessing me with the strength to overcome challenges.

Throughout this week, I delved into the world of chord voicings, incorporating octave chords, and focusing on minor 7th harmony scales. These techniques added depth and complexity to my playing, allowing me to explore different tonalities and textures. By experimenting with new chord structures and scales, I was able to expand my musical vocabulary and enhance my playing style. This exploration not only challenged me but also inspired me to push the boundaries of my creativity.

One of the highlights was the creation of an original musical idea. I spent hours crafting a melodic motif that resonated with me on a deep level. This creative process was both fulfilling and exhilarating, as I allowed my imagination to run wild and express my emotions through music. Recording this musical idea was a cathartic experience, allowing me to capture the essence of my creativity in its purest form. Thank you, Jesus, for inspiring me and guiding me through this creative journey.

As I worked on refining my musical idea, I realized that the tune I had created embodied elements of contemporary jazz. The fusion of intricate chord progressions, subtle harmonies, and melodic phrasing gave the composition a modern and sophisticated feel. I immersed myself in the world of contemporary jazz, drawing inspiration from the genre's rich history and innovative spirit. This tune demonstrated my growth as a musician and my ability to adapt to different styles and genres.

In conclusion, Guitar Stroke Recovery Week 13 was a transformative experience filled with growth, creativity, and gratitude. I am proud of the progress I have made, and I am excited to continue pushing the boundaries of my musical journey. Through dedication, passion, and faith, I have discovered new techniques, honed my skills, and unleashed my creativity. Thank you, God, for blessing me with the gift of music and guiding me through this remarkable journey of self-discovery and musical exploration.

Recovery Week 14
I Am Still Pushing Forward

*They took palm branches and went out to meet him,
shouting, "Hosanna! Blessed is he who comes in the name of
the Lord!"*

—John 12:13

https://youtu.be/84Or_LKoF78

What a rewarding week filled with dedication, focus, and determination as I continue to work on my timing and pick control. Despite the trials I have faced along the way, I am still pushing forward and remain committed to regaining my skill and passion for playing the guitar.

I have been preparing to play "Hosanna" by Paul Baloche at church this Sunday. As I practiced this beautiful and heartfelt worship song, I found myself immersed in its melody and lyrics, feeling a sense of peace and connection with God. I have been pouring my heart and soul into perfecting the chords and transitions, ensuring that my worship execution on Sunday in church will be nothing short of exceptional.

In addition to my own practice sessions, I have reached out to my family and friends for their support and prayers. Knowing I have a strong network of loved ones who are cheering me on and lifting me up in prayer has been incredibly encouraging and uplifting. Their words of encouragement and positivity have fueled my determination to succeed and have reminded me that I am not alone on this journey.

For my video guitar stroke recovery practice and recording this week, I decided to get creative and push myself outside of my comfort zone. I challenged myself to come up with an original musical idea that would showcase my skills and creativity. I experimented with beautiful guitar chords, emotional expressive lead scales, and melodic ideas, resulting in a unique and captivating composition. I recorded this original piece using two separate guitar lines, layering them together to create a rich and dynamic sound.

As I look back on Week 14, I am filled with a sense of pride and accomplishment. Despite the setbacks and obstacles I have faced, I have persevered and continued to push myself to new heights. I am grateful for the progress I have made and the growth I have experienced both as a musician and as a person. I am more determined than ever to keep moving forward and to keep striving for excellence in my music.

In conclusion, this week has been a week of growth, dedication, and creativity. I am grateful for the progress I have made and the support I have received from my loved ones. As I continue on this journey, I am filled with a sense of optimism and excitement for the future. I am still pushing forward, and I know with hard work and positivity, I will achieve my goals and rediscover my love for playing the guitar. Thank you, God, for guiding me on this journey and for blessing me with the strength to overcome any challenges that come my way.

Recovery Week 15
"Hosanna" by Paul Baloche

...and you killed the Author of life, whom God raised from the dead. To this we are witnesses.

—Acts 3:15

https://youtu.be/NQXyYXos5fw

As I entered Week 15, I found myself faced with both challenges and progress. The iconic worship song "Hosanna" by Paul Baloche served as the soundtrack to my week, reminding me of the power of praise and the healing it can bring. Despite encountering some bad notes here and there, I continued to push forward, focusing on improving my hand and wrist movement for better coordination.

I noticed that my hand and wrist were feeling stiffer and more swollen than usual. This discomfort ebbed and flowed, at times hindering my practice sessions. I realized the importance of listening to my body and taking breaks when needed to prevent exacerbating the issue. While frustrating, I remained hopeful that with time and continued dedication, my mobility would improve.

Despite the physical setbacks, I also experienced moments of progress and breakthroughs. As I delved deeper into the intricacies of "Hosanna," I found myself connecting with the music on a deeper level. The lyrics resonated with my journey, reminding me to turn my eyes toward hope and embrace the yearning of my heart for healing. Each note I played became a prayer, lifting me up and pushing me forward.

Navigating the ups and downs of recovery is no easy feat. It requires perseverance, patience, and a willingness to push past limitations. While some days may feel discouraging, I remind myself that every small step forward is a victory. Whether it's mastering a difficult chord progression or simply picking up the guitar when I feel uninspired, every effort contributes to my overall progress.

Music has always been a source of inspiration and solace for me, especially during challenging times. "Hosanna" served as a beacon of hope, reminding me of the healing power of praise and worship. As I immersed myself in the melody and lyrics, I found comfort in the words and a renewed sense of determination to overcome my current obstacles.

As Easter approaches, I am reminded of the ultimate sacrifice and triumph of Jesus Christ. His resurrection symbolizes new life, renewal, and hope for a brighter future. I draw strength from this message, knowing that just as Christ overcame death, I too can overcome the challenges I face in my recovery journey.

Final thoughts, Week 15 of my recovery has been a mix of highs and lows. While I continue to grapple with stiffness and swelling in my hand and wrist, I am also making strides in my playing and finding inspiration in the music I create. Remember to take each day as it comes, celebrate the victories no matter how small, and never lose faith in the healing power of music. The journey may be long and laborious, but with dedication and a heart full of praise, anything is possible. Keep strumming, keep singing, and keep believing in the power of hope. As I look toward Easter and the promise of new beginnings, I am filled with hope and determination to keep pushing forward. Praise is indeed rising, and my eyes are turning toward a brighter future. Have a blessed Easter. ♫♫

RECOVERY WEEK 16
Pushing Myself Toward Recovery

"Built on the foundation of the apostles and prophets, Christ Jesus himself being the cornerstone." This verse describes Jesus as the most important stone in a building, holding all the parts together to form a holy temple.

—Ephesians 2:20

https://www.youtube.com/watch?v=BexVDuMO_2s

Are you ready to hear about my guitar recovery journey in Week 16? I am still pushing myself to get back to where I was before the stroke, and this week brought some unexpected surprises. Let's dive into the details of my progress and setbacks as I continue to work on my guitar skills post-stroke.

This week, I decided to focus more on my rhythm hand motion while practicing. I found that using more rhythm in my playing helped me stay in the groove and keep a steady beat. Surprisingly, I was able to play with more fluidity and control, which boosted my confidence and motivated me to continue pushing myself.

Have you ever surprised yourself by exceeding your own expectations in a challenging situation? For me, the answer is yes. This week's practice session with the song "Cornerstone" by Hill Song reminded me of why Jesus Christ is the cornerstone of my faith. Despite the challenges I faced, I found joy in the music and the message behind it, which pushed me to smile more and enjoy the process instead of focusing solely on concentration.

During this week's practice, I challenged myself to play octave chords and attempted to play harmony guitar melody lines. It was not easy at this stage of my recovery, but I refused to let that hold me back. I pushed myself to try new techniques and push the boundaries of my current capabilities. While it was challenging, I found satisfaction in the progress I made, no matter how small.

What techniques have you tried that seemed difficult at first but eventually became easier with practice? For me, the answer is playing octave chords and harmony melody lines that seemed daunting at first, but with perseverance and dedication, I was able to make progress and improve my skills. It just goes to show that pushing yourself out of your comfort zone can lead to significant growth and development.

As I move forward in my recovery, I am excited to see where my dedication and hard work will take me. Despite the impediments I face, I am determined to continue pushing myself and improving my guitar skills. Each new week brings new opportunities for growth and progress, and I am eager to tackle them head-on.

This week was filled with surprises, challenges, and more breakthroughs. By being assertive to try new techniques and practice with enthusiasm, I was able to exceed my own expectations and move one step closer to achieving my goals. I am grateful for the progress I have made so far and look forward to continued growth in the weeks ahead.

RECOVERY WEEK 17
"This Is Amazing Grace"
by Phil Wickham

Who breaks the power of sin and darkness? Whose love is mighty and so much stronger? The King of glory, the King above all kings!

—Phil Wickham

https://www.youtube.com/watch?v=sIiqwFy8HUc

This week, I tackled the iconic song "This Is Amazing Grace" by Phil Wickham. Despite facing some trials with my right-hand limitations, I powered through and reinvented parts of the song to make it work. It was not easy, but with the grace of God, I was able to record five different guitar parts. One of the challenges was playing the melody guitar line a third apart, which pushed my wrist and hand even more. Let me share with you my experience and insights.

To me, playing "This Is Amazing Grace" was more than just a musical endeavor—it was a spiritual experience. As I strummed the chords and picked the notes, I felt a sense of connection with God. The lyrics of the song resonated with me on a deeper level, reminding me of the grace and love that has sustained me through this challenging time. I truly felt thankful to God for giving me the strength and determination to continue on this journey of recovery.

One of the biggest encounters I faced was navigating the intricate guitar parts with my right-hand limitations. I had to get creative and find alternate ways to play certain sections of the song. Despite the initial struggles, I persevered and was able to overcome this obstacle. It was a reminder that with dedication and faith, anything is possible.

I found myself reinventing certain parts of the song to accommodate my physical boundaries. I had to think outside the box and come up with new approaches to playing the music. This process not only tested my musical skills but also forced me to push past my comfort zone. In the end, I was able to create a unique interpretation of "This Is Amazing Grace" that reflected my journey of recovery.

As I reflect on Week 17, I am filled with gratitude for the progress I have made and the obstacles I have overcome. I am humbled by the support and encouragement I have received from my loved ones and the strength I have found in my faith. Playing "This Is Amazing Grace" was a testament to the power of perseverance and the grace of God. Thank you, Jesus, for guiding me through this journey.

In conclusion, Week 17 of my expedition was a challenging yet rewarding experience. Playing "This Is Amazing Grace" by Phil Wickham pushed me to my limits but ultimately strengthened my resolve. I am grateful for the opportunity to share this journey with you and to witness the healing power of music and faith. As I look ahead to the next week, I am filled with hope and determination to continue pressing forward. Thank you for joining me on this incredible journey. Let's strum for life together.

Recovery Week 18
"Come Thou Fount, Come Thou King" by Gateway Worship

*Come, Thou Fount, come, Thou King; Come, Thou precious
Prince of Peace, Hear Your bride, to You we sing, come,
Thou Fount of our blessing.*

—Gateway Worship

https://www.youtube.com/watch?v=0uwT581ixHw

Hey there, fellow guitar enthusiasts and Stroke Warriors! Can you believe I am already in Week 18 of my guitar stroke recovery journey? Time sure does fly when you're having fun. This week, I dove into "Come Thou Fount, Come Thou King" by Gateway Worship. It's another challenging piece, but with dedication, I am confident I will get through and learn this beautiful up-tempo song. Let me delve into the details of this week's practice session.

First and foremost, I want to take a moment to thank God for another fantastic practice week. Each week brings new challenges and victories, and I am grateful for the progress I continue to make. While practicing "Come Thou Fount, Come Thou King," I realized that I need to smile more. Music is such a beautiful gift, and it's essential to enjoy the process fully. So, as I tackle this piece, I am reminding myself to let the joy of music shine through with a big smile. Thank you, Jesus, for guiding me on this musical journey.

In my practice session this week, I explored the different guitar tunings used in traditional Scottish and Irish pipe music. Guitar 1 was in regular tuning, while Guitar 2 was in DADGAD tuning. This contrast provided a unique sound that enhanced the overall performance of "Come Thou Fount, Come Thou King." By experimenting with various tunings, you can create depth and richness in your music.

Again, one of the highlights of this week's practice was exploring the various voicings used in traditional Scottish and Irish pipe music. These guitar chord voicings add a distinctive flair to the music, capturing the essence of the Celtic sound. Incorporating these unique guitar chord voicings into my playing helped me experiment and elevate my practice performance and hopefully create a truly authentic musical experience for listeners.

As I continue to dissect "Come Thou Fount, Come Thou King," it's essential for me to pay attention to the intricate details of the piece. Each note, chord, and strumming pattern plays a crucial role in bringing the music to life. By delving deeper into the music, I can fully understand its complexities and nuances, allowing the practice performance to have precision and emotion.

Week 18 was filled with challenges and triumphs. By embracing the music, thanking God for His guidance, and smiling through the process, I can conquer any obstacle that comes my way. "Come Thou Fount, Come Thou King" by Gateway Worship may present its challenges, but with dedication and practice, I know I will master it. Keep strumming, keep smiling, and keep making beautiful music. Until next week, rock on!

Recovery Week 19
More Challenges, More Progress!

*Come, let us sing for joy to the LORD; let us shout aloud to
the Rock of our salvation.*

—Psalm 95:1

https://www.youtube.com/watch?v=r7QicXHZSkU

I give all praise to God for this week's uplifting stroke recovery. Week 19 has been a significant milestone in my journey toward regaining control and strength in my right hand. With determination and perseverance, I have continued to push myself to try more challenges and incorporate new techniques into my practice sessions.

This week, I have pushed myself to try more challenging exercises to further strengthen my right hand. I have focused on exercises that require a combination of both pick and finger techniques to improve dexterity and coordination. By incorporating these challenges into my practice routine, I have noticed a significant improvement in the strength and control of my right fingers.

One of the key aspects of this week's practice was the incorporation of more pick and finger techniques. By combining these two techniques, I have been able to explore new sounds and dynamics on the guitar. It has been a rewarding experience to see my right hand gradually gaining more control and precision with each practice session.

As I continue to practice and push myself to try new challenges, I can feel my right fingers getting stronger and gaining more control. The increased wrist movement has also been a significant improvement, allowing me to achieve a more fluid and dynamic playing style. I am grateful for the progress I have made so far and look forward to continuing this journey toward full recovery.

This week, I had the pleasure of practicing an original tune that brought me great joy. The upbeat feeling of the tune made my heart smile, and I enjoyed experimenting with scales and fun guitar chords. It was a refreshing change of pace from the usual exercises and helped me tap into my creativity and musical expression.

Overall, Week 19 of my voyage has been a transformative experience. With dedication and the guidance of God, I have been able to make significant progress in strengthening my right hand and improving my playing technique. I am excited to see what challenges and breakthroughs the coming weeks will bring. Thank you, Jesus, for this journey of healing and growth.

Recovery Week 20
Learning "We Praise You"
by Matt Redman

*He also said, "Blessed be the Lord, the God of Shem; and let
Canaan be his servant."*

—Genesis 9:26

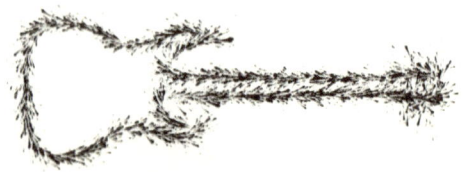

https://www.youtube.com/watch?v=haLqsQTi7QU

Thank you, Jesus, for your healing powers, both mentally and physically.
As I continue my journey Week 20 has been a significant milestone for
me, I had the opportunity to learn the great Christian song "We Praise
You" by Matt Redman.

Playing this song has been a truly uplifting experience for me. Not only
did it allow me to thank Jesus for my progress, but it also challenged me
to improve my wrist and finger control. The innovative guitar chords and
lead guitar parts a third apart added a new layer of complexity to my
playing, pushing me to improve my skills even further.

Throughout the week, I focused on working on my timing and mastering
the four different guitar parts in the song. This meant ensuring that each
part complemented the others seamlessly, creating a harmonious blend of
music. It was a challenging yet rewarding process, and I am grateful for
the opportunity to challenge myself in this way.

As I have said many times, I am truly thankful for the progress I have made throughout my guitar stroke recovery journey. Each week brings new challenges and achievements, pushing me to grow and develop as a guitarist. The support and guidance of my loved ones, along with my faith in Jesus, have been instrumental in my recovery process.

To me, learning "We Praise You" by Matt Redman has been a significant milestone in my guitar recovery. It has allowed me to challenge myself, improve my skills, and express my gratitude to Jesus for his healing powers. I look forward to continuing my progress in the weeks to come, with a renewed sense of determination and faith in my abilities.

RECOVERY WEEK 21
Embracing a New Sound

Lift up a song, strike the tambourine, play the sweet-sounding harp and lyre.

—Psalm 81:2

https://www.youtube.com/watch?v=xP1K2a6A35I

In my 21st week I decided to shift gears and explore a different musical style. I delved into the realm of 1960s-style blues rock, aiming to challenge myself and push the boundaries of my playing abilities. This week was all about honing my right-hand technique while keeping up with the intricate movements of my left hand. Although not perfect, it was a rewarding week of practice, and I am grateful for every moment of progress. Thank you, Lord Jesus, for guiding me on this journey.

One of the highlights was my experiment with infusing a psychedelic sound into my playing. Drawing inspiration from the music era of the 1960s, I sought to create a captivating experience through intricate guitar phrases and dual guitar leads. While it was a challenge to step out of my comfort zone, I embraced the opportunity to explore new sounds and techniques. Pushing myself to play something different not only kept me motivated but also helped me grow as a musician.

Playing in a style that was unfamiliar to me was both exhilarating and daunting. The freedom to explore new musical territories allowed me to break free from routine and discover hidden facets of my creativity. As I navigated through the psychedelic soundscape, I encountered moments of uncertainty and self-doubt. However, with each note I played, I gained confidence in my abilities and learned to trust my instincts. It was a reminder that growth often stems from embracing the unknown and stepping outside of one's comfort zone.

As I reflect on my journey through Week 21, I am filled with gratitude for how far I have come. Each practice session is a testament to my commitment to overcoming challenges. The road to recovery may be tiresome, but with faith and perseverance, I am confident I will continue to make strides toward regaining my musical prowess. I am thankful for the opportunity to share my progress and experiences with others, knowing that my journey may inspire and encourage those facing similar obstacles.

In conclusion, Week 21 was marked by exploration, growth, and gratitude. By delving into a new musical style and challenging myself to play something different, I expanded my horizons and tapped into my creativity. Embracing the unknown and stepping outside of my comfort zone allowed me to push past limitations and achieve new heights in my playing. As I continue on this path of recovery, I am filled with hope and optimism for the future. With each strum of the guitar, I am reminded of the healing power of music and the joy of embracing growth.

Remember, progress is not measured by perfection but by the willingness to learn and grow. Keep pushing yourself, stay inspired, and never lose sight of the passion that drives you forward. Strumming for life!

RECOVERY WEEK 22
Learning to Play "Glorious Day" by Passion

You called my name, And I ran out of that grave, Out of the darkness, Into Your glorious day.

—Passion

https://www.youtube.com/watch?v=GT_jQUpWZDA

I challenged myself to learn a new and complex song: "Glorious Day" by Passion. This Christian song is not only beautiful but also technically challenging, especially the lead melody portion. Despite the difficulties, I embraced the process with gratitude and determination, pushing my limitations and trusting in God along the way.

With this expedition, I have come to rely on my faith in God for strength and progress. Each week brings new challenges, both physically and mentally, but I know with God by my side, I can overcome anything. As I tackle the intricate melodies and difficult chord progressions of "Glorious Day," I am reminded of the power of faith in guiding me through even the toughest of times.

Learning the lead melody of "Glorious Day" was a true test of my musical abilities. Not only did it require precision and dexterity in my fretting hand, but it also challenged the strength and coordination of my strumming hand. As I practiced day in and day out, I felt the familiar frustration of hitting wrong notes and fumbling through difficult passages. But with each mistake, I learned and grew stronger, inching closer to mastering the song.

Despite the challenges I faced, I reminded myself that perfection is not the goal, progress is. "Glorious Day" may not have sounded flawless during my practice sessions, but each small improvement added up to a significant leap forward in my guitar playing journey. I embraced the imperfections, knowing they were all part of the learning process and essential for my growth as a musician.

As I look back on Week 22 of my stroke recovery, I am filled with gratitude for the progress I have made. Learning "Glorious Day" was a milestone in my journey, a moment where I pushed beyond my comfort zone and reached new heights. I am thankful for the opportunity to challenge myself, to grow, and to make music that brings joy and inspiration to others.

My week was a challenging but a rewarding experience. Learning "Glorious Day" by Passion pushed me to my limits, both musically and mentally, but with diligence, I was able to overcome the obstacles. I am excited to see what the next weeks will bring and how I will continue to grow as a musician. Thank you, Jesus, for guiding me through this journey of recovery and music.

RECOVERY WEEK 23
A Major Pentatonic Scale
and Colorful Chords

"O come, let us sing unto the Lord: let us make a joyful noise to the rock of our salvation." The first three verses of Psalm 95 are a call to worship that praises God.

—Psalm 95:1

https://www.youtube.com/watch?v=1Mu1GigPSAs

Thank you, Jesus, for pushing me forward, I am thrilled to share my progress with you all. I have been focusing on developing more independent wrist movements and exploring different musical ideas to enhance my playing. This week, I practiced an interesting melody using the A major pentatonic scale and incorporated some colorful guitar chords to add depth and mystery to my music. Overall, it has been a blessed week filled with musical exploration and growth.

During Week 23 of my guitar resilience path, I spent a significant amount of time working with the A major pentatonic scale. This scale has a bright and uplifting sound, making it perfect for creating melodic lines and solos. By practicing various scales regularly, I have noticed a significant improvement in my finger dexterity and ability to navigate the fretboard with ease.

To add an adventurous and mysterious touch to my musical ideas, I decided to experiment with colorful guitar chords this week. These chords introduced new harmonic possibilities and added rich textures to my playing. By incorporating unconventional chord voicings and progressions, I challenged myself to think outside the box and explore different tonalities. This creative experimentation has not only expanded my musical palette but also pushed me to step out of my comfort zone and try new things.

In addition to exploring new scales and chords, I have been working diligently on developing more independent wrist movements in my playing. This has been a crucial aspect of my guitar stroke recovery journey, as it allows me to play more fluidly and expressively. By focusing on wrist control and relaxation, I have noticed a significant improvement in my overall technique and tone. This week, I dedicated extra time to exercises that target wrist mobility and strength, and I can already feel the difference in my playing.

As I reflect on my 23rd week, by incorporating the A major pentatonic scale, colorful chords, and focusing on wrist movement, I have continued to push the boundaries of my playing and grow as a musician. Each week presents new challenges and opportunities for learning, and I am excited to see where this journey takes me next. Thank you, Jesus, for guiding me on this path of musical exploration and growth.

RECOVERY WEEK 24
Finding Musical Inspiration

Sing to the LORD a new song; sing to the LORD, all the earth.

—Psalm 96

https://www.youtube.com/watch?v=b3XcImm400Q

Happy Father's Day to all those great fathers out there! Today, I want to share my experience because I created another interesting melody to practice this week, focusing on increasing stronger hand strength. Though it's not perfect, I had an enjoyable time practicing this new piece all week. I am grateful for the progress I've made and give thanks to Jesus for pushing me further.

This past week, I delved into creating original musical ideas that have broadened my knowledge as a musician. Exploring new melodies and rhythms has been beneficial not only for my stroke recovery but also for my overall growth as a guitarist. Through consistent practice and dedication, I have been able to see tangible improvements in my ability to play the guitar with confidence.

One of the key benefits I've experienced from creating original music is the sense of fulfillment and creativity it brings. By challenging myself to come up with unique musical ideas, I have been able to push the boundaries of my comfort zone and expand my musical repertoire. This has not only enhanced my stroke recovery journey but has also made me a more well-rounded musician.

Developing wrist control and hand strength has been crucial in my guitar stroke recovery process. By focusing on exercises and melodies that require precision and dexterity, I have been able to improve my overall technique and playing ability. Practicing regularly has allowed me to build endurance and stamina, enabling me to play for longer periods without fatigue.

As I continue to navigate through my recovery journey, I am reminded of the importance of perseverance and determination. Playing the guitar has always been a source of joy and comfort for me, and I am grateful for the opportunity to strum away life's challenges. With each strum, I am reminded of the resilience and strength within me, driving me to keep moving forward.

This stroke recovery journey has been filled with musical inspiration and growth. Through creating original melodies and focusing on wrist control and hand strength, I have been able to see significant progress in my playing abilities. I am excited to continue exploring new musical ideas and pushing myself to new heights as a musician. Thank you, Jesus, for guiding me on this path of recovery and musical discovery. Happy Father's Day to all! Keep strumming for life and never stop pursuing your passion for music. Most importantly this week, thank you, Dad, for inspiring me to never give up, I miss you every day. Wishing everyone a blessed and musical journey ahead!

Recovery Week 25
Overcoming Challenges
Through Music

You are the one above it all, I stand in awe; You're the God
over all I know, no higher name, no greater throne, You
stand alone; You're the God over all I know.

—Vertical Worship

https://youtu.be/fyBTKzi96Gs

God has truly blessed me this week as I continue my journey of relearning how to play the guitar. It has been a challenging but rewarding road, and I am forever grateful for the progress I have made. This week, I focused on practicing the song "Over All I Know" by Vertical Worship, and it has truly been a powerful experience.

It's amazing how music has a way of weaving through the ups and downs of life, isn't it? Despite the challenges of tightening wrist control, mastering pick control for string skipping, and struggling with timing during Recovery Week 25, "Over All I Know" was like a loyal companion, helping me navigate through it all. I hope my hard work and dedication truly paid off, showing that even imperfect attempts lead to growth and improvement. Here's to the power of music and unwavering determination!

Throughout this week, I faced numerous challenges in my guitar playing. From struggling with wrist control to feeling frustrated with timing, there were moments where I felt like giving up. However, each time I picked up my guitar and played "Over All I Know," I was reminded of the power of music to heal and inspire.

One of the biggest victories this week was overcoming my struggles with string skipping. This technique has always been difficult for me, but through dedicated practice and focused effort, I was able to improve significantly. "Over All I Know" provided the perfect foundation for me to work on this skill, and I am proud of the progress I have made.

Music has a unique ability to touch our hearts and souls in ways that words alone cannot. Whether we are facing challenges or celebrating victories, music has the power to uplift us and carry us through even the darkest times. "Over All I Know" by Vertical Worship is a perfect example of a song that not only entertains but also inspires and motivates.

As I played this song throughout the week, I felt a sense of peace and comfort wash over me. The lyrics spoke to my soul, reminding me that even in my weakest moments, there is always hope and strength to carry on. Music truly is a gift from God, and I am grateful for the healing power it has brought into my life.

In closing, I want to express my gratitude to the one who has guided me through this journey of guitar recovery. Thank you, Jesus, for blessing me with the talent and determination to overcome my challenges. Thank you for the gift of music, which has been my constant companion in times of joy and sorrow. I am excited to see what the future holds as I continue to grow and learn through my guitar playing. Through the power of music and faith, we can overcome any challenge that comes our way. Thank you, Jesus, for always being by our side. Thank you, Jesus, for everything.

RECOVERY WEEK 26
Practicing Double Stops with Etta James's "I'd Rather Go Blind"

Be joyful in hope, patient in affliction, faithful in prayer.
—Romans 12:12

https://youtu.be/cKeAobbo4D4

Have you ever experienced a moment when you felt like your heart was meant to be seen? Well, I had that exact feeling this week as I practiced playing double stops with an excellent song by the legendary Etta James. As I delved into the smooth and soulful sounds of "I'd Rather Go Blind," I couldn't help but thank Jesus for guiding me on this musical journey.

Starting off Week 26 of my guitar stroke recovery, I decided to try something new and challenge myself by incorporating double stops into my practice routine. Double stops, where you play two notes simultaneously, can add depth and richness to your playing, and I wanted to explore this technique further.

Jamesetta Hawkins, known professionally as Etta James, was a powerhouse in the world of music. Her soulful voice and captivating performances have inspired countless musicians, including myself. "I'd Rather Go Blind" is one of her classic songs that beautifully showcases her vocal prowess and emotional depth.

As I sat down with my guitar, I focused on mastering the double stops in "I'd Rather Go Blind." I paid close attention to the intervals between the notes and worked on blending them seamlessly together. It was a challenging yet rewarding experience as I felt myself growing as a musician.

Music has a way of touching our souls and connecting us to something greater than ourselves. As I immersed myself in the music of Etta James, I couldn't help but feel a sense of gratitude and awe for the beauty of music. It was a reminder that music is a gift that should be cherished and shared with others.

In conclusion, Week 26 of my guitar stroke recovery journey was filled with new challenges and musical inspiration. Playing double stops with Etta James's "I'd Rather Go Blind" was an enriching experience that pushed me out of my comfort zone and allowed me to grow as a musician. Thank you, Jesus, for showing me the way and guiding me on this musical path.

So next time you pick up your guitar, why not challenge yourself with a new technique or learn a classic song that inspires you? Remember, music is a journey that is meant to be shared and enjoyed. Thank you, Jesus, for guiding us on this musical adventure—strumming for life!

Recovery Week 27
Enjoying Progress and Growth

This is God's way of saying carry on and live life to the fullest.

—Actor James Woods

https://youtu.be/jQ6QWJ4HUF8

As a believer in the healing power of Jesus, I am grateful for another week of progress in my stroke recovery. This week has been particularly rewarding as I explored learning a beautiful Christian song by Josh Baldwin titled "Evidence." Despite facing some challenges, such as incorporating slide guitar techniques into the song, I feel blessed to see how far I have come since the beginning of my recovery. Thank you, Lord, for guiding me and pushing me onward on this musical path.

Learning a new song always comes with its own set of challenges, but it is through overcoming these hurdles that we grow and improve as musicians. "Evidence" by Josh Baldwin presented me with the opportunity to work on my slide guitar skills, something I had not explored much before. While it was challenging at first, I welcomed the chance to expand my musical abilities and add a new dimension to my playing.

Music has always been a source of inspiration and comfort for me, especially during challenging times like my stroke recovery. The lyrics of "Evidence" speak of the endless presence of God in our lives and the reassurance that He is always with us, even in our darkest moments. As I delved into the song and immersed myself in its message, I felt a renewed sense of faith and hope.

In any recovery journey, I always say, it is important to celebrate even the smallest victories along the way. This week, I found joy in mastering the slide guitar parts of "Evidence" and being able to play them smoothly and confidently. These seemingly small accomplishments serve as reminders of how far I have come and motivate me to keep pushing forward toward full recovery.

Through the ups and downs of my guitar stroke recovery, one thing remains constant—my gratitude for the progress I have made and the resilience that keeps me going. I am thankful for the gift of music and the healing power it holds, allowing me to express myself and connect with others in meaningful ways. With each strum of the guitar strings, I feel the presence of Jesus guiding me and filling me with strength.

As I wrap up another week of practice and reflection, I am filled with a sense of anticipation for what lies ahead on this journey. I am excited to continue learning new songs, exploring different genres, and honing my skills as a guitarist. With Jesus by my side, I know I can overcome any challenge and achieve great things in my recovery. Thank you, Lord, for the progress and growth I have experienced this week.

My guitar journey continues to be a testament to the healing power of music and the omnipresent support of Jesus. Each new song I learn, like "Evidence" by Josh Baldwin, brings me closer to full recovery and reminds me of the strength that lies within me. As I look ahead to the weeks to come, I am filled with hope and determination to keep pushing forward, knowing that with faith and perseverance, anything is possible.

RECOVERY WEEK 28
The Challenge

Give your burdens to the Lord, and he will take care of you.
He will not permit the godly to slip and fall.

—Psalm 55:22

https://youtu.be/X3Xns4m8Nj0

This week's practice was indeed very challenging for me. I could feel the progress in my fingers, but my pick hand felt like it was being pushed to its limits. Despite not achieving perfection in my recordings, I am grateful for the progress I have made so far. The process of recovering from a stroke has involved various challenges, but overall, I appreciate the resilience and determination that have supported this journey. As I reflect on this week's practice, I am reminded of the importance of fortitude in the face of adversity.

In times of struggle, it is important to remember that Jesus knows our needs and is always there to guide us through. Through prayer and faith, we can find the strength and courage to overcome any obstacles that come our way. Healing and recovery take time, but with Jesus by our side, we can face each challenge with hope and determination. This week's practice may have been difficult, but I know with Jesus's help, I can continue to progress and grow as a guitarist.

Recovering is not an easy journey; recovery requires patience, dedication, and a willingness to push through the pain and frustration. This week's practice was a reminder of the importance of persistence in the face of adversity. Even when things seem tough, it is crucial to keep pushing forward and never give up on your dreams. With each strum of the guitar strings, I am reminded that progress is possible, as long as I remain dedicated to my recovery journey.

As I look back on my journey, I am amazed at how far I have come. From the early days of struggling to hold a pick to now being able to play more complex chords and melodies, I can see the progress I have made. While I still have a long way to go before I reach my ultimate goal, I am proud of the determination and perseverance that have brought me this far. Each new week brings new challenges, but I am confident that with Jesus's guidance, I can continue to make strides in my recovery.

Despite the difficulties I faced, I am grateful for the progress I have made and the lessons I have learned along the way. With Jesus by my side, I know I can continue to work toward my goal of full recovery. As I look ahead to the coming weeks, I am filled with hope and determination to keep pushing forward. Guitar stroke recovery is a long and arduous process, but with faith in myself and Jesus, I know I can overcome any obstacles that come my way.

Recovery Week 29
Unveiling a Slow and Dreamy Tune

*...who sing idle songs to the sound of the harp and like
David invent for themselves instruments of music...*

—Amos 6:5

https://youtu.be/jLGf8kdWbx4

I encountered an interesting and challenging practice session that pushed me to new limits. This week's practice was truly a test of my determination to overcome the obstacles in my path. The tune I worked on was unlike any other, with a slow and dreamy vibe that required me to connect minor triads, mainly focusing on A minor within the key of G major.

One thing that stands out about this particular style of music is how deceptively easy to play it may appear at first glance. The nuances and subtle intricacies hidden within the slow and dreamy melody require a deep level of understanding and mastery to truly bring out its beauty. It was a challenge that tested both my technical skills and my ability to convey emotion through my playing.

As I explored the music, I couldn't help but reflect on the blessings in my life. The tune served as a reminder to shift my focus from what I lack to the abundance of blessings that surround me. It was a moment of gratitude and humility, as I recognized the hand of God in guiding me through my recovery journey. With a heart full of thanks, I whispered,

"Thank You, Jesus—I repent of focusing on the things I don't have instead of the blessings You have given me. Amen."

This week's practice was more than just a musical exercise; it was a lesson in perseverance and growth. The slow and dreamy tune pushed me out of my comfort zone, forcing me to confront my weaknesses and work on areas that needed improvement. With each note played, I felt a sense of progression and development, knowing that every challenge I faced was shaping me into a stronger and more skilled musician.

As I reflected on the week's practice and the emotions it evoked, I found myself wondering, *What title would best capture the essence of this slow and dreamy tune?*

In conclusion, the 29th week of my guitar stroke recovery was evidence of my dedication and passion for music. The slow and dreamy tune challenged me in ways I never imagined, pushing me to new heights of skill and understanding. As I continue on this musical journey, I am grateful for the lessons learned and the growth experienced. The journey may be long and challenging, but with each stroke of the guitar, I am one step closer to reaching my ultimate goal—to fully recover and reclaim my musical prowess.

RECOVERY WEEK 30
Finding Blues Bliss

I will sing a new song to you, O God!

—Psalm 144:9

https://youtu.be/N1VZCiTusDw

In Week 30 I focused on practicing a slow and easy blues lead with an emphasis on phrasing and pick-hand control. Using the D minor pentatonic scale as my foundation, I explored adding additional flat notes to the scale to create more interest and depth in my playing. The goal was to develop a unique and curious blues phrasing style that would set me apart as a guitarist.

As I delved into the intricacies of blues phrasing, I encountered both challenges and rewards. The slow tempo of the blues lead allowed me to really focus on each note and how it connected to the overall melody. I experimented with different rhythms and accents, trying to inject my own personality and emotions into the music. It was a process of trial and error, but with each repetition, I could feel myself growing more comfortable and confident in my phrasing abilities.

One aspect of my practice this week that I paid special attention to was pick-hand control. The way I attacked each note and the dynamics I employed had a significant impact on the overall sound of the blues lead. I worked on varying the intensity of my picking hand to create a more dynamic and expressive performance. It was a subtle but crucial element that added depth and richness to my playing.

As I navigated through the challenges of blues phrasing and pick-hand control, I found solace and motivation in the words of Galatians 6:9, "Let us not become weary in doing good, for at the proper time we will reap a harvest if we do not give up." This verse reminded me of the importance of perseverance and determination in the face of obstacles. It served as a source of inspiration and encouragement, pushing me to give my best effort in every practice session.

As I reflect I am filled with a sense of pride and accomplishment. The progress I have made in refining my blues phrasing and improving my pick-hand control is a testament to my dedication and passion for music. With each passing week, I am getting closer to reaching my goal of becoming a skilled and expressive guitarist. I am excited to see what the future holds and to continue pushing myself to new heights in my musical journey.

In conclusion, Week 30 was a tough yet rewarding experience. By focusing on blues phrasing and pick-hand control, I was able to further develop my skills and grow as a guitarist. The words of Galatians 6:9 served as a source of inspiration and encouragement, motivating me to keep pushing forward despite any setbacks. As I look ahead to the coming weeks, I am filled with excitement and resolve to continue honing my craft and becoming the best musician I can be.

RECOVERY WEEK 31
Overcoming Challenges with Resilience and Determination

Sing to him, sing praise to him; tell of all his wonderful acts.

—1 Chronicles 16:9

https://youtu.be/r1oAqJ-n7mc

Welcome to Week 31, this week was truly a challenge, focusing on improving pick control and exploring slow and melodic guitar phrases with a captivating back rhythm. As I reflect on the progress I have made, I draw inspiration from the words of Philippians 4:13, "I can do all this through him who gives me strength." Let me dive into the highlights and learnings of this week's practice.

The focus this week was on enhancing pick control, a fundamental skill for any guitarist. It required precision and finesse to produce clean and articulate notes. Despite the initial struggles, the process of tackling this challenge was undeniably rewarding. Playing slow and melodic guitar phrases allowed for a deeper understanding of rhythm and timing, leading to a more expressive and emotive playing style.

During practice sessions, it became evident how crucial it is to maintain a balanced approach to both technical proficiency and musicality. By incorporating interesting melodic back rhythms, the songs came alive with a unique character and depth. It was a testament to the importance of exploring different musical elements to enhance the overall sound and impact of the performance.

As the week progressed, the results began to speak for themselves. The dedication to consistent practice and willingness to push through challenges resulted in noticeable improvements in pick control and overall playing ability. It was a reminder that progress is a gradual journey, requiring willpower and a positive mindset to overcome obstacles along the way.

During Week 31, my commitment to never give up remained steadfast. Every moment of frustration or setback was viewed as an opportunity for growth and learning. This mindset shift allowed for a more resolute approach to guitar practice, reinforcing the belief that success is achievable with patience and persistence.

The journey to mastering pick control and melodic guitar phrases is a testament to the strength and dedication required to excel in music. The quote from Philippians 4:13 serves as a guiding light, reminding us that with faith and perseverance, anything is possible.

As Week 31 draws to a close, it's clear that the guitar stroke recovery journey is a continuous evolution of skill, passion, and personal growth. The challenges faced along the way serve as opportunities for development and refinement, paving the way for greater musical achievements in the future. I will carry the lessons learned from this week forward, embracing the journey with enthusiasm. Remember, the tide will turn, and success is within reach for those who persevere.

Recovery Week 32
Melodic Country Lead Exploration

Therefore, as you received Christ Jesus the Lord, so walk in him, rooted and built up in him and established in the faith, just as you were taught, abounding in thanksgiving.

—Colossians 2:6-7

https://youtu.be/UD9-mF9JVwY

In Week 32 I decided to test myself by trying a new technique—a melodic country lead. This involved combining arpeggios with the D major scale, creating a unique and intricate sound that pushed me out of my comfort zone. Despite the difficulty, I did not give up, knowing that every new challenge is an opportunity for growth and improvement.

The melodic country lead is a technique that requires precision, accuracy, and a deep understanding of music theory. By combining arpeggios with the D major scale, players can create a beautiful and melodic sound that is both challenging and rewarding. This technique pushes the boundaries of traditional guitar playing, allowing for creative expression and exploration of new sounds and styles.

As I dug into the world of melodic country guitar lead playing, I faced numerous trials and difficulties along the way. From mastering the finger placements to understanding the intricate relationship between arpeggios and scales, every step presented a new hurdle to overcome. However, I reminded myself of the words from Matthew 19:26: "With man this is impossible, but with God all things are possible." This gave me the strength to push through the difficulties and keep going, no matter how tough it seemed.

After hours of practice, I finally started to see progress in my melodic country lead technique. The notes began to flow more smoothly, the transitions became more seamless, and the overall sound became more cohesive. The reward of persistence and hard work was evident in the music I was creating, and I felt a sense of accomplishment and satisfaction unlike any other.

For those looking to explore the world of melodic country lead, here are a few tips to help you on your journey:

1. Start slow and gradually increase the tempo as you become more comfortable with the technique.

2. Practice consistently and regularly to build muscle memory and improve your overall skill level.

3. Experiment with different chord progressions and scales to create unique and interesting melodies.

4. Don't be afraid to make mistakes—they are part of the learning process.

5. By following these tips and staying persistent, you too can master the art of creating beautiful and captivating music.

Week 32 of my guitar stroke recovery was a challenging but worthwhile experience as I explored into the world of melodic country lead. By combining arpeggios with the D major scale, I expanded my musical horizons and pushed myself to new heights. Through perseverance and dedication, I was able to overcome obstacles and see real progress in my playing. So, remember, with God, all things are possible—even mastering the most intricate and challenging guitar techniques.

Recovery Week 33
Mixing Mixolydian Scales and Rhythm Fills

Is anyone among you in trouble? Let them pray. Is anyone happy? Let them sing songs of praise.

—James 5:13

https://youtu.be/j6vG8ZMz-Uw

I experienced a great breakthrough learning a better understanding Mixolydian scales with rhythm fills based on chord shapes. I sensed that recovering from a stroke helped me to focus extra with relearning to play the guitar. This week's practice was all about getting my right wrist moving again after the setback I experienced last week. Despite the challenges, I tried to stay positive and remember the words from Isaiah 41:10, "So do not fear, for I am with you; do not be dismayed, for I am your God. I will strengthen you and help you; I will uphold you with my righteous right hand."

One of the techniques I focused on this week was incorporating Mixolydian scales into my practice routine. Mixolydian scales have a unique sound that adds a jazzy and bluesy flavor to my playing. By practicing these scales, I challenged myself to explore new tonalities and expand my musical vocabulary. While it was tricky at first, I found that with perseverance and dedication, I was able to make significant progress throughout the week.

In addition to working on Mixolydian scales, I also experimented with incorporating rhythm fills based on chord shapes into my playing. Rhythm fills add texture and dynamics to my guitar playing, making my music more interesting and engaging. By combining these fills with chord shapes, I was able to create a more dynamic and layered sound that pushed me out of my comfort zone. It was a challenging but ultimately rewarding experience that helped me grow as a musician.

Throughout this week's practice sessions there were moments when I felt frustrated and discouraged, wondering if I would ever fully recover from my stroke. However, I reminded myself of the importance of keeping a positive mindset and believing in my ability to overcome obstacles. By staying focused and determined, I was able to push through the difficulties and make progress in my guitar recovery journey.

I am reminded of the importance of embracing the journey, no matter how challenging it may be. Every setback and obstacle I face is an opportunity for growth and learning. By pushing myself out of my comfort zone and trying new techniques, I am constantly evolving as a musician and as a person. I am grateful for the progress I have made so far and excited to see where this journey will take me next.

Week 33 was a mix of challenges, setbacks, and breakthroughs. By incorporating Mixolydian scales and rhythm fills into my practice routine, I pushed myself to new limits and expanded my musical horizons. With a positive mindset and dedication to my craft, I am confident I will continue to make progress in my guitar recovery journey. Stay tuned for more updates on my musical journey and remember, with perseverance and passion, anything is possible.

RECOVERY WEEK 34
Playing "Way Maker"

*Way maker, miracle worker, promise keeper, light in the
darkness, my God, that is who You are.*

—Leeland

https://youtu.be/srysAnc63V4

I had to work extra hard this week—thank you, Jesus. This week, I focused on playing a wonderful Christian song titled "Way Maker." It's a great and powerful song that I thoroughly enjoyed learning, despite its challenges. In addition, I continued to work on improving the movement of my right wrist. I also wanted to give a big thank you to my camera girl, the lovely Ms. Lisa, for her support and encouragement throughout this journey.

This week, I dedicated my practice sessions to mastering the chords and strumming pattern of "Way Maker." The song's uplifting lyrics and beautiful melody inspired me to push through any difficulties that arose. As I strummed the guitar strings and sang along, I could feel a sense of peace and joy wash over me. It was a truly rewarding experience to be able to play such a meaningful song.

While learning "Way Maker," I encountered some challenges with the intricate chord changes and rhythm of the song. However, I persevered and practiced diligently to overcome these obstacles. With each passing day, I noticed improvement in my ability to play the song with more confidence and accuracy. It was a testament to the power of persistence and dedication in the journey of guitar playing.

Throughout the week, I continued to focus on enhancing the movement of my right wrist while strumming the guitar. This particular aspect of playing the guitar has been a point of emphasis for me in recent weeks, as I strive to improve my overall technique and sound quality. By practicing various exercises and drills, I have been able to strengthen my wrist and achieve a smoother and more controlled strumming motion.

I want to express my sincere gratitude to Ms. Lisa, my beautiful wife, who has been my dedicated camera girl and constant source of encouragement. Her presence during my practice sessions has motivated me to push myself further and strive for excellence in my guitar playing. I am truly thankful for her support and guidance throughout this journey of my guitar stroke recovery.

In conclusion, Week 34 of guitar stroke recovery has been a significant milestone in my musical journey. Learning to play "Way Maker" and focusing on improving my right wrist movement have been key highlights of this week's progress. I am grateful for the challenges and successes that have come my way, as they have all contributed to my growth as a guitarist. I look forward to the continued improvement and exploration of new musical avenues in the weeks to come.

Recovery Week 35
Embracing the Joy of Music

*My flesh and my heart may fail, but God is the strength of
my heart and my portion forever.*

—Psalm 73:26

https://youtu.be/0lfIxApjwE8

Thank you, God, for blessing me. My guitar journey has been a truly remarkable one this week. As I reflect on the progress I have made in Week
35, I am overwhelmed with gratitude for the gifts of music and healing
that have been bestowed upon me. In this week's guitar stroke recovery
post, I will share the highlights of my week, the challenges I faced, and
the joy that music has brought into my life.

Wow, Week 35, and I am still moving forward, thank you, Jesus! This
week, I dug into the world of slow country rock, drawing inspiration from
the legendary band Pure Prairie League and their talented guitarist Vince
Gill. I worked on an original tune in this style, focusing on double stops,
playing thirds, and crafting melodic guitar lead lines. Despite the inevitable mistakes and missed notes, the progress I made was truly uplifting.

One of the most rewarding aspects of Week 35 was witnessing the return
of my musical creativity. As I explored new techniques and experimented

with different sounds, I felt a sense of liberation and joy. The process of creating an original tune allowed me to express myself in ways that words cannot capture. Music truly has the power to heal and uplift the spirit.

While Week 35 brought many moments of joy and inspiration, it was not without its challenges. There were times when frustration threatened to derail my progress, but I persevered with intense focus. Every missed note and every stumble served as a reminder of the resilience and strength that reside within me.

As I look back on the past week, I am filled with a sense of pride and accomplishment. The small victories—mastering a tricky passage, nailing a challenging riff, or finding the perfect tone—all added up to a week of immense growth and progress. It is important to celebrate these achievements, no matter how small they may seem.

As I prepare to begin Week 36 of my guitar stroke recovery journey, I do so with a heart full of gratitude and a mind open to new possibilities. Music has been my constant companion, guiding me through the darkest days and uplifting me in times of joy. I look forward to the weeks ahead with excitement and anticipation, knowing that each day brings new opportunities for growth and discovery.

In conclusion, Week 35 of my guitar stroke recovery has been proof of the power of music and the human spirit. Through creativity, determination, and a deep love for music, I have overcome obstacles, celebrated victories, and embraced the joy that music brings into my life. As I continue on this journey, I am filled with gratitude for the blessings that have been bestowed upon me. Thank you, God, for guiding me through this incredible journey.

Recovery Week 36
Practicing "Goodness of God" by Bethel Music

Behold, God is my salvation; I will trust and will not be afraid; for the Lord God is my strength and my song, and He has become my salvation.

—Isaiah 12:2

https://youtu.be/FEZ1TZ6I_pE

Are you a guitar enthusiast looking for some inspiration in your practice routine this week? Well, let me share with you my experience with practicing "Goodness of God" by Bethel Music and Jenn Johnson. This beautiful song not only challenged me as a guitar player but also touched my heart with its powerful message. Keep reading to learn about my guitar stroke recovery journey with this tune and how I added my own twist to make it truly special.

When I first decided to tackle "Goodness of God," I knew it wouldn't be an easy task. The intricate chords and melodies required precision and dedication to master. However, as I delved deeper into the song, I found myself falling in love with its lyrics and melody. Each strum of the guitar brought me closer to understanding the goodness of God in a whole new light.

To truly capture the essence of "Goodness of God," I decided to record three guitar parts to bring out a full, rich sound. Each part harmonized with the others, creating a beautiful tapestry of music that showcased the beauty of the song. By layering the guitar parts, I was able to add depth and dimension to the overall sound, making the song come alive in a whole new way.

In addition to the three guitar parts, I wanted to add a unique twist to the song. I introduced twin guitar leads playing a third part, creating an interesting dynamic that added flair to the overall composition. This unexpected element brought a new level of excitement to the song, making it stand out even more.

To further enhance the song, I decided to add guitar lead fills in the bridge and chorus sections. These guitar fills added a sense of fluidity and movement to the music, creating a seamless transition between the different parts of the song. The intricate melodies danced across the strings, weaving a mesmerizing tapestry of sound that captivated the listener's ear. Overall, this was an amazing week for my guitar stroke recovery with exciting trials. Thank you, God.

In conclusion, my experience with practicing "Goodness of God" by Bethel Music and Jenn Johnson was both challenging and rewarding. Through dedication and passion, I was able to bring this beautiful song to life in a way that honored its message and essence. By recording three guitar parts, adding twin guitar leads, and incorporating lead fills, I was able to create a rendition that I hope did justice to the original. Thank you, God, for the gift of music and the ability to share your goodness through it.

RECOVERY WEEK 37
Exploring Jazz Blues Sounds

Speaking to one another with psalms, hymns, and songs from the Spirit. Sing and make music from your heart to the Lord.

—Ephesians 5:19

https://youtu.be/9lB3QiF_12k

This week, I decided to switch things up a bit and plunge into the world of jazz blues. I wanted to broaden myself by incorporating sliding chords and intricate scales to create a unique fusion of blues and jazz sounds. While my practice session and recording were far from perfect, with some missed notes and occasional hiccups, I firmly believe that pushing boundaries and trying new things is essential for growth as a musician.

Playing jazz blues requires a different approach compared to traditional blues music. It involves more complex chord progressions and an understanding of jazz scales and improvisation techniques. For this practice session, I focused on the G7, C9, and D9 chords to create a rich and engaging sound palette.

To capture the essence of jazz blues, I incorporated sliding chords into my playing. Sliding into chords adds a subtle yet impactful touch to the music, creating a smooth transition between notes and enhancing the overall dynamics of the piece. It's a technique that requires precision and control, but the payoff in terms of sound quality is well worth the effort.

In jazz blues, scales play a crucial role in adding depth and emotion to the music. I spent time experimenting with different scales to find the right balance between complexity and simplicity. By playing thought-out scales, I was able to create a sense of tension and release in my improvisation, elevating the overall mood of the piece.

Maintaining a bluesy vibe while incorporating jazz elements is a delicate balancing act. I aimed to infuse my playing with the raw emotion and soulful expressions that are characteristic of blues music, while also incorporating the sophisticated harmonies and rhythms of jazz. It's a challenging task, but one that allows for endless creativity and experimentation.

Throughout this practice session, I encountered a few hiccups and imperfections in my playing. Some notes were slightly off, and there were moments of hesitation and uncertainty. However, I firmly believe that imperfections are a natural part of the creative process. They serve as learning opportunities and reminders of the importance of perseverance and dedication in pursuing musical excellence.

In conclusion, my exploration of jazz blues in Week 37 of my guitar stroke recovery journey has been both challenging and rewarding. By stepping outside my comfort zone and trying new techniques, I have expanded my musical horizons and deepened my understanding of different genres. While the road to recovery may have its bumps and obstacles, the thrill of discovery and growth makes it all worthwhile. Thank you, God, for guiding me through this musical journey of self-discovery and exploration. Here's to many more weeks of progress, creativity, and inspiration in my recovery.

RECOVERY WEEK 38
Embracing Slow Jazzy Blues and the Path to Progress

And when Jesus entered Peter's house, he saw his mother-in-law lying sick with a fever. He touched her hand, and the fever left her, and she rose and began to serve him. That evening they brought to him many who were oppressed by demons, and he cast out the spirits with a word and healed all who were sick.

—Matthew 8:14–16

https://youtu.be/mOPI4ikz760

Thank you, God, for giving me the faith and strength to overcome the challenges of my guitar stroke recovery journey. This week marks the 38th week of relearning to play guitar after a stroke, and I am still making gains. It hasn't been easy, but I refuse to give up on my passion for music and playing the guitar.

This week, I decided to stick with the slow jazzy blues theme in my practice sessions. I have always been drawn to the smooth, soulful sounds of blues music, and I believe it can help me improve my finger placement, timing, and overall technique. Despite struggling with these aspects, I know that consistent practice will eventually lead to progress.

In my practice sessions, I focused on playing a series of guitar techniques, including double stops, one-third intervals, and smooth melodic playing. These techniques require precision and control, which are areas that I need to strengthen in my playing. It may be challenging, but I am willing to put in the effort to refine my skills to relearn to play guitar.

Despite the setbacks and frustrations faced this week, I refused to give up. I reminded myself that progress takes time and effort, and that every mistake is an opportunity to learn and grow. I will continue to practice diligently and stay committed to my recovery journey.

In summary, the recovery process has involved fluctuations, but there is a continued commitment to progress. With faith, strength, and perseverance, I know I can overcome any obstacles that come my way. Thank you for following my journey, and I hope my story inspires others to never give up on their dreams. Let's keep making progress, one chord at a time. Remember, the road to recovery may be long and challenging, but with persistence and dedication, anything is possible. Keep strumming, keep believing, and never give up on your passion for music.

RECOVERY WEEK 39
Creating a Bluesy Sound

For I will restore health to you, and your wounds I will heal," declares the Lord, "because they have called you an outcast; It is Zion for whom no one cares!

—Jeremiah 30:17

https://youtu.be/7EStI-c6p8w

Thank you, God, for so many blessings; I pray for all Stroke Warriors. In this week's recovery journey, I focused on playing an original musical idea on my guitar. I aimed to create a bluesy, smokey sound with a rock feel, working on careful finger placement on the fretboard to establish a smoother sound. To achieve this, I layered the recording with two guitars, one for rhythm and the other for lead playing.

For my Week 39 recovery, I decided to experiment with creating a bluesy sound on my guitar. With a focus on finger placement and layering different guitar tracks, I aimed to challenge myself innovatively while also working on refining my techniques.

To create a bluesy sound on the guitar, I believe it's essential to pay close attention to finger placement on the fretboard. Please spend the time to ensure that each note is played with precision and feeling, as this is key to capturing the authentic bluesy vibe. I like to experiment with different chord progressions and scales to find the right balance between smokiness and rock feel.

Here is another interesting tip, when layering guitar tracks, consider assigning different roles to each track. For example, one guitar can be used for rhythm playing to establish a solid foundation, while the other can take on the lead role for more intricate melodies and solos. Also, I experimented with panning and effects to create a sense of depth and space in my recordings.

Here is what I learned this week: the bluesy sound is a fundamental aspect of guitar playing that adds soul and emotion to music. By mastering the bluesy feel, you can infuse your guitar playing with authenticity and expressiveness. Whether you're playing a slow ballad or a high-energy rock track, integrating blues elements can elevate your sound and captivate listeners.

I am dedicated to pushing boundaries and exploring new musical ideas during my guitar stroke recovery. By focusing on creating a bluesy sound with a rock feel, this not only challenged me creatively but also honed my technical skills. Through careful finger placement and layered guitar tracks, I aimed to establish a unique and captivating sound that resonates. Whether you're a beginner or a seasoned player, experimenting with different styles and techniques can help you discover your musical voice and grow as a guitarist.

Recovery Week 40
Improvising in a Minor Key

Music is a form of expression that allows individuals to convey their praises, love, and gratitude. It can enhance moments of reflection, encourage others, or even soothe the mind and soul.

https://youtu.be/H-9iGK8c_dQ

Music is a powerful tool that can be used for worship, expression, and healing. As a guitarist, I have found that playing music not only allows me to connect with my emotions but also helps me strengthen my right hand, which was affected by a stroke. This week, I challenged myself by improvising in a minor key, playing through minor chord progressions and using the minor pentatonic scale for fill licks.

Music has always played a significant role in worship. Whether it is through hymns, contemporary worship songs, or instrumental music, we use music to express our praises, love, and gratitude to God. As I continue on my journey of stroke recovery through relearning guitar, I have found that music not only enhances my worship experience but also serves as a form of physical therapy.

In order to improve my right-hand technique, I have been experimenting with different approaches to playing the guitar. This week, I focused on improvising in a minor key, which presented its own set of challenges. By playing through minor chord progressions, I was able to familiarize myself with the unique sound and feel of the minor key.

To add depth and complexity to my improvisation, I used notes from the minor pentatonic scale as fill licks. These short melodic phrases helped me create interesting and dynamic musical ideas while also improving my technical abilities. While my improvisation was not perfect, I enjoyed the process of trying new things and pushing myself beyond my comfort zone.

During my journey of recovering from a stroke, I have developed a profound appreciation for the process of learning and evolving as a musician. Each week presents new challenges and opportunities for me to improve my playing and strengthen my right hand. By embracing new techniques and pushing myself to try new things, I am able to see progress and feel a sense of accomplishment.

In summary, music serves various purposes including worship, expression, and healing. By incorporating new techniques and challenging ourselves as musicians, we can continue to grow and improve our skills. As I continue my guitar stroke recovery journey, I am grateful for the opportunity to use music as a form of therapy and self-expression. Thank you, Jesus, for guiding me on this path of healing and growth. Amen!

RECOVERY WEEK 41
Improving Timing and Creativity

My lips will shout for joy, when I sing praises to you; my soul also, which you have redeemed.

—Psalm 71:23

https://youtu.be/gAst_LYVY38

During Week 41 I embraced a new challenge that required me to step outside of my comfort zone. I decided to focus on playing a slow, soulful rhythm in the style of G major, incorporating several bluesy fill licks. This not only tested my technical skills but also encouraged me to improvise and be more creative in my playing.

One key aspect that this week's challenge helped me with was improving my timing, especially with my right-hand picking. The slow tempo of the rhythm forced me to pay close attention to the placement of each note and to ensure that my strumming was consistent and precise. As I practiced, I could feel myself becoming more in tune with the rhythm and developing a better sense of musicality.

Beyond just focusing on technical skills, this challenge also allowed me to explore my creativity and find new ways to express myself through music. By incorporating bluesy fill licks into the rhythm, I was able to add my own personal touch to the music and experiment with different phrasing and dynamics. It was incredibly rewarding to see how these small embellishments could completely transform the feel of the music and add depth to my playing.

As I reflected on my progress at the end of the week, I couldn't help but feel grateful for the opportunity to grow and learn through the guitar stroke recovery process. Each new challenge pushes me to stretch myself and discover new aspects of my playing that I never knew existed. I am constantly amazed by the power of music to heal and inspire, and I am thankful for the chance to continue on this journey.

In conclusion, Week 41 of my recovery has been a truly enriching experience. Through focusing on timing and creativity, I have been able to take my playing to new heights and explore the depths of my musical potential. I am excited to see where this journey will take me next and look forward to the challenges and growth that lie ahead.

RECOVERY WEEK 42
Pushing Boundaries with Slow Country Music

Grace that flows like a river washing over me. Fount of heaven, love of Christ, overflow in me.

—Hannah Hobbs and Hillsong Worship

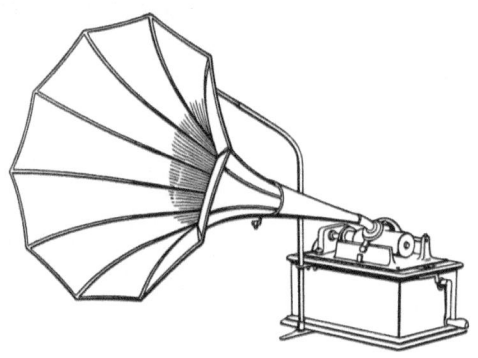

https://youtu.be/znQT7nSIi54

This week, I decided to push the boundaries of my playing by tackling a slow country music tune. The goal? To make the guitar sound like a pedal steel, using guitar voicings with double and triple unison bends and unique strumming techniques. But that wasn't all, I also added another guitar to the recording to play a country-style rhythm.

Trying to make a guitar mimic the sound of a pedal steel is no easy feat. Pedal steel guitars have a unique tone that comes from the pedals and levers that change the tension of the strings while the player is performing. To replicate this sound on a standard guitar, I had to get creative with my techniques. By experimenting with double and triple unison blends, I was able to achieve a similar twang and sustain that is characteristic of pedal steel guitar playing.

In addition to focusing on creating a pedal steel sound, I also had to pay close attention to the rhythm of the music. Country music is known for its distinctive rhythms, often featuring a strong backbeat and lively strumming patterns. By adding another guitar to play a country-style rhythm, I was able to enhance the overall feel of the song and created a more authentic country music experience.

Throughout my recovery journey, I learned the importance of experimentation and creativity in music. By pushing the boundaries of my playing and taking on new challenges, I not only improved my technical skills, but I also slowly regained some my past guitar playing. Also, this week's recovery practice expanded my musical horizons. Playing a slow country music tune may have been challenging, but it also provided me with an opportunity to grow as a musician and explore new ways of expressing myself through my guitar again.

Again, as I reflect on my experience playing a slow country music tune, I am so very proud of the progress I have made and the skills I am redeveloping. By challenging myself to make the guitar sound like a pedal steel and incorporating country-style rhythm into my playing, I have demonstrated to myself my never-give-up commitment with pushing boundaries and exploring new musical avenues. The journey may be long and challenging, but with dedication, creativity, and a passion for music, I know with the grace of God that I can continue to grow and improve as a reborn guitarist, version 2.0. As I continue on my recovery journey, I remain committed to embracing challenges, experimenting, and growing as a musician. Thank you, Jesus, for setting me free and for being my Savior and rescuer.

RECOVERY WEEK 43
A Milestone Reached!

Practice these things, immerse yourself in them, so that all
may see your progress.

—1 Timothy 4:15

In Week 43 of my guitar stroke recovery journey, I experienced a significant milestone that filled me with excitement and gratitude. Although I didn't record a video this week, I played guitar at church for the first time in over two years since my stroke. This experience marked a crucial step forward in my recovery, and I couldn't be more grateful for this achievement.

After a long hiatus, playing the guitar in a church setting was a dream come true for me. The familiar melodies, the sense of community, and the spiritual connection all came together in a beautiful moment of musical expression. As I strummed the strings and poured my heart into the music, I felt a sense of peace and joy wash over me.

In moments like these, I am reminded of the power of faith and perseverance. With a heart full of gratitude, I thanked Jesus for guiding me through this challenging journey of recovery. As the verse from Matthew 9:35 reminds us, Jesus went about healing every sickness and disease among the people. In my own journey, I have experienced the healing power of music and faith, and for that, I am truly thankful.

Looking back on the past weeks of recovery, I can see how far I have come. Each strum of the guitar, each chord progression mastered, has been a step toward healing and renewal. While the road ahead may still be long and challenging, I am filled with hope and determination to continue pushing forward, one chord at a time.

In the midst of recovery, it's important to celebrate even the smallest victories. Whether it's mastering a new chord, playing a beloved song, or simply finding joy in the act of music-making, each moment of progress is worth commemorating. By acknowledging and celebrating these small victories, we can stay motivated and inspired on our journey toward full recovery.

As I reflect on my experience of playing guitar at a place of worship, I am filled with a sense of accomplishment and gratitude. Faith plays a crucial role in the recovery process, providing individuals with the strength and courage needed to navigate through difficult times. Believing in something greater than oneself can act as a guiding force, offering solace and hope during moments of despair. Personally, integrating faith into my recovery journey has enabled me to find meaning and purpose in the face of adversity. It has instilled in me a sense of resilience and optimism, motivating me to persist in my efforts toward improvement.

Again, playing at church has filled me with gratitude and renewed determination to keep moving forward. With each strum of the strings, I am reminded of the healing power of music and the guiding hand of Jesus. Thank you for being a part of this incredible journey with me.

RECOVERY WEEK 44
Spirituality Plays a Role in Your Recovery Process?

Heal me, O Lord, and I shall be healed; save me, and I shall be saved; for thou art my praise.

—Jeremiah 17:14

I did not document my practice this week with a video journal, but I want to recount the challenges and victories of my journey. Through perseverance and faith, I have been able to embrace hope and life after a stroke.

Recovering from a stroke is not an easy feat. It comes with physical pain, emotional turmoil, and spiritual longing. As a Stroke Warrior, I navigate through these challenges with determination and resilience. This week, I focused on strengthening my right hand and wrist movement through practicing songs like "Hosanna," "Your Name," "More Like Jesus," and "Endless Praise." Each chord strummed is a testament to my dedication to regaining my musical abilities. It was not easy, but with the support of my loved ones and my deep faith, I found the strength to push through the pain and limitations. I embraced each small improvement as a victory and sought solace in music, a powerful healer for the mind and soul.

My relationship with God has been a guiding light throughout my journey. I found comfort in prayer and sought peace in worship. Through music, I connected with a higher power, allowing me to find healing, not just physically but also spiritually.

Returning to the church stage to play guitar filled me with a sense of joy and fulfillment. It was a reminder of the person I was before the stroke and a glimpse of the person I am becoming through perseverance and faith. Music has the power to heal, and through my presentations, I hope I am not only recovering but also inspiring others on their own journeys.

As I reflect on my guitar stroke recovery journey, I am grateful for the progress I have made and the lessons I have learned. Through dedication, faith, and the support of my community, I have found hope and life after a life-altering event. The path to recovery may be challenging, but with a positive mindset, anything is possible. Amen to that!

Recovery Week 45
Guitar Recovery Challenges

The Lord is my rock and my fortress and my deliverer, my God, my rock, in whom I take refuge, my shield, and the horn of my salvation, my stronghold.

—Psalm 18:2–6

As a guitarist, every week brings new challenges and triumphs. This week, I had the privilege of playing in church on Sunday morning after a week of dedicated practice. It was a time of growth and learning, and I am so grateful for the opportunity to share my music in worship. Join me on this journey of guitar recovery as I reflect on my experiences and the songs I prepared to play.

This week presented me with some unique challenges in my guitar recovery journey. Specifically, I focused on strengthening my right rhythm hand to ensure smooth and consistent playing. The songs I prepared for Sunday morning Here for You, How Good Is He, Goodness of God, and Endless Praise—required precision and control. Despite the difficulties, I approached each practice session with determination and perseverance, knowing that each chord and strum brought me one step closer to achieving my musical goals.

There is something truly special about playing music in a church setting. The opportunity to use my talents to praise and worship Jesus fills my heart with joy and gratitude. As I strummed my guitar on Sunday morning, I felt a sense of connection and peace that can only come from serving God through music. The words of Nehemiah 9:5 rang true in my heart: "Blessed be your glorious name, and may it be exalted above all blessing and praise." It was a reminder of the power of music to uplift and inspire, and I am so thankful for the chance to share my gift with others.

While I was fully immersed in my practice sessions this week, I unfortunately did not make a video vlog of my progress. Although I usually enjoy documenting my journey and sharing it with others, I decided to focus solely on honing my skills and preparing for Sunday morning. However, I will make sure to capture my next practice sessions to give you a glimpse into my guitar recovery process.

Playing in church on Sunday morning was a true blessing, and I am thankful for the opportunity to share my music with others. As I continue on this musical journey, I am reminded of the power of perseverance and dedication in achieving my goals. Thank you for joining me on this adventure and may we all continue to praise and worship through the gift of music.

Recovery Week 46
Playing Guitar in Church and Overcoming Challenges

For I consider that the sufferings of this present time are not worth comparing with the glory that is to be revealed to us.

—Romans 8:18

I had another amazing opportunity to play guitar in church. It was a challenging week of practicing, making mistakes, and pushing through, but ultimately, it was a rewarding experience. Here is a breakdown of the songs I prepared and played live in church this morning.

I did not make a video journal of my practice this week, but the hours spent relearning to play guitar were crucial in preparing for today's worship. I focused on four songs: "You Alone Are God" in Bb, "How Good Is He" in Bb, "Hope Has Come (Behold Him)" in G, and "To Our God" in G.

Choosing the right songs for a church service is important, as they need to resonate with the congregation and create an atmosphere of worship. Each song presented its own set of challenges, from chord changes to complicated strumming patterns. However, I was determined to overcome these obstacles and deliver a meaningful worship experience for all.

This morning, on the church stage with my guitar in hand, I felt a mix of nerves and excitement. The familiar melodies of the songs filled the church, and I could feel the presence of God as I played. Despite a few mistakes and moments of fatigue in my pick hand, I was able to push through and deliver a heartfelt performance.

Isaiah 41:10, "So do not fear, for I am with you; do not be dismayed, for I am your God. I will strengthen you and help you; I will uphold you with my righteous right hand," is a powerful reminder of God's faithfulness and strength, which carried me through the challenges of playing guitar in church.

In conclusion, playing guitar in church this morning was a humbling and uplifting experience. Despite the mistakes and challenges, I faced during practice, I was able to push through with determination and faith. Music has a way of connecting people to God and each other, and I am grateful for the opportunity to share my gift with the congregation. Hallelu - jah, Hallelu - jah, Hallelu - jah!

Recovery Week 47
Peace of God

May mercy, peace, and love be multiplied to you.

—Jude 1:2

Are you feeling challenged in your journey toward experiencing God's peace? It takes a mixture of humility and courage to truly let go and seek beyond the mere abilities of our own understanding. This week, as I tackled learning new songs for church, I found that the process of working on my picking and strumming right-hand technique was the best therapy I could have asked for.

This week, I didn't make a video journal of my practice sessions. Instead, I decided to focus more on learning to play the guitar again. As I delved into the melodies of the songs I played on Sunday. This Is Amazing Grace," "Peace On Earth," "Hope Has Come (Behold Him)," and "Your Love, Oh Lord"—I could feel a sense of tranquility washing over me. It's amazing how music has the power to heal and uplift the soul.

Music has a way of touching our hearts and minds in ways that words alone cannot. When we immerse ourselves in playing an instrument, we tap into a realm of creativity and expression that goes beyond mere words. This week, as I focused on my right arm and hand movements while playing the guitar, I could sense my brain making new connections. It's truly remarkable how music can help us heal and grow in ways we never thought possible.

In times of uncertainty and strife, it's easy to feel overwhelmed and anxious. However, as I meditated on the lyrics of the songs I played this week, I was reminded of the verse from Philippians 4:7, "And the peace of God, which surpasses all understanding, will guard your hearts and your minds in Christ Jesus." Music has a way of bringing us closer to God and helping us experience His peace in a deeper way.

As I reflect on this week's guitar journey, I am grateful for the opportunity to experience God's peace through music. The process of learning new songs for church has not only challenged my musical abilities but has also brought a sense of healing and wholeness to my soul. I am reminded that with God's peace, anything is possible. Thank you, Jesus, for this peace that surpasses all understanding.

RECOVERY WEEK 48
Finding Joy in the Journey

You will show me the path of life; In Your presence is fullness of joy; At Your right hand are pleasures forevermore.

—Psalm 16:11

As I sat down to practice, I realized that joy and happiness are not the same thing. While happiness can be self-generated, joy is a deep-seated feeling that comes from the Holy Spirit being active in your life.

One of the challenges I faced this week was learning to play songs that required me to use both my guitar pick and fingers simultaneously. As any musician knows, practicing a song in the comfort of your own home is quite different than performing it live in front of an audience. Despite the difficulty, I persevered and was able to play these songs with the help of the Holy Spirit.

Throughout the week, I found myself praying for the ability to master the picking technique required for these songs. As I played in church today, I realized that the joy I felt was not something I could manufacture on my own. It was a gift from the Holy Spirit, guiding me through the music and filling me with a sense of peace and contentment.

As I revisit Galatians 5:22–23, reminding me that the fruit of the Spirit includes love, joy, peace, patience, kindness, goodness, faithfulness, gentleness, and self-control, I felt a renewed sense of hope and faith in my journey toward recovery.

While I did not document my practice sessions through video this week, I focused on reconnecting with the joy of playing guitar. Each strum of the strings and every chord change brought me closer to the music and allowed me to express myself in ways words cannot capture. It was a reminder that joy is not found in perfection but in the journey of growth and learning.

In conclusion, this week's guitar stroke recovery practice was a testament to the power of faith and the presence of the Holy Spirit in my life. Through challenges and triumphs, I have learned to trust in the process and find joy in the music. As I continue on this journey, I am grateful for the lessons learned and the joy experienced along the way.

RECOVERY WEEK 49
Finding Joy in Music and Mistakes

He rules the world with truth and grace, and makes the nations prove the glories of His righteousness, And wonders of His love...

—"Joy to the World" *by* Isaac Watts

https://youtu.be/hmza77-H9CM

Are you a musician who has faced setbacks due to health issues? Recovery can be a challenging journey, but finding joy in music can make all the difference. In Week 49 of my guitar stroke recovery, I had the opportunity to play at church and experience the beauty of making music, despite the challenges I faced.

Playing in church today was a reminder that music is a gift that transcends perfection. Even though my pick hand was not collaborating with my left hand as well as I would have liked, I felt blessed to be able to share my love for music with others. Making mistakes is a natural part of the learning process, and it's important to remember mistakes do not define our worth as musicians.

The songs we played at church today were a beautiful reminder of the power of music to uplift and inspire. "Come Thou Fount, Come Thou King," "Great Is Thy Faithfulness," and "Hope Has Come (Behold Him)" filled the sanctuary with melodies of praise and worship. Each chord and lyric carried a message of hope and love, reminding us of the beauty of God's grace.

In addition to playing at church, I have been working on a new "TuneZ" that includes interesting rhythmic fills that can be played between chords. These guitar fills add depth and complexity to my playing, allowing me to experiment with different textures and tones. They can also be used as guitar fills when playing lead, adding a dynamic element to my music and to yours as well.

As I played and sang in church, I was reminded of the words from Luke 2:13–14: "Glory to God in the highest heaven, and on earth peace to those on whom His favor rests." This message of peace and glory resonated with me, filling my heart with gratitude and joy. Music has a way of touching our souls and connecting us to something greater than ourselves.

In Week 49 of my guitar stroke recovery, I learned the importance of finding joy in music, even in the midst of challenges and imperfections. Playing at church reminded me of the power of music to inspire, uplift, and connect us to something greater than ourselves. Despite the mistakes I made, I felt grateful for the opportunity to share my love for music with others. As I continue on my recovery journey, I am committed to embracing the beauty of music and finding joy in every note I play.

Recovery Week 50
Merry Christmas!

Jesus sits on His throne, next to God, and intervenes on your behalf. Pray to Jesus for your help in all you need.

—Matthew 7:7–11

https://youtu.be/aMQCVkgdY2U

As Christmas approaches, I find myself reflecting on the past year and all the blessings that have come my way. This is my second Christmas since I suffered a stroke, and I am filled with gratitude for the progress I have made in my recovery journey.

One of the key aspects that have kept me going during this challenging time is my faith in God. I believe that He has shown me a new path to start playing guitar again, and this ever-learning journey is still moving forward. I am truly thankful for all the miracles and blessings that have come my way.

Recovering from a stroke has been the hardest thing I have ever had to do, both physically and mentally. The journey has been filled with ups and downs, victories and setbacks, but through it all, I have felt the hand of God guiding me and giving me strength.

Along the way, I have had the privilege of meeting other stroke survivors who have shared their own stories of triumph and perseverance. Their courage and determination have inspired me to keep pushing forward, no matter how difficult the road may seem.

As we celebrate the birth of Jesus this Christmas, I encourage you to take a moment to reflect on the incredible sacrifice He made for us. Jesus left the glory of heaven to be born in a humble manger, to live a life of service and sacrifice, and ultimately to die for our sins. His love knows no bounds, and I am forever grateful for the gift of salvation that He offers.

Music has played a significant role in my recovery journey, particularly as I have been relearning how to play the guitar. I have found that immersing myself in music has brought me joy, peace, and a sense of accomplishment. This week, I have been working on a new TuneZ, a blend of major and minor pentatonic riffs, with a touch of a blues-style lead. It may not be perfect, but I enjoyed every moment of recording it. I have even ventured into playing the bass guitar, exploring new sounds and techniques.

As I continue my recovery journey, I find comfort in knowing that Jesus sits on His throne, interceding on my behalf. I put my trust in Him, praying for strength, healing, and guidance in all that I do. His love and grace sustain me, and I am confident that with His help, I can overcome any obstacles that come my way.

This Christmas, as we celebrate the birth of Jesus, let us remember the true meaning of the season. Let us give thanks for all the blessings in our lives, for the gift of recovery, and for the hope that Jesus offers. May His love and grace fill your heart with peace and joy this holiday season. Amen!

RECOVERY WEEK 51
Embracing New Beginnings

*Therefore, prepare your minds for action, keep sober in spirit,
fix your hope completely on the grace to be brought to you at
the revelation of Jesus Christ.*

—Peter 1:13

https://youtu.be/RuE7J6CyeNQ

As we welcome the New Year with open arms, it is a time for reflection, gratitude, and setting new goals. For those on a journey of recovery, like me, the start of a new year presents an opportunity to renew our commitment to our health and well-being. This week, I had the pleasure of playing my guitar in church and it was a truly uplifting experience.

Playing the guitar has always been a source of joy and comfort for me and being able to share that gift with others is a true blessing. In church, we played some beautiful songs including "Blessed Assurance," "Way Maker," "Build My Life," and "You Are My Strength." Each note resonated with meaning and brought us closer to God through music.

As I continue my journey toward full recovery from a stroke, I am constantly working on improving my fine motor skills. This week, I focused on gaining more motion in my affected right hand and practicing useful triads that can be applied in various playing styles. While it may not be perfect, playing the guitar and improving my skills bring me great joy and a sense of accomplishment.

The New Year symbolizes a fresh start, a blank canvas waiting to be painted. It is a time to prepare our minds and hearts for the journey ahead, keeping our spirits sober and our hope fixed on the grace that awaits us. As we step into the unknown of the new year, we are reminded of our ability to reshape our lives and make positive changes.

Peter 1:13 reminds us to prepare our minds for action and fix our hope on the grace brought to us through Jesus Christ. As I navigate the ups and downs of recovery, I am constantly reminded of the importance of faith and perseverance. My guitar playing serves as a form of worship and connection to the divine, allowing me to express my gratitude and praise through music.

In conclusion, the New Year offers us a chance to start anew, to set intentions, and to embrace the journey ahead. For those on a path of recovery, like me, it is a time to renew our commitment to healing and growth. As we move forward with faith and determination, may we all find joy, peace, and fulfillment in the days to come. Always remember that the New Year is a time for growth, reflection, and gratitude. May your journey toward recovery be filled with hope, strength, and the sweet sound of music. Happy New Year!

RECOVERY WEEK 52
Finding Joy in Playing Guitar in Church

May the God of hope fill you with all joy and peace in believing, so that by the power of the Holy Spirit you may abound in hope.

—Romans 15:13

This week, I reached a key point in my guitar stroke recovery. I'm grateful to play again and reflect on my progress. Playing worship songs in church reminded me of the blessing of praising God through music.

God has truly blessed me this week as I continue to relearn how to play the guitar. The joy and fulfillment I experience when strumming the strings and worshipping through music are beyond compare. Each chord, each note, is a testament to God's grace and healing power in my life. Through the songs I play, I offer my praise, my thanksgiving, my love to Him who has held me through it all.

Here is a list of the beautiful songs we played:

1.   "Here I Am to Worship" (E)

2.   "Speak Jesus" (E)

3.   "More Like Jesus" (G)

4.   "Holy and Anointed One" (G)

"Praise Him with trumpet sound; praise Him with lute and harp! Praise Him with tambourine and dance; praise Him with strings and pipe! Praise Him with sounding cymbals; praise Him with loud clashing cymbals!" (Psalm 150:3–5)

The beauty of music lies in its ability to transcend language and touch the deepest parts of our souls. As I strum my guitar in church, I feel a connection with God that words alone cannot express. The melodies, the harmonies, the rhythms all come together to form a symphony of praise and worship that elevates my spirit and brings me closer to the divine.

Playing guitar in church holds a special place in my heart, as it allows me to express my faith, my gratitude, and my love for God through music. It is a form of worship, a way for me to connect with God on a deeper level and to share the gift of music with others. Each strum of the guitar strings is a prayer, each note is a hymn of praise, and each song is a declaration of my faith in Him who gives me strength and healing.

In conclusion, playing guitar in church is not just a musical performance, but a spiritual experience that fills my heart with joy and gratitude. It is a reminder of God's presence in my life and a testament to His faithfulness and grace. As I continue on this journey of guitar stroke recovery, I am filled with hope and thanksgiving for the gift of music and the ability to worship Him in spirit and in truth. Remember to play with all your heart and soul, for when we worship God, we worship Him with all that we are.

RECOVERY WEEK 53
Praise and Progress

*Jesus went throughout Galilee, teaching in their synagogues,
proclaiming the good news of the kingdom, and healing
every disease and sickness among the people.*

—Matthew 4:23

https://youtu.be/vxBn5JCNOj4

Reflecting on my guitar journey, I'm grateful for the progress each week. Playing in church has been healing and rewarding. In Week 53, we played challenging songs that helped me improve my guitar skills. Here are the highlights of this week's musical journey.

During this past week's church service, we played a beautiful selection of songs that allowed me to showcase my progress on the guitar. The songs included "Come Thou Fount, Come Thou King" in the key of C, "Yet Not I, but Through Christ in Me" in the key of C, "I Speak Jesus" in the key of E, and "Savior King" in the key of E. Each song presented a unique challenge and opportunity for me to grow in my guitar playing abilities.

One of the exciting developments in Week 53 was the addition of a new video TuneZ in the key of B. In this video, I focused on incorporating soulful blues lead phrases that were inspired by the major and minor pentatonic scales. While the performance may not have been perfect, it provided a great workout for my right picking hand, which has been affected by the stroke. Despite the challenges, I am grateful for the opportunity to continue to hone my skills and share my music with others.

As I reflect on my journey of recovery, I am reminded of the words of Matthew 4:23, which speak of Jesus's healing ministry in Galilee. Just as Jesus healed every disease and sickness among the people, I am filled with hope and faith that I too can experience healing and restoration through my music. The power of music to heal and uplift the spirit is truly a blessing that I am grateful to experience each week.

Praise God for all the recovery I have received so far. Each week brings new challenges and opportunities for growth, and I am thankful for the progress I have made on this musical journey. The inspiration of scripture, and the healing power of music, I am encouraged to continue on this path of recovery. Thank you for joining me on this journey of praise and progress.

RECOVERY WEEK 54
Overcoming Challenges and Building Resilience

Let your light shine before men, that they may see your good works, and glorify your Father which is in heaven.

—Matthew 5:16

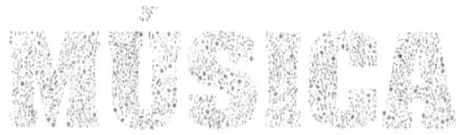

https://youtu.be/xdqvpxQwnrY

Reflecting on my stroke recovery and guitar relearning journey, I realize the strength of the human spirit. Weekly challenges for my right side persist, but I am determined to overcome them. This week, attending church online, I was inspired by the youth in the praise band, reminding me that dedication and practice make anything possible.

One of the biggest challenges I have encountered in my guitar stroke recovery is adapting to the changes in my right-side picking hand. Simple tasks like strumming and picking that used to come naturally now require a significant amount of focus and practice. However, I have come to embrace these challenges as opportunities for growth. By facing each obstacle head-on and working diligently to overcome them, I am building resilience and strength both physically and mentally.

Navigating through the struggles of stroke recovery has taught me valuable lessons about perseverance and determination. Every mistake or setback I encounter serves as a steppingstone toward improvement. By embracing the learning process and not being afraid to make mistakes, I am able to grow and develop my skills as a guitarist. As the saying goes, what doesn't kill you makes you stronger.

One of the key aspects of stroke recovery is learning from mistakes and using them to your advantage. Each time I face a challenge or make a mistake while practicing, I take the opportunity to reflect on what went wrong and how I can improve. By analyzing my mistakes and making adjustments, I am able to progress and become a better musician. It is through these setbacks that I am able to truly appreciate the journey of recovery and the strength that comes from overcoming obstacles.

The verse from Isaiah 41:10, "So do not fear, for I am with you; do not be dismayed, for I am your God," serves as a source of inspiration and comfort during my guitar stroke recovery journey. I have found that my faith keeps me motivated. As I continue to face challenges and navigate through struggles, I hold onto the belief that I am not alone in this journey and that there is strength in overcoming obstacles.

In conclusion, my guitar stroke recovery has involved challenges, struggles, and growth. By facing each obstacle with determination and resilience, I am able to make progress and continue to pursue my passion for music. As I navigate through the ups and downs of recovery, I am reminded of the power of faith, perseverance, and the strength that comes from overcoming obstacles. With each strum of the guitar, I am one step closer to reclaiming my skills and embracing the journey ahead. Amen.

RECOVERY WEEK 55
A Wonderful Day at Church

I hope to come to you soon, but I am writing these things to you so that, if I delay, you may know how one ought to behave in the household of God, which is the church of the living God, a pillar and buttress of the truth.

—Timothy 3:14–15

I am sorry I did not make a video journal of my practice this week. What a wonderful day at church. I played some songs with huge pick-hand challenges. Even though I could not use a speedy, smooth pick hand, I used some new alternative methods to make it work, Amen! Here are the songs we played this morning: "Just as I Am" (A), "To Our God" (G), "Only King Forever" (Bb), and "It Is Well" by Austin Stone (Bb).

In Week 55 of my recovery process, I faced some significant challenges with my pick hand while playing at church. Despite the limitations I encountered, I refused to be discouraged and instead embraced the opportunity to explore new techniques and approaches to overcome these obstacles.

One of the key lessons I learned during this recovery week was the importance of adaptability and creativity in the face of adversity. Instead of dwelling on what I couldn't do with my pick hand, I focused on finding alternative methods to achieve the desired outcome. By experimenting with different picking styles and grips, I was able to make the songs work in a way that felt authentic and fulfilling.

As a musician, I draw inspiration and strength from my faith, using music as a powerful tool for praise and worship. Again, the songs we played at church, including "Just as I Am," "To Our God," "Only King Forever," and "It Is Well," serve as powerful reminders of the divine presence in our lives. Through music, we can connect with something greater than ourselves and find solace and comfort in times of challenge and hardship.

In moments of struggle and doubt, it is essential to remember that we do not have to face our battles alone. The verse from Psalm 121:1–2 reminds us to lift our eyes to the mountains and seek help from the Lord, the Maker of Heaven and Earth. By reaching out for assistance, whether from a musical mentor, a supportive community, or through prayer and reflection, we can find the strength and guidance needed to overcome barriers and continue moving forward on our journey of recovery.

As I reflect on my experience at church during Week 55, I am filled with gratitude for the opportunity to play music, despite the challenges I faced with my pick hand. By embracing creativity, faith, and a willingness to seek help when needed, I was able to overcome obstacles and find joy in the music we shared. By maintaining a positive attitude, I am confident I will continue to make progress on my path to recovery and inspire others to do the same.

RECOVERY WEEK 56
Reflecting on My Progress

*As you come to him, a living stone rejected by men but in
the sight of God chosen and precious, you yourselves, like
living stones, are being built up as a spiritual house, to be a
holy priesthood, to offer spiritual sacrifices acceptable to God
through Jesus Christ.*

—1 Peter 2:4–5

I didn't make a video journal of my practice this week due to extra PT
and OT. Nonetheless, as I played guitar in church today, I noticed an
improvement in my skills.

This morning, as I strummed the chords and played along with the worship band, I felt more confident and in control of my playing. I was able
to hit the right notes at the right time, and my fingers seemed to move
more smoothly across the strings. It was a small victory, but it was important to me.

After the service, as I listened to our pastor deliver a brilliant message, I
found myself contemplating the role of music in worship. I wondered,
does a guy with a guitar really improve church worship? It's a question
that has been debated for years, especially among the older members of
the congregation. While guitars, choirs, pianos, and pipe organs can enhance the worship experience, they are not the essence of worship itself.

True worship goes beyond the music; it is about encountering and glorifying God. As Scripture says, worship is for the greater glory of God, and our focus should always be on Him, not on the instruments we use. As I continue on my journey of recovery and rehabilitation, playing the guitar has become both physical therapy and a spiritual practice for me. It allows me to express myself creatively and connect with something greater than myself. Each week, I strive to improve my skills and bring joy to those around me through my music.

In conclusion, while guitars can play a valuable role in church worship, the true essence of worship lies in our hearts and our intentions. As I reflect on my progress in Week 56 of my recovery journey, I am grateful for the opportunity to use my music to glorify God and inspire others. Each strum of the guitar brings me one step closer to healing, both physically and spiritually. Remember, it's not about the instrument but the heart behind the music that truly matters in worship. Let the music flow from your soul and let it be a source of healing and comfort for yourself and others. Embrace the journey of recovery and let the power of music guide you toward strength and inspiration.

RECOVERY WEEK 57
Overcoming Post-Stroke Symptoms and Finding Strength

What then, brothers? When you come together, each one has a hymn, a lesson, a revelation, a tongue, or an interpretation. Let all things be done for building up.

—1 Corinthians 14:26

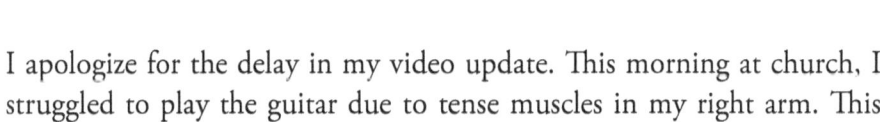

I apologize for the delay in my video update. This morning at church, I struggled to play the guitar due to tense muscles in my right arm. This stiffness is a symptom of my post-stroke spasticity.

After experiencing a stroke, it is common for muscles to stiffen up and become tight, leading to spasticity. Spasticity is related to muscle tone and can make simple movements, like playing the guitar, challenging. In my case, the involuntary contractions in my muscles make it difficult to control my movements and play with precision.

To manage spasticity and improve muscle flexibility, regular stretching with a wide range of motion is essential. Before I play the guitar, I need to make sure to include stretching exercises in my warm-up routine. By keeping my muscles limber and relaxed, I can prevent the stiffness and tension that affect my performance.

During moments of frustration and difficulty, I often turn to Scripture for guidance and strength. As 2 Timothy 3:16 reminds me, all Scripture is inspired by God and offers valuable teachings for correction and training. Additionally, Isaiah 41:10 provides reassurance that God is with me, offering strength and support through challenging times. These verses serve as a source of comfort and encouragement as I navigate through the ups and downs of my recovery journey.

Throughout my Guitar Stroke Recovery Week 57, I have come to realize the importance of patience, persistence, and self-care. By understanding the effects of post-stroke symptoms like spasticity and taking proactive steps to address them, I can work toward improving my guitar playing skills and overall well-being. As I continue to learn and grow from these experiences, I am grateful for the support and encouragement of those around me. Together, we can overcome obstacles and achieve our goals one strum at a time. Remember to take care of yourself and seek support when needed. Your recovery journey is unique, but you are never alone in facing its challenges. Keep strumming and stay strong!

RECOVERY WEEK 58
A Glorious Morning to Play Guitar in Church

Let us therefore come boldly unto the throne of grace, that we may obtain mercy and find grace to help in time of need.

—Hebrews 4:16

https://youtu.be/CAKG3D_pHEk

I found myself facing a glorious morning as I prepared to play guitar in church. Even though I am relearning to play the guitar, I remained dedicated and hung in there with the best of them. Despite making a few mistakes along the way, I embraced them as opportunities to learn and improve. Through it all, I am grateful for God's grace, even at times when I feel undeserving.

As I navigated through the songs for church, my right hand, affected by stroke, presented its own set of challenges. However, I persevered and focused on getting more movement and control. Each strum and chord change felt like a small victory, reminding me of the progress I have made in my recovery journey.

This week, I dedicated myself to practice, honing my skills and familiarizing myself with the songs for the church service. Despite the setbacks caused by my stroke, I remained determined to push myself and improve my guitar playing abilities. Every strum, every note, and every chord change were a step closer to my goal of fully recovering and playing with confidence once again.

With each practice session, I found myself growing stronger both physically and mentally. The challenges posed by my stroke did not deter me but rather fueled my determination to overcome them. I embraced imperfections and mistakes as part of the learning process, knowing that every setback was an opportunity to grow and become a better musician.

As I reflect on my journey, I am filled with gratitude for the progress I have made and the support I have received along the way. Despite the hurdles I have faced, I have remained resilient and focused on my goal of regaining my guitar playing abilities. The setbacks only served to strengthen my resolve and deepen my appreciation for the gift of music. Trust in God!

Week 58 of my guitar stroke recovery journey was a reminder of the power of perseverance and determination. Despite the challenges and setbacks, I remained dedicated to my goal of relearning to play the guitar and honing my skills. Through practice, patience, and a positive mindset, I am certain I will continue to make progress and eventually return to playing with confidence and joy.

RECOVERY WEEK 59
A Curious Musical Journey

The beginning of wisdom is this: Get wisdom. Though it cost all you have, get understanding.

—Proverbs 4:7

God has blessed me so much this week with relearning to play guitar, and I am forever grateful. This week's journey of practicing guitar and preparing for church was truly a unique and challenging experience. As I reflect on the events of the past week, I can't help but share the curious challenges I faced and the valuable lessons I learned.

Practicing guitar this week was a mix of excitement and frustration. As I tried to play the songs for church, I encountered a curious experience that left me feeling mentally fatigued. The praise band members were supportive, but I couldn't shake off the brain fog that seemed to cloud my thinking.

After consulting with my doctors and doing some research, I learned that fatigue is a common issue after experiencing a stroke. This physical and mental exhaustion can vary from person to person but can leave you feeling drained and lacking energy. I realized the importance of taking regular breaks and listening to my body's needs.

According to the Stroke Foundation, there are some strategies that can help manage fatigue after a stroke:

1. Plan regular rest breaks throughout the day.

2. Take moments to sit in silence or practice deep breathing.

3. Break large tasks into smaller, manageable chunks.

4. Allow yourself to take short naps or lie down when needed.

Despite the challenges of the week, I was determined to play the songs for church on Sunday morning. We performed "O Come to the Altar," "The Rock Won't Move," "Firm Foundation," and "None But Jesus." The experience of playing these songs live was both humbling and gratifying, knowing that I overcame my struggles to share my music with others.

As I continue my guitar stroke recovery journey, I am grateful for the progress I have made. I hope to incorporate video clips in future posts to share my musical journey with others. While the sound mix may not be perfect yet, I am excited to continue improving and growing as a guitarist.

In conclusion, this week's guitar practice and church performance have been a valuable learning experience for me. Despite the challenges of brain fog and fatigue, I am grateful for the support of the praise band and the opportunity to share my music with others. I look forward to the continued progress in my guitar stroke recovery journey and hope to inspire others facing similar challenges. Remember, with belief in yourself and God, anything is possible.

Recovery Week 60
Finding Inspiration Through Music

My lips will shout for joy when I sing praises to you; my soul also, which you have redeemed.

—Psalm 71:23

https://youtu.be/PcjXH12nPUk

Recovering from my stroke, I found music to be a powerful healer. Playing guitar in church is an honor that brings me joy and spiritual fulfillment. Each week, I receive four songs via email and eagerly learn them, deepening my connection with God.

Music has always had a profound impact on my life, but its significance took on a whole new meaning after my stroke. I found solace in the melodies, and as I learned to play each song, I felt a sense of accomplishment and purpose. The act of strumming the guitar strings and producing beautiful music became a form of therapy for me, both physically and emotionally. The rhythm and melodies helped to rewire my brain and improve my motor skills, while the lyrics served as a source of inspiration and encouragement.

Despite my physical limitations, I refused to let my stroke define me or restrict my passion for playing the guitar. With unwavering faith in God and a determined spirit, I continued to practice and improve my skills. Each note I played was a testament to my resilience and determination to overcome adversity. I learned to adapt and find alternative ways to play, proving that with faith and perseverance, anything is possible.

To my fellow Stroke Warriors, I offer these words of encouragement: Stay strong, never give up, and do not let anyone tell you what you can or cannot do. Our journeys may be different, but our determination and courage unite us in our fight for recovery. Let us continue to inspire one another, celebrate each other's victories, and support each other through the challenges. Together, we are warriors, and together, we are unstoppable.

Through this challenging journey of recovery, I have learned to trust in God's plan and timing. He has guided me through the darkest moments and lifted me up when I felt defeated. Playing guitar in church has become a way for me to connect with God on a deeper level, expressing my gratitude and praise through music. As I play each song to the best of my ability, I am reminded of God's grace and endless love for me.

In conclusion, playing guitar in church on Sunday mornings has been a transformative experience for me, both physically and spiritually. It has allowed me to find healing, purpose, and inspiration in the midst of adversity. I am grateful for the opportunity to use my passion for music to glorify God and share my journey of recovery with others. As I continue to learn and grow, I am reminded that with faith, determination, and a positive mindset, anything is possible. Trust in God, stay strong, and never give up. Amen.

RECOVERY WEEK 61
A Journey Toward Healing and Inspiration

Come to me, all who are weary and burdened, and I will give you rest.

—Matthew 11:28

https://www.youtube.com/watch?v=KWBvhTrUAjs

Every small step in stroke recovery is a victory. Week 61 of my guitar recovery journey highlights progress, challenges, and inspirations. Join me in exploring determination, support, and faith amidst adversity.

One of the key factors in stroke recovery is the presence of a strong support system. Whether it's family, friends, or healthcare professionals, having people by your side to cheer you on can make all the difference. Jo Ann Glim, thank you for inviting me to your podcast. What an honor to share my stroke story and be a part of your dedication to sharing other Stroke Warriors' stories of resilience and hope. Your podcast program has become a source of inspiration for many, including Stroke Warriors and those battling traumatic brain injuries and neurodegenerative conditions.

In the midst of adversity and challenges, it's easy to feel alone and isolated. But as we navigate the twists and turns of life, we are reminded that our hearts are meant to be seen, our stories meant to be shared. In the journey of stroke recovery, every moment of progress is proof of the strength and resilience within us. The verse from Hebrews 4:16, "Let us then with confidence draw near to the throne of grace, that we may receive mercy and find grace to help in time of need," serves as a beacon of hope for Stroke Warriors on their recovery journey. By tapping into their faith and inner strength, individuals can navigate the ups and downs of stroke recovery with courage and tenacity. So let us continue to press forward, with faith as our guide and music as our healer, knowing that we are never truly alone. Every strum of the guitar, every beat of our hearts, brings us one step closer to healing and hope. Let us embrace the journey, knowing that our hearts are meant to be seen, shining bright with courage and determination.

It's often said that shared pain is half the pain, and shared joy is double the joy. When individuals come together to share their experiences, they create a sense of community and solidarity that can be incredibly empowering. The stories highlighted by Jo Ann Glim and others like her serve as a reminder that we are never alone in our struggles. Together, we can find the strength to keep moving forward, one step at a time.

Music has long been known for its therapeutic effects on the mind and body. For many stroke survivors, playing an instrument like the guitar can be a form of rehabilitation and self-expression. As I experience the progress of Week 61 unfolding, I am reminded of the healing power of music and the ways in which it can bring pleasure and comfort during difficult times.

As Week 61 of the guitar stroke recovery journey comes to a close, again I am reminded of the resilience, determination, and hope that have carried me this far. Through the support of others, the healing power of music, and the strength of faith, we all can continue to press forward, one chord at a time. Thank you, Jo Ann Glim, for shining a light on the stories of Stroke Warriors and inspiring us all to keep fighting. May we all find grace and mercy in our time of need, and may our hearts continue to be seen, shining bright with courage and resilience.

RECOVERY WEEK 62
Playing Guitar in Church Again

Be watchful, stand firm in the faith, act like men, be strong.

—1 Corinthians 16:13

https://youtu.be/vjuHfBDeFLs

After my stroke, it's been rewarding to play guitar in church again. By working on hand exercises and wrist movements, I'm retraining my brain for better mobility.

As a stroke survivor, it's crucial to keep a close eye on how your hand and wrist are moving and feeling. Damage to the brain can affect specific muscles in the body, leading to issues with hand and wrist positioning. By examining my movements and focusing on controlled exercises, I am gradually improving my dexterity and coordination.

Recovery from a stroke requires persistence, patience, and belief in oneself. By practicing controlled movements and exercises regularly, you can retrain your brain to regain lost motor skills. It's important to stay committed to your recovery journey and have faith in your ability to overcome challenges.

One of the key components of my recovery journey has been my strong relationship with God. Spending time in prayer and seeking His guidance has provided me with the strength and resilience to face the obstacles in my path. As the psalmist said, "Bless the Lord, O my soul, and forget not all His benefits."

This morning, the praise band played some beautiful songs in church that uplifted my spirit. We sang "Glorious Day," "Blessed Assurance," "Way Maker," and "Jesus Paid It All." The music filled the sanctuary with joy and praise, reminding me of the healing power of worship.

After church, I recorded a video of myself playing an easy melodic lead on the guitar. I focused on using suspended (sus) chords to create a harmonious sound without the need to think about scales. Music has been a significant aspect of my life, and I have shared a tune for your consideration.

Recovering from a stroke is a challenging journey, but with dedication, perseverance, and faith, it is possible to regain lost abilities. By focusing on hand and wrist exercises, monitoring movement, and staying connected to God through prayer, I am making progress in my recovery. Playing the guitar in church again has been a rewarding experience that reminds me of the healing power of music and faith.

RECOVERY WEEK 63
Inspiration to Never Give Up

The steadfast love of the Lord never ceases, his mercies never come to an end; they are new every morning; great is your faithfulness.

—Lamentations 3:22–23

https://youtu.be/3dsQ3i7uTvU

In Week 63 of my stroke recovery and guitar relearning, I marveled at my progress. This week's improvement feels absolutely incredible, like once again playing lead guitar in church. Moments like these fill me with awe and remind me that through God, anything is truly possible.

One of the highlights of this week was my incredibly productive practice sessions. I noticed a significant improvement in my timing when playing guitar chords and scales. This newfound sense of rhythm and precision is incredibly encouraging and motivates me to keep pushing forward. It's moments like these that remind me why I never gave up on my passion for music.

Above all, I hope my journey can serve as inspiration for others who may be facing their own challenges. Whether it's a musical setback like mine or any other obstacle in life, I want to show that perseverance and faith can lead to incredible breakthroughs. So, if you're feeling discouraged, remember that every small step forward is a victory worth celebrating.

As I look back on this week, I am filled with gratitude for the progress I have made. It's a reminder that with dedication, hard work, and a whole bunch of faith, anything is possible. So, keep strumming those chords, playing those scales, and never give up on your dreams. Who knows what miracles are waiting just around the corner?

RECOVERY WEEK 64
A Palm Sunday to Remember

They took palm branches and went out to meet him,
shouting, "Hosanna!" "Blessed is he who comes in the name
of the Lord!" "Blessed is the king of Israel!"

—John 12:13

https://youtu.be/-ZFkzVg2gzc

Week 64 of guitar stroke recovery was a remarkable milestone filled with notable achievements. The joy of playing the guitar in church on Palm Sunday, a cherished celebration for Christians worldwide, added an extra layer of excitement and meaning to the journey.

Palm Sunday marks the beginning of Holy Week, a time when Christians commemorate the events leading up to Jesus's crucifixion and resurrection. On this day, we remember Jesus's triumphant entry into Jerusalem, where he was greeted by a crowd waving palm branches and shouting "Hosanna!" The significance of this event was beautifully explained by our pastor, reminding us of the humble yet powerful nature of Jesus's arrival.

Playing guitar in church on Palm Sunday was a truly humbling experience. Despite the challenges I still face with my affected arm and hand, I was determined to give my best in honoring this special day. The praise band played inspiring songs that captured the essence of the occasion, and I had the opportunity to showcase my skills with a challenging lead solo and intricate chord voicings.

Despite the difficulties I still face with my recovery, I am grateful for the progress I have made in Week 64. With each strum of the guitar, I feel a renewed sense of hope and determination to overcome the obstacles in my path. As I continue to trust in the process and in the healing power of music, I am confident that I will reach new heights in my recovery journey.

As we wrapped up our worship session on Palm Sunday, I felt a sense of gratitude and joy in my heart. The words of Zechariah rang true in my mind: "Rejoice greatly, O daughter of Zion! Shout aloud, O daughter of Jerusalem! Behold, your king is coming to you." In that moment, I felt truly blessed to be able to share my gift of music with others and to praise the Lord through my guitar playing.

Week 64 of my guitar stroke recovery journey was truly a memorable one. Playing guitar in church on Palm Sunday was a great honor and a reminder of the healing power of music and faith. As I continue to make progress with my playing, I am filled with hope and gratitude for the journey ahead. Amen!

RECOVERY WEEK 65
Celebrating Easter and Resurrection

And God raised the Lord and will also raise us up by his power.

—1 Corinthians 6:14

https://youtu.be/FcnIhNTFalU

In Week 65 of my guitar stroke recovery, I celebrate Easter, marking Jesus Christ's resurrection three days after his crucifixion. This occasion fills me with deep reflection, immense gratitude, and a sense of renewal as I honor his ultimate sacrifice. It is a powerful reminder of hope and perseverance, inspiring me to continue my journey with faith and determination.

Easter is a time to celebrate Jesus Christ's triumph over death. His resurrection signifies the eternal life that is granted to all who believe in Him. It is a time of hope, faith, and love as we rejoice in the victory of light over darkness. Amen!

In church I had the honor playing wonderful music this morning, filling the air with joy and inspiration. However, amidst the celebration, I found myself struggling with my right hand and wrist movement. It was a reminder of the challenges I still face on this journey of recovery.

This week, my practice focused on relearning to strum with a more fluid up and down motion. It was a task that required patience and perseverance, but I know that with dedication, I will continue to improve. I plan to dedicate more time to this technique in the coming weeks, determined to conquer this obstacle.

During a recent discussion with a health provider, I was offered a unique perspective on my condition. The analogy of the brain as a freeway, with signals passing freely like cars on a highway, resonated with me. After a stroke, however, this flow is disrupted, creating a "major traffic jam" that hinders the brain's ability to communicate with the muscles. It was a simple yet powerful explanation that helped me better understand the challenges I face in my recovery. Just like a congested highway, my goal is to clear the "traffic jam" in my brain and restore the smooth flow of signals. It is a process that requires dedication, hard work, and unwavering belief in my ability to overcome. As Jimi Hendrix once sang in his iconic song "Crosstown Traffic," I am navigating through the challenges, determined to find my way back to full strength.

To my fellow Stroke Warriors, I offer words of encouragement and solidarity. Let us rise up together, fueled by the belief in the Resurrection of Jesus Christ. Just as He triumphed over death, we too can overcome the obstacles in our path. Amen!

In conclusion, the journey of guitar stroke recovery is filled with highs and lows, challenges and triumphs. As we celebrate Easter and the Resurrection, let us draw strength from the eternal message of hope and renewal. With faith, perseverance, and a steadfast spirit, we can conquer any obstacle that comes our way. Keep strumming, keep believing, and remember that we are all warriors in this journey of recovery. Amen!

RECOVERY WEEK 66
Being a Stroke Survivor and Relearning to Play Worship Lead Guitar

Let us come before him with thanksgiving, and make a joyful noise unto him with psalms.

—Psalm 95:2

https://youtu.be/EbNWP4noOjY

As a stroke survivor, relearning to play lead guitar properly can be a challenging and slow process. In my 66th week of recovery, I am determined to regain the full function of my fingers, hand, and wrist in order to continue serving my worship team effectively. With consistent practice and dedication to rehabilitation exercises, I am seeing improvements in my hand recovery, although it remains one of the slowest aspects to return after a stroke.

Hand function is often slow to return after a stroke because the hands are distal to the midline of the body, farthest from the brain and spinal cord. This distance can make it more difficult for the brain to re-establish connections with the hand muscles, leading to delays in recovery. Despite these challenges, I am committed to pushing through the frustrations and setbacks to regain full use of my hands for playing guitar.

Playing lead guitar in a worship setting requires a high level of skill and precision. It is not just about playing the notes correctly but also about expressing the emotions and message of the music through your playing. By relearning proper guitar technique, I am able to convey the worship songs with greater conviction and passion, leading the congregation in a meaningful worship experience.

While the road to recovery may be long and arduous, I am constantly reminded of the verse from Psalm 101:1, "I will sing of your love and justice; to you, LORD, I will sing praise." This serves as a constant source of inspiration and motivation to keep pushing forward, even when faced with setbacks. I am learning to embrace the growth that comes from adversity and trust in the process of healing.

As I continue in my journey of stroke recovery and relearning to play worship lead guitar, I am keeping my eyes on the future. Perhaps my experiences will lead me down a new path, such as becoming a physical therapist to help others on their own recovery journeys. With faith, determination, and a heart full of worship, I am confident I will overcome any obstacles that come my way.

In conclusion, being a stroke survivor and relearning to play worship lead guitar properly is a deeply personal and transformative journey. It requires patience, dedication, and a willingness to push beyond one's limits. Through it all, I am grateful for the opportunity to serve my congregation and lead them in worship, using my music as a vessel for God's love and grace.

RECOVERY WEEK 67
Keeping It Real

*Keep your thoughts continually fixed on all that is authentic
and real, honorable and admirable, beautiful and respectful,
pure and holy, merciful and kind.*

—Philippians 4:8–9

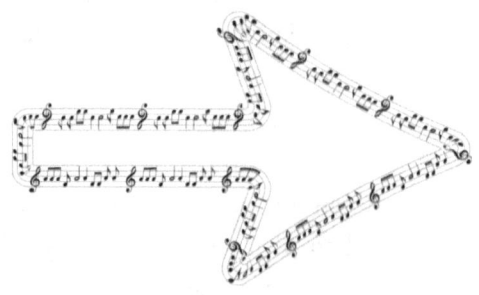

https://youtu.be/zCOLcDf4UAI

Playing guitar in church on Sunday is a truly exhilarating experience, filled with both mental and physical challenges that make the journey incredibly rewarding. It's about overcoming negativity, cultivating understanding, and embodying compassion. Although it can be tough, the unwavering commitment to perfecting guitar skills fuels a deep sense of purpose and joy.

I recently came across an article titled "LSU Rehabilitating Stroke Patients Through Adaptive Guitar," which discussed the potential benefits of music in improving motor function and altering brain function in healthy individuals. Playing guitar, in particular, requires coordination of both arms, making it an ideal activity for stroke survivors. Can music-based approaches enhance clinical movement rehabilitation outcomes for stroke survivors? According to the article, the answer is a resounding yes.

The research mentioned provides hope for all of us Stroke Warriors. As Jeremiah 17:14 says, "Heal me, O Lord, and I shall be healed; save me, and I shall be saved, for you are my praise."

I made a promise to myself when starting these guitar recovery posts that I would not compromise my thoughts or ideas. It's important to stay true to yourself and your journey, no matter what challenges may come your way. Each step forward, no matter how small, is a victory worth celebrating. As I navigate through Week 67 of my guitar stroke recovery, I am reminded of the importance of perseverance and dedication. Each strum of the guitar serves as a reminder of how far I have come and how much further I have yet to go. It's a journey filled with ups and downs, but ultimately, it is a journey of hope and healing.

Recovering from a stroke is not just a physical battle but a mental and emotional one as well. It requires vulnerability and courage to face the challenges head-on and embrace the journey ahead. It's okay to feel frustrated, scared, or overwhelmed at times. These feelings are a natural part of the healing process. By opening up about my own struggles and triumphs, I hope to inspire others who may be going through similar experiences. Together, we can find strength in vulnerability and support one another on our individual paths to recovery.

In conclusion, the path to guitar stroke recovery is filled with challenges and successes, but ultimately, it is a journey of hope and healing. By staying true to yourself, finding strength in vulnerability, and embracing the power of music, you can overcome any obstacle that comes your way. Keep strumming, keep believing, and most importantly, keep going. The best is yet to come.

RECOVERY WEEK 68
Celebrating Stroke Recovery Stories
During International Stroke Month

*"But I will restore you to health and heal your wounds,"
declares the LORD, "because you are called an outcast, Zion
for whom no one cares."*

—Jeremiah 30:17

https://youtu.be/Yi4yCBZGLyI

As I strum my guitar strings in church this week, I am filled with gratitude for my journey to recovery after suffering a stroke. The month of May marks International Stroke Month, a time dedicated to raising awareness about stroke prevention, treatment, and supporting stroke survivors. Join me as I share insights on stroke signs and symptoms, the importance of timely treatment, and the impact strokes have on individuals and their loved ones.

It has been a long and challenging road to recovery, but here I am, standing strong and playing lead guitar in church during Guitar Stroke Recovery Week 68. Each strum of my guitar fills me with joy and reminds me of how far I have come since that fateful day when I experienced a stroke. While the journey was tough, my determination to overcome the odds has fueled me every step of the way.

The signs of a stroke are crucial to recognize, as every second counts in seeking medical help. Remember the acronym FAST—Face drooping, Arm weakness, Speech difficulty, Time to call 911. If you or someone you know shows these signs, do not hesitate to seek immediate medical attention. Strokes can happen to anyone at any age, and knowing the signs can save lives and prevent long-term disability.

I have learned, time is of the essence when it comes to strokes. Nearly two million brain cells die each minute a stroke remains untreated, emphasizing the importance of rapid access to medical treatment. Seeking help promptly can make the difference between full recovery and permanent disability. Remember, stay alert to the signs, act fast, and never underestimate the power of timely intervention.

Here are some sobering facts about strokes that underscore the urgency of raising awareness and promoting preventive measures:

1. Eighty percent of all strokes are preventable through healthy lifestyle choices.

2. Stroke is the fifth leading cause of death in the US and a major cause of severe disability.

3. One person dies from a stroke every four minutes on average.

4. Over 795,000 people experience strokes annually in the US.

5. Strokes are responsible for almost 130,000 deaths among the 800,000 Americans who die from cardiovascular disease each year.

To all the stroke survivors and their loved ones, remember to stay strong and never give up. Your resilience and determination are a powerful reminder that hope and recovery are possible. Together, let us raise awareness, support one another, and strive to prevent strokes from impacting more lives. Stay strong, stay resilient, and never lose faith in the power of healing.

In conclusion, Guitar Stroke Recovery Week 68 has been a celebration of perseverance, hope, and the unwavering spirit of stroke survivors. As I strum my guitar in church, I am reminded of the journey that has brought me to this moment of gratitude and reflection. Let us continue to support one another, raise awareness, and advocate for stroke prevention and treatment. Together, we can make a difference and inspire others to never give up in the face of adversity. Stay strong, Stroke Warriors!

RECOVERY WEEK 69
A Blessed Weekend Getaway

With man this is impossible, but with God all things are possible.

—Matthew 19:26

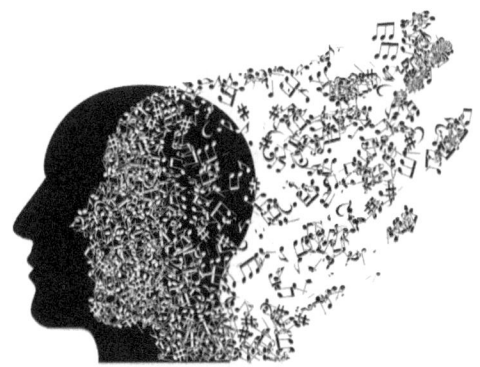

https://youtu.be/NUX63jmR1gk

In this weekly vlog, I will share my experience of a special weekend getaway to Auburn, Alabama, as part of my ongoing recovery from a stroke. Despite the challenges I have faced, I am grateful for the love and support I have received from my loved ones, as well as the strength I have found in connecting with other Stroke Warriors along the way.

What a blessed and special weekend. My querida and I traveled to Auburn for a short getaway to watch a baseball game at Samford Stadium-Hitchcock Field at Plainsman Park. It was a refreshing change from the routine of daily life and a much-needed break from the challenges of my stroke recovery journey. As we cheered on our favorite team, LSU, surrounded by the energy of the game, I felt a sense of normalcy that I had been missing for so long. The thrill of the crowd, the cheers and chants, all added to the experience and lifted my spirits in a way that words cannot describe.

I cannot help but feel overwhelmed with gratitude for the blessings in my life. From the love and mercy of God guiding me through my recovery to the loyal support of my family and friends, I am truly fortunate. Their encouragement and prayers have been a source of strength and motivation, helping me navigate through the toughest days. I am also immensely grateful for the camaraderie and support I have found among fellow Stroke Warriors. Sharing our struggles and triumphs, we have formed a fellowship. Together, we are fighting against the odds, refusing to let a stroke define us or limit our potential.

One of the highlights of the weekend was my attempt to play the guitar again, captured in a video link shared above, just a quick recap of my journey. Despite the setbacks, I am determined to keep going, never giving up on my passion. With the love and support of my querida, Lisa, I am inspired to continue my journey of recovery with unwavering determination and faith.

As I reflect on the weekend getaway to Auburn, I am reminded of the words from Isaiah 41:10, reassuring me of the strength and support I have in my journey. With every step forward, I am filled with gratitude for the blessings in my life and the continual love and support that surrounds me. The weekend was truly a reminder of the fortitude that lies within us, guiding us through the toughest of times.

In conclusion, the weekend getaway to Auburn, Alabama, was a testament to the power of faith, love, and resilience in overcoming life's challenges. As I continue on my stroke recovery journey, I am filled with gratitude for the blessings in my life and the unwavering support that surrounds me. With every step forward, I am reminded that with faith and determination, anything is possible.

RECOVERY WEEK 70
A Great Morning at Church as Mother's Day approaches!

She opens her mouth with wisdom, and the teaching of kindness is on her tongue.

—Proverbs 31:26

https://youtu.be/TakdtYjAwgw

Welcome to the Week 70 update of Charlie's Guitar Stroke Recovery! This week was bursting with excitement as I share my incredible experience playing lead guitar at church, celebrate the heartfelt significance of Mother's Day, and continue my relentless journey toward recovery. Join me in this story of unwavering strength, boundless resilience, and steadfast faith. Let's dive into this inspiring adventure together!

I enjoyed playing lead guitar at church, marking another milestone in my road to recovery. Despite the challenges I face, I continue to grow stronger with each passing week, thanks to the unwavering faith and determination that has filled my heart. As I strum the strings of life with my guitar in hand, I can't help but feel a sense of peace and joy that only music can bring.

As Mother's Day approaches, I deeply reflect on the significance of this special holiday. I fondly remember my own mother, a strong and loving woman who created a safe and nurturing home for her family. Though she is no longer with me, her memory lives on in my heart, as I celebrate the love and sacrifices of all mothers around the world.

According to Adam Augustyn, Mother's Day originated from the practice of allowing people to visit their home parishes and mothers on Laetare Sunday during the Middle Ages. In Britain, this tradition evolved into Mothering Sunday, which later inspired the modern-day celebration of Mother's Day. It serves as a reminder to cherish and honor the maternal figures in our lives, past and present.

On this special day, I encourage everyone to embrace the spirit of Mother's Day and express gratitude to the women who have shaped and nurtured your life. Whether it's a heartfelt hug, a kind gesture, or a simple phone call, let us show our appreciation for the selfless love and care that mothers provide. Remember, a mother's love knows no bounds.

In his video vlog, I captured the essence of the songs played at church, showcasing my blessed passion for music and the healing power it brings. I have to include a newfound flexibility in my wrist, a sign of progress in this recovery journey. With faith as my guide and music as my solace, I continue to navigate the challenges of stroke recovery with grace and resilience.

As I conclude this week's update, we are reminded of the importance of faith, family, and music in a journey toward healing. Through unwavering spirit and dedication, we can aspire to never lose hope and always believe in the power of resilience. Join me next week for another installment of Charlie's Guitar Stroke Recovery series, as I continue to hopefully witness the unfolding story of strength, courage, and triumph.

RECOVERY WEEK 71
A Testimony of Faith

A joyful heart is good medicine.

—Proverbs 17:22

https://youtu.be/7_toNVrxhxA

The journey has been filled with numerous challenges, but my recovery in guitar playing has seen remarkable progress. This morning, I played the guitar in church and felt deeply grateful for the chance to share the joy of music again.

Our heavenly Father works everything together for the greatest good in the long run, even if that good requires difficult times. The presence of pain and suffering does not negate the goodness of God. God's presence is what helps carry us through pain and suffering, and I have truly felt His presence guiding me through each step of my recovery journey.

This week, I am reminded of the term "heart language," which has multiple meanings, including a language that is a source of identity and a language for deep communication. Speaking from the heart includes having good intentions, being confident, and softening your throat, eyes, chest, and heart. According to the Seed Company, who accelerates the work of Bible translation by connecting local field partners around the world with investors, resources, and training, in an article titled, "What's a Heart Language, and Why Does It Matter?" "When one believes God speaks in the language of his or her heart, it makes all the difference. And it has power beyond mere words."

This week's song preparation for playing guitar at church was extremely challenging, with guitar picking and strumming rhythms. However, through the power of music, I have found healing and strength to overcome these challenges. Music has a way of reaching deep into our hearts and souls, connecting us to something greater than ourselves.

Relearning to play the guitar after a stroke has been one of the biggest challenges of my life, but it has also been a journey filled with victories and blessings. Each week, I am reminded of the progress I have made and the hurdles I have overcome, and it fills me with a sense of pride and gratitude.

In conclusion, my guitar stroke recovery journey has been a testament to the power of faith and the healing nature of music. I am grateful for this opportunity to share my story and inspire others to never give up on their dreams, no matter how challenging the road may seem. Thank you, Jesus, for guiding me through this journey and allowing me to once again share my music with the world.

RECOVERY WEEK 72
A Reflection

After they prayed, the place where they were meeting was shaken. And they were all filled with the Holy Spirit and spoke the word of God boldly.

—Acts 4:31

https://youtu.be/MjKw9HzUt4s

As I strummed the chords on my guitar during the church service, I couldn't help but be reminded of the encouraging words I had read recently: "At my lowest, God is my hope," "At my darkest God is my light," "At my weakest God is my strength," and "At my saddest God is my comforter." These words resonate with me deeply, as they have been my guiding light throughout this recovery process. Unfortunately, I cannot remember where I learned this or read this, but these words have provided me great inspiration.

This past weekend was a time of reflection and gratitude as we celebrated Pentecost and honored our fallen heroes on Memorial Day. Pentecost, a Christian holiday that commemorates the descent of the Holy Spirit upon the Apostles, holds a special place in my heart. It was a reminder of the power of faith and the importance of community in times of celebration and hardship.

Memorial Day, on the other hand, is an American holiday that pays tribute to the men and women who have made the ultimate sacrifice while serving in the US military. It is a time to reflect on the bravery and selflessness of our military personnel and to honor their memory.

Playing the guitar in church has always been a source of solace and joy for me, and being able to do so again after my stroke is a true testament to the power of music in healing. Music has a way of uplifting the spirit and bringing people together, and I am grateful for the opportunity to share my gift with others once again.

As I reflect on Week 72 of my guitar stroke recovery journey, I am filled with a sense of hope and gratitude. The support of my church community, the power of prayer, and the healing properties of music have all played a crucial role in my recovery. I am reminded that even in the darkest times, there is always a glimmer of light to guide us through.

In conclusion, the road to recovery may be long and challenging, but with faith, determination, and the support of loved ones, anything is possible. As I continue on this journey, I am filled with hope for the future and am grateful for the blessings in my life. Remember, even in the darkest of times, there is always a glimmer of light to guide us through. Keep strumming those chords and never lose sight of the hope that lies within.

RECOVERY WEEK 73
A Memorable Trip to Nashville

The Lord is my strength and my song, and he has become my salvation; this is my God, and I will praise him, my father's God, and I will exalt him.

—Exodus 15:2

Week 73 of my recovery was certainly one for the books, as my sweetheart Lisa and I decided to take an overnight trip to Nashville, Tennessee, and attend a show at the iconic Grand Ole Opry. Despite the challenges, we were determined to make the most of our time together and create lasting memories.

The moment we arrived in Nashville the vibrant music scene and southern hospitality immediately lifted our spirits. From exploring the local music venues to indulging in delicious southern cuisine, every moment was a reminder that life is meant to be lived to the fullest, stroke recovery or not.

One of the most rewarding aspects of my recovery journey has been the unwavering support of my loved ones, especially my dear Lisa. Throughout our time in Nashville, she remained by my side, providing encouragement and strength during moments of fatigue or uncertainty. Together, we proved that a stroke does not define our ability to enjoy life's pleasures and adventures.

With advancements in medical research, stroke survivors now have a better understanding of neuroplasticity and the brain's ability to heal and adapt over time. Week 73 served as a reminder that progress is ongoing, and setting new goals plays a crucial role in maintaining momentum and motivation throughout the recovery journey.

As I look back on the milestones I have achieved since my stroke, I am reminded of the resilience and determination that have carried me through difficult times. It is essential for stroke survivors to celebrate their progress, no matter how small, and continue to push themselves toward new challenges and aspirations.

Through prayer and faith, my sweetheart and I found solace and comfort during our trip to Nashville. The quote from 2 Corinthians 12:9, "My grace is all you need, for my power is the greatest when you are weak," resonated deeply with us, serving as a reminder that we are never alone in our struggles.

Week 73 of my guitar stroke recovery journey was a testament to the power of resilience, love, and faith. By embracing each moment with gratitude and determination, I was able to overcome challenges and create lasting memories with my sweetheart in Music City. As I continue to navigate the ups and downs of recovery, I am filled with hope and optimism for the future. Together, with the support of my loved ones and the grace of our Lord, I am confident that I will continue to make progress and live life to the fullest.

Recovery Week 74
A Testimony of Faith and Healing

Be devoted to one another in love. Honor one another above yourselves.

—Romans 12:10

https://youtu.be/QDYwhYOiJCk

What a great time in church this Sunday. Thank you, Pastor Lindsey Murphy, for a great message. Yesterday, Saturday evening, I had the honor and privilege to celebrate David and Joyce Smith's 50th golden wedding anniversary—what a fantastic evening, what an inspiration to the dedication of marriage and true love. As David and Joyce were giving their closing statements, David said something that just hit me, "Always pray for your spouse." This statement got me thinking, do I truly understand what he is trying to tell us. David, thank you for opening up my eyes. Marriage is an institution ordained by God from the very beginning. The bond in marriage is so strong and powerful. God is the only one we can turn to for help in keeping our marriages intact. For Christians, there is no more powerful weapon that we have access to than prayer. Prayer is one of the most tangible and powerful ways you can love your spouse. This is why we must constantly pray for our significant other. This truth is the same when life has sudden changes, when one spouse has a medical emergency, for example a stroke. If we have constant prayer in our marriage, we can survive these surprising life changes, Amen!

Prayer is a vital tool in any marriage. It allows couples to connect on a spiritual level, seek guidance from a higher power, and support each other through life's challenges. When one spouse is facing a health crisis, such as a stroke, prayer can provide comfort, strength, and hope. It can also help the couple navigate the uncertainties and difficulties that come with the recovery process.

I believe playing guitar in church has been a source of joy and healing for many individuals. It allows them to express their faith through music, connect with others in the congregation, and find solace in times of need. For someone recovering from a stroke, playing guitar can also provide physical and cognitive benefits. It helps improve dexterity, coordination, and concentration, while also boosting mood and reducing stress.

As someone who has experienced the effects of a stroke firsthand, I can attest to the power of music in the healing process. Playing guitar in church has not only helped me regain strength in my right hand but has also improved my cognitive function by helping with brain fog. It has been a form of therapy that has allowed me to connect with others, express myself creatively, and find hope and inspiration in the midst of adversity.

In conclusion, prayer and music can be powerful tools in the recovery process, whether it's from a health crisis like a stroke or the challenges of marriage. By incorporating these practices into our daily lives, we can find strength, support, and healing during life trials. So let us continue to pray for our spouses, seek solace in music, and trust in the power of faith to guide us through the journey of recovery and renewal.

RECOVERY WEEK 75
Thanking God for Strength and Progress

Rejoice in hope, be patient in tribulation, be constant in prayer.

—Romans 12:12

https://youtu.be/rgwroUe4OB4

This journey has been incredibly challenging, but through unwavering faith and relentless perseverance, I have made remarkable progress. It is my fervent hope that my story ignites a spark of inspiration in others who may be facing similar obstacles in their lives.

As I reflect on celebrating Father's Day in church this week, I am reminded of the importance of faith in God during challenging times. My father taught me never to give up. Dad, I miss you every day. The many stories I have read about overcoming obstacles and having unwavering faith in God after a stroke have inspired me to seek God's guidance in my own recovery journey. Instead of dwelling on the past or lamenting what I can no longer do, I am choosing to trust in God and focus on making the most of my life right now. These are the values my father has taught me.

The loss of movement on the right side of my body has not deterred my love for playing guitar, especially in church. With God's guidance, I am determined to overcome this obstacle. I have learned that God wants us to turn to Him and ask for guidance on how to navigate our challenges. By giving thanks in all circumstances, we align ourselves with God's will for our lives. Relearning to play guitar has been a difficult but rewarding journey. Despite the challenges, I recorded a new musical idea last night that showcases a cheerful guitar melody and lead lines. It was a challenging process, but the end result is a testament to God's grace and mercy. The video attached to this week captures my progress and serves as a reminder of the power of faith and tenacity in overcoming obstacles. I hope my music can bring joy and inspiration to others who may be facing their own struggles.

As I continue on my journey toward full recovery, I am grateful for the guidance of God, and the opportunity to share my story through music. Embarking on this daring journey of relearning the guitar after a stroke, I am wholeheartedly committed to entrusting myself to God's divine plan, knowing that His guidance led me to once again playing guitar in church. As I navigate this path with audacious faith and unwavering determination, I hope to inspire others to confront their own challenges with valor, faith, and a heart filled with gratitude. Each day, I am blessed to witness God's strength propelling me forward, inching closer to my cherished goal. With each note strummed, I find myself immersed in a symphony of gratitude for God's enduring love and unfaltering support throughout this awe-inspiring journey.

Recovery Week 76
Stroke Warriors Stay Strong!

A new command I give you: Love one another. As I have loved you, so you must love one another.

—John 13:34

https://youtu.be/Om0xZgmY2tg

As a member of the Stroke Warriors community, I have found happiness and strength in coming together with my fellow survivors to support each other on our journey to recovery. This week, I had a breakthrough in my rehabilitation process that I want to share with all of you—the power of music, specifically playing the guitar, in speeding up my recovery.

Music has always been a big part of my life, even before my stroke. I have always found comfort and joy in playing the guitar, and this week I decided to bring my passion for music into my rehabilitation process. I stepped up my game, started playing the guitar during my therapy sessions, and the results were incredible. Not only did it improve my motor skills and coordination, but it also lifted my spirits and gave me a sense of normalcy in the midst of my recovery journey.

One of the highlights of my recovery week was playing the guitar in church. I have been a part of the church praise band for years, even before my stroke, and being able to pick up my guitar and strum, play guitar fills, and guitar leads again with the hymns was a truly uplifting experience. Not only did it improve my playing dramatically, but it also brought a sense of peace and joy to my heart. Being surrounded by fellow Christians who have supported me throughout my recovery journey was incredibly encouraging, and I felt truly blessed to be a part of such a loving and supportive community.

Recovery from a stroke is not easy, and there are many challenges along the way. However, being a part of the Stroke Warriors community has taught me the importance of staying strong and persevering through the tough times. We may face disagreements and conflicts along the way, but it is important to remember that we are all unique individuals with our own perspectives and viewpoints. Loving one another, even when we don't see eye to eye, is something that Jesus commanded us to do, and it is a principle that I hold dear in my heart.

In conclusion, playing the guitar this week has been a truly transformative experience in my stroke recovery journey. It has not only improved my motor skills and coordination but has also been a blessing from God. Being a part of the church community has also been a source of strength and support, and I am grateful for the love and encouragement I have received from my fellow Stroke Warriors. As we continue on this journey together, let us remember to stay strong, love one another, and keep strumming those guitars for life!

Stroke Warriors, let's stay strong and keep playing on! Stroke Warrior Strong!

RECOVERY WEEK 77
Overcoming Emotional
Challenges After a Stroke

For the LORD your God is the one who goes with you to
fight for you against your enemies to give you victory.

—Deuteronomy 20:4

https://youtu.be/PK2uoFeaTdA

This Sunday marked a significant milestone in my recovery journey. The absence of the praise band members at church due to summer vacations reminded me of the progress I have made and the challenges I have overcome filling in gaps in the music. As I prepare for a trip to Maine to visit family, I am filled with a sense of determination and gratitude for how far I have come.

Again this Sunday was a bit different, as the praise band was missing band musicians due to summer vacations. While I missed their presence, I found solace in attending the service and pushing my musical abilities. So I reflect, my stroke has confined me to my home and the local area for the past couple of years as I focused on healing and recovery. However, the time has come for me to step out of my comfort zone and embrace new experiences. Planning a trip to Maine is a significant step toward reclaiming normalcy in my life, and I ask for prayers for strength and guidance.

A stroke is a sudden and shocking event that can have a profound impact on every aspect of your life. It is not uncommon to experience a range of emotions, including shock, denial, anger, grief, and guilt. Each individual's journey through emotional recovery is unique, but it is essential to acknowledge and address these feelings to prevent them from becoming overwhelming. Ignoring emotional distress can hinder physical and mental recovery, making it vital to seek support and coping mechanisms. It is crucial to recognize and express your emotions openly, as bottling them up can lead to further difficulties. Talking to loved ones or seeking professional counseling can help in processing and understanding your emotions. Surround yourself with a strong support system of family, friends, and healthcare professionals who can offer encouragement and guidance during difficult times. Participating in therapies, both physical and emotional, can aid in your overall recovery and provide a sense of purpose and progress.

To my fellow Stroke Warriors, I stand in solidarity with you as we navigate the challenges of stroke recovery. It may feel like an uphill battle at times but remember that you are not alone on this journey. Together, we can overcome emotional hurdles and emerge stronger and more resilient. Let us continue to support each other and trust in our ability to conquer adversity. Your perseverance and determination are an inspiration to us all, and I believe that with faith and resilience, victory is within reach. Amen.

In conclusion, overcoming emotional challenges after a stroke is a crucial part of the recovery process. By acknowledging and addressing your feelings, seeking support, and actively engaging in therapy, you can pave the way for a more fulfilling and successful recovery journey. Remember that you are not alone in this battle, and with determination and faith, you can conquer any obstacle in your path. Stay strong, stay positive, and never give up. You are a Stroke Warrior, and victory is yours to claim.

RECOVERY WEEK 78
Overcoming Challenges and Staying Strong

Those who trust in the LORD will renew their strength; they will soar on wings like eagles; they will run and not grow weary; they will walk and not faint.

—Isaiah 40:31

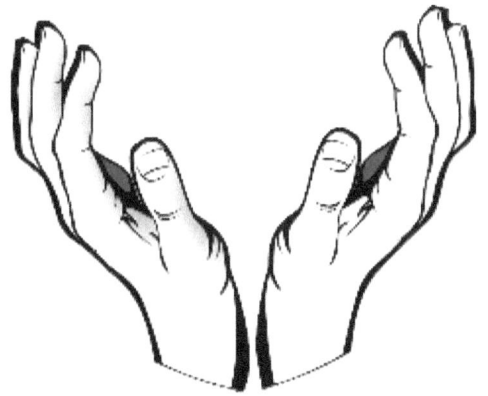

https://youtu.be/GqOiR_5YH5w

What a fantastic week it has been! I had the opportunity to spend time with my sweetheart in Maine and reconnect with my older brother and family. However, I must admit that I missed playing guitar in church yesterday. But I refuse to let my stroke dictate my life with limitations. To my fellow Stroke Warriors, I want to remind you that we are capable of achieving anything we set our minds to, even if it means taking a different approach. Stay strong, my friends, we've got this!

I faced a self-imposed setback this week when I realized I will be missing playing guitar in church. It was a moment of self-discovery of how much I love playing there. This became a time of self-reflection, reminding myself of the progress I have made on my recovery journey and how playing guitar in church has speeded up my recovery. Most importantly, I am now in the beautiful state of Maine with my sweetheart enjoying the time with my older brother George and my cousins focused on the opportunities that lay ahead. I am learning to embrace challenges with resilience and determination, knowing that every transactional moment is just a steppingstone toward a greater comeback. As I embarked on my journey to Maine, I couldn't help but feel a sense of excitement and anticipation. Being surrounded by loved ones and familiar faces brought me a sense of comfort and joy. While I may have missed playing the guitar in church, I didn't let that dampen my spirits. I am learning to embrace change and adapt to new circumstances, knowing that every experience holds valuable lessons and opportunities for growth.

One of the greatest blessings in life is the power of connection and support from loved ones. As I spent time with my family in Maine, I was reminded of the unwavering love and encouragement that surrounds me. My older brother, in particular, has been a pillar of strength and inspiration throughout my recovery journey. His belief in me and unfaltering support have been instrumental in helping me stay positive and motivated.

To my fellow Stroke Warriors, I want to remind you that you are not alone in this journey. We may face challenges and setbacks, but together, we are stronger. Let's continue to support and uplift each other, celebrating every small victory and milestone along the way. Remember, we can do anything we set our minds to, even if it means taking a different path. Stay strong, my friends, and keep pushing forward. We've got this!

As I reflect on this week's experiences, I am filled with gratitude for the love and support that surrounds me. While I may have missed playing the guitar in church, I am reminded of the resilience and determination that fuel my recovery journey. I am learning to embrace change, adapt to new circumstances, and lean on the power of connection and support from loved ones. To my Stroke Warriors, I want to encourage you to stay strong and keep pushing forward. Together, we can overcome any challenge that comes our way. Stay resilient, stay positive, and never lose sight of the strength that lies within you.

RECOVERY WEEK 79
Always Reflecting on My Journey: A Family Affair

Lord, be gracious to us; we long for you. Be our strength every morning, our salvation in time of distress.

—Isaiah 33:2

https://youtu.be/iHLuMIVBGZg

Stroke recovery is a challenging journey that can be made easier with the support of family members. In my case, the support of my Maine family has played a crucial role in my rehabilitation process, particularly my wife, Lisa. The positive impact of family support on the physical and psychosocial well-being of stroke patients cannot be overstated. I would like to share my personal experience of my Miane vacation trip and how my Maine family support has contributed to my ongoing recovery and functional improvement.

Family members, especially spouses, provide a strong pillar of support during the challenging times of stroke recovery. Their encouragement, care, and presence can make a significant difference in the patient's recovery journey. My wife, Lisa, has been by my side every step of the way, assisting me in various aspects of my rehabilitation.

Family support not only benefits the patient but also helps alleviate the stress and burden on caregivers. In my case, Lisa has been actively involved in my recovery process, which has provided her with a sense of purpose and involvement in my healing journey. This shared responsibility has helped us navigate the challenges of stroke recovery together.

As a musician, I have found solace in playing music during my stroke recovery and relearning to play after my stroke. Music has a therapeutic effect on the mind and body, helping me stay positive and motivated throughout the rehabilitation process. I have been working on a musical idea using the "flatties" in the A minor pentatonic scale and the F major scale, which has been a source of creative expression for me.

In conclusion, the support of my Maine family has been instrumental in my stroke recovery journey. Their love, encouragement, and presence have fueled my progress and motivated me to keep pushing forward. I am grateful to have such a strong support system by my side, especially Lisa, who has been my rock throughout this challenging time. Family support truly makes a difference in the recovery and well-being of stroke patients, and I am fortunate to have experienced its positive impact firsthand.

RECOVERY WEEK 80
Resilience, Faith, and Music

...speaking to one another with psalms, hymns, and songs from the Spirit. Sing and make music from your heart to the Lord.

—Ephesians 5:19

https://youtu.be/lAAxq3LMZIo

Reflecting on past experiences of mental confusion, muscle spasms, and spasticity challenges highlights the persistence required for recovery. The recovery process has involved various obstacles, but with consistent effort and a positive approach, progress has been achieved each day.

The first few week's post-stroke were a whirlwind of emotions and physical challenges. From the debilitating muscle spasms to the frustration of non-working limbs, the hospital nights were long and arduous. However, the impressive support of nurses and medical staff provided comfort and encouragement during this difficult time. These experiences served as a stark reminder of the fragility of life and the power of perseverance in the face of adversity.

As I navigate through the ups and downs of recovery, I am reminded of the importance of maintaining a curious mindset. The willingness to learn and explore new possibilities has been a driving force in my rehabilitation journey. By visualizing a positive future and setting goals for progress, I am able to stay motivated and focused on the road ahead.

There is a saying that resonates deeply with me there are three types of people in this world: those who make things happen, those who watch things happen, and those who wonder what happened. I choose to be among those who take action and make a difference in their own lives. Through hard work, dedication, and a relentless pursuit of recovery, I am determined to overcome the challenges that lie ahead.

In times of struggle and uncertainty, faith has been my guiding light. I am grateful for the strength and support I have received from my faith in Jesus Christ. His presence has been a source of comfort and inspiration as I continue on this journey of recovery.

In addition to faith, music has played a significant role in my healing process. As I experiment with different musical ideas and scales, I revel in the creative expression that music allows. The connection between music and the mind is a powerful tool in promoting healing and well-being.

I have been exploring a new song idea that incorporates the use of flatties in the A minor pentatonic scale and the F major scale. This creative experimentation has been a source of inspiration during my recovery process. Music has the power to uplift the spirit and transcend the limitations of the physical body.

Through faith, determination, and the healing power of music, I continue to make strides toward recovery. The journey is far from over, but with each passing day, I am reminded of the resilience and strength that lies within. As I look toward a brighter future, I am filled with hope and optimism for what lies ahead.

Recovery Week 81
Overcoming Challenges and Finding Inspiration

He himself bore our sins in his body on the tree, that we might die to sin and live to righteousness. By His wounds you have been healed.

—1 Peter 2:24

https://youtu.be/osDJmZ_0RlQ

For all my Stroke Warrior guitar players or any musical instrument warriors who have faced setbacks in your playing due to health issues, have you ever wondered if it's possible to regain your skills and get back to playing the way you used to? I would like to explore with you the journey of guitar players who have overcome physical obstacles and found inspiration to keep moving forward in their musical pursuits. I know their stories have inspired me to never give up strumming for life.

When facing a health issue that affects your ability to play guitar, it's common to go through a range of emotions. From frustration and sadness to determination and hope, the process of recovery can be a challenging one. It's important to acknowledge and accept these emotions while also staying focused on the goal of getting back to playing guitar.

For me, playing lead guitar in church every Sunday has been a source of motivation and strength, and the same is true for many other musicians on their road to recovery. The power of music, combined with faith and tenacity, can help individuals push through the physical and emotional barriers that may come with regaining their guitar-playing abilities.

Dave Mustaine and Pat Martino are just two examples of guitar players who have overcome significant health challenges to continue pursuing their passion. By dedicating themselves to intense physical therapy and rehabilitation, they were able to relearn how to play the guitar and ultimately return to the stage. Their stories serve as a reminder that perseverance and hard work can lead to incredible results.

1. **Dave Mustaine** is one of the Metal world's most prominent and influential guitar players. Dave's radial nerve caused radial neuropathy, also known as Saturday night palsy, which left him with greatly decreased motor skills and strength in his left arm and hand. During this time Dave disbanded Megadeth and began to undergo intense physical therapy five days a week. After months of rehabilitation and painstaking practice, Dave retaught himself how to play the guitar and restarted Megadeth.

2. **Pat Martino** is one of the most respected jazz guitar players and composers of all time. In 1980, Pat experienced a violent seizure that left him hospitalized. A CT scan finally revealed Pat's seizures, headaches, and psychiatric problems where the result of an abnormal blood vessel mass called an arteriovenous malformation in his left temporal lobe. The scan also revealed that the arteriovenous malformation had begun to hemorrhage and would cost Pat his life unless he underwent brain surgery where 70 percent of his temporal lobe would be removed. Due to Pat's resilience, he regained a significant amount of his guitar-playing ability during this time, though it took him quite a few years more to regain the level of proficiency he had before his surgery. So bottom line, although Pat forgot how to play the guitar, he never stopped working to regain his skill. Even when faced with setbacks or obstacles, it's essential to keep working toward your

goals. Pat Martino's journey to regain his guitar playing abilities after brain surgery teaches us that progress may take time, but with dedication and persistence, anything is possible. So, keep pushing forward, keep practicing, and never stop striving for progress in your musical journey.

In conclusion, recovering from a health issue that affects your guitar playing can be a challenging journey, but with determination, hard work, and the right mindset, it is possible to overcome these obstacles. Drawing inspiration from the stories of musicians who have faced similar challenges and come out stronger on the other side can help you stay motivated on your own path to recovery. Remember, the journey may be long and difficult, but the joy of playing music again will make it all worth it in the end. Keep strumming, keep practicing, and never give up on your passion for the guitar!

RECOVERY WEEK 82
Overcoming Challenges

So, faith comes from hearing, and hearing through the word of Christ.

—Romans 10:17

https://youtu.be/wq2mQeamBYs

What a great day in church playing lead guitar and having great fellowship. When I first had my stroke, the whole right side of my body was paralyzed. My brave and strong wife called 911 right away, which gave me a greater chance for recovery due to the speed to the hospital.

As I reflect on this journey and playing guitar in church today, it brings me back to what my first neurologist in North Huntsville Alabama said to me on our initial visit. He bluntly told me that I would never play the guitar again. This news was unacceptable, and I refused to accept defeat. I sought out a new neurologist, who told me something that changed my perspective entirely. He said I could do anything I wanted, and playing the guitar was entirely up to me.

I'm nowhere near 100 percent yet, but I've regained enough to play the songs and even play solos, leads, and fills in the church music. Thank You, Jesus! Despite the challenges and setbacks, I continue to push forward on my journey of recovery and redemption. This journey is not just a physical battle but a mental and emotional one as well.

This positive recovery is not solely attributed to medical professionals but rather to a higher power. Our God, Our Savior Jesus Christ, Our Holy Spirit, and my faith played significant roles in this miraculous journey. I believe this is a testament to the resilience of the human spirit and the power of belief in overcoming seemingly insurmountable obstacles.

In the face of doubt and adversity, emotional intelligence played a crucial role in my journey of recovery. The ability to remain resilient, positive, and determined in the face of challenges is a testament to the power of emotional intelligence. Stroke recovery is not just about physical recovery but also about mental and emotional strength in the face of adversity.

In conclusion, Week 82 for me and hopefully inspiring for others, is optimistically a tale of resilience, faith, and determination. Despite facing significant challenges and doubt from medical professionals, I managed to persevere and return to my passion for playing the guitar. I hope this serves as a powerful reminder that with faith, determination, and emotional intelligence, anything is possible. So, next time someone tells you that you can't do something, remember it is entirely up to you to push forward and overcome. Amen!

RECOVERY WEEK 83
A Journey of Faith and Resilience

I can do all this through Him who gives me strength.

—Philippians 4:13

BE YE GRATEFUL

https://youtu.be/9ZzEoTJD9xQ

As a boy growing up on Aquidneck Island (Middletown) in Rhode Island, I developed a passion for sports, particularly hockey and baseball. However, I also had a lot of curiosity about playing guitar, and I will never forget the day I finally got one of my own. I discovered a new love. I devoted hours to honing my skills and eventually found myself performing in bands. Despite facing challenges along the way, my determination never wavered. This journey of self-discovery led me to reflect on the source of my unwavering drive.

Where does this inner fire come from? It seems that when you have a deep passion for something, no obstacle is too great to overcome. This rings especially true for those of us who have experienced a stroke. As Stroke Warriors, we refuse to let adversity define us. We push forward, striving to reclaim our passions and lead fulfilling lives.

In the words of the legendary B. B. King, the key is to start "slow and easy." By gradually pushing ourselves to add new challenges to our playing, we continue to grow and evolve. Each small victory is evidence of our strength and tenacity. It is this commitment to our craft that fuels our recovery and propels us toward our goals.

Throughout this journey, I have found comfort in faith. I believe that God has a plan for each of us, tailored to our unique strengths and abilities. He sees beyond our physical limitations, focusing instead on the purity of our souls and our dedication to Him. In times of struggle, prayer serves as a guiding light, providing comfort and strength as we navigate our recovery journey.

As a demonstration of the power of persistence and determination, I invite you to watch a video of a jam session where I explore different chord voicings and melodies. With each note, I am reminded of the progress I have made and the challenges I have overcome. I hope this musical journey serves as inspiration for others embarking on their own path to recovery.

In conclusion, the journey of stroke recovery is not easy, but it is marked by resilience, faith, and resolute determination. As we face each day with courage and conviction, we move one step closer to reclaiming our passions and leading fulfilling lives. Remember, slow and steady wins the race, and with faith as our guide, we can overcome any obstacle that stands in our way. Let us continue to support and uplift one another on this journey of healing and self-discovery.

RECOVERY WEEK 84
Overcoming Setbacks and Finding Strength in Unity

The Lord is my strength and my shield; my heart trusts in him, and he helps me. My heart leaps for joy, and with my song I praise him.

—Psalm 28:7

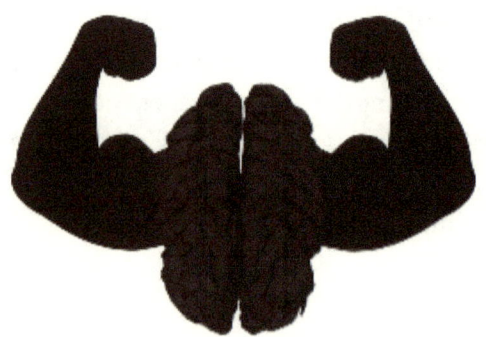

https://youtu.be/F9N2PaKhhrc

It has been a rollercoaster ride of emotions, but through it all, I have come to a unique conclusion that life is crazy but interesting at the same time.

Being a stroke survivor, there is always the challenge of imagining how I am going to take one more step forward. It hasn't been easy, but I am grateful for the progress I have made so far. With experience and self-discovery, I have learned to deal with setbacks and use them as stepping-stones to future success.

One of the biggest stumbling blocks for me on this journey was removing the negative stories I had been telling myself. Thoughts like *it's too hard, it can't be done*, or *it's too complicated* were holding me back. I had to make a conscious effort to replace these negative thoughts with more positive ones, such as pausing, reflecting, learning, growing, and turning to prayer for guidance.

As stroke survivors, it is important for us to work together as a team toward our recovery goals. Whether it's playing guitar again or simply offering an encouraging word, we can support each other on this challenging journey. This reminds me of a quote I heard in church today from Tecumseh. Tecumseh was a Shawnee chief and warrior who promoted resistance to the expansion of the United States onto Native American lands. A very persuasive orator, he said, "A single twig breaks, but the bundle of twigs is strong." So, if we are alone in our recovery we are like that single twig, but if we band together, we are the bundle of twigs that is strong. When we come together, we become strong in the face of adversity. Amen!

Yes, being a stroke survivor is full of setbacks, failures, obstacles, and challenges. But setbacks are not the true focus of our life; they are a critical part of it. They redirect us toward our true path, reminding us of where we should be heading. Instead of throwing us off track, setbacks guide us toward our ultimate destination.

In my journey, I have learned to embrace progress and improvement, no matter how small. Recognizing challenges and areas for growth is the first step toward making positive changes. For example, I recently played guitar in church and noticed that the sound mix was off. Instead of ignoring it, I saw it as a challenge for improvement and progress.

Embarking on this week's journey of relearning guitar in recovery was undoubtedly an adventurous challenge, but oh, the rewards that followed were nothing short of exhilarating! As I strummed the strings and played with determination, weaving intricate guitar fills and soul-stirring leads, I felt a surge of creativity and joy coursing through me. The moment of sharing these wonderful Christian songs in church, enriching the music with my newfound skills, was a truly magical experience. It was a harmonious blend of overcoming obstacles and basking in the sweet satisfaction of progress, reminding me that every challenging note conquered leads to a melody of accomplishment and fulfillment.

As I navigate through Week 84 of my guitar stroke recovery, I am reminded that life is indeed a crazy and interesting journey. Through setbacks and challenges, I have found strength in unity and growth in embracing progress. As I continue on this path toward healing and renewal, I am grateful for the support of my fellow stroke survivors and the lessons learned along the way. Together, we are stronger. Remember, setbacks are not the end of the road; they are simply redirections guiding us toward our true path. Embrace the challenges, support each other, and continue to grow and learn on this journey toward healing and renewal. Together, we are stronger than we could ever be alone.

RECOVERY WEEK 85
A Celebration of Strength and Gratitude

My flesh and my heart may fail, but God is the strength of my heart and my portion forever.

—Psalm 73:26

https://youtu.be/EOySaPFbLds

As I reflect on the past three years since my stroke, I am filled with a mix of emotions. Should I celebrate the progress I have made or dwell on the challenges I have faced? The answer is clear to me—it is a time for celebration!

According to Merriam-Webster, to celebrate is to mark an occasion with festivities or deviations from routine. In my case, it is a chance to celebrate being a stroke survivor and a warrior. I am grateful for the support of my family, friends, and the unwavering strength of my wife, Lisa, who has been my rock throughout this journey.

It is also a time to express my gratitude to God for His grace and for guiding me through the darkest moments of my recovery. I am thankful for the Holy Spirit, whose presence has been a source of comfort and strength.

In the aftermath of my stroke, I lost the use of my right side and the ability to play the guitar, a passion of mine. However, through hard work and determination, I have regained my strength and am now back to playing lead guitar in church. This is a testament to the power of perseverance and faith.

Alongside physical recovery, I have also found a stronger voice within me, one of hope, empathy, and resilience. This voice has been shaped by the challenges I have faced and the triumphs I have celebrated. I am grateful for the opportunity to share my story and inspire others on their own journey to recovery.

With this week's guitar recovery video, the praise band played some wonderful songs this Sunday morning. Here are some video clips from church this week. The audio mix needs some improvement, which means some audio areas need fine-tuning and there are issues with synchronization between the video and audio.

In conclusion, celebrating my stroke recovery Week 85 is a reminder of the strength and resilience that lie within me. It is a time to be grateful for the progress I have made and the support I have received along the way. Through faith, determination, and the love of those around me, I continue to move forward on my journey to healing and wholeness. Remember, your strength is an inspiration to others. Keep playing your lead guitar and shining your light as a beacon of hope and courage. The celebration of recovery is a testament to the power of resilience and the unwavering support of loved ones. You are a Stroke Warrior, a survivor, and a living example of the triumph of the human spirit. Keep strumming those chords of strength and gratitude, for your music is a gift to the world.

RECOVERY WEEK 86
Celebrating My Progress and Recognizing My Heroes

And we know that for those who love God all things work together for good, for those who are called according to his purpose.

—Romans 8:28

https://youtu.be/ImylY0Q2exY

As I celebrate a winning year as a stroke survivor and a Stroke Warrior, I continue to reflect on the individuals who have had a significant impact on my recovery journey. In this weekly series, I want to highlight the importance of occupational therapists and physical therapists in helping patients regain their independence and improve their overall quality of life. Today, I want to shine a light on a young and inspiring occupational therapist, Lauren Lindquist, who played a pivotal role in my journey to reclaiming my passion for playing the guitar.

One of the key lessons that Ms. Lindquist taught me was the importance of occupational therapy in considering all aspects of a patient's life, not just their immediate physical challenges. She took the time to get to know me on a deeper level, understanding my passion for playing the guitar and recognizing the void it left in my life after my stroke. Through her encouragement and personalized therapy goals, I found the courage to pick up my guitar again, despite the initial pain and fear of failure.

Ms. Lauren Lindquist's approach to therapy was not just about physical rehabilitation but also about empowering her patients to regain their independence and pursue their passions. By understanding my lifestyle, habits, and emotional well-being, she helped me overcome the barriers that were holding me back from reconnecting with my guitar and, in turn, with myself.

Occupational therapy goes beyond just improving physical mobility. It also has profound emotional and social impacts on patients' lives. By working with occupational therapists like Ms. Lindquist, patients can regain a sense of purpose, confidence, and joy in their daily activities. Through personalized care and holistic support, occupational therapists play a crucial role in helping individuals rebuild their lives after experiencing a stroke or other life-altering events.

Ms. Lauren Lindquist's dedication to her patients and her unwavering optimism have transformed my outlook on recovery and inspired me to pursue my passion for music again. Her impact on my life serves as a testament to the profound difference that occupational therapists can make in the lives of stroke survivors and individuals facing physical challenges.

In closing, I want to express my deepest gratitude to Ms. Lauren Lindquist and all the occupational therapists who work tirelessly to help patients like me rediscover their strength, independence, and passion for life. Through their compassionate care and support, they truly are our heroes in the journey to recovery. As I continue to strum my guitar and embrace the joy of music once again, I am reminded of the power of therapy, dedication, and belief in the possibility of renewal after adversity. Thank you, Ms. Lauren Lindquist, for changing my life and helping me find my way back to my old friend, my guitar.

Recovery Week 87
Celebrating Three Years of Survival and Warriors!

And the prayer of faith will save the one who is sick, and the Lord will raise him up. And if he has committed sins, he will be forgiven.

—James 5:15

https://youtu.be/PFncXQ_mcWU

Dear readers, welcome to another week of my guitar stroke recovery journey! As I reflect on another year as a stroke survivor and a Stroke Warrior, I am filled with immense gratitude for the blessings that have come my way. Today, I want to shine the spotlight on a special hero in my recovery journey—the incredible physical therapist, Ashley Mooney Silva.

Physical therapists play a crucial role in the rehabilitation journey of individuals recovering from strokes. They possess a deep understanding of the human body and its ability to heal and adapt. By analyzing movement patterns, habits, and limitations, they are able to tailor a customized care plan that addresses the specific needs of each patient.

Ashley Mooney Silva is not just a physical therapist; she is a beacon of hope and healing for her patients. With her infectious personality and compassionate bedside manner, Ashley goes above and beyond to ensure that her patients receive the best possible care. She is a true making-the-body-move expert, dedicated to improving the quality of life for those under her care.

One of the things that sets Ashley apart is her keen eye for detail. She meticulously evaluates her patients' conditions and designs treatment plans that focus on improving mobility, managing pain, and restoring function. Through prescribed exercises, hands-on therapy, and patient education, Ashley empowers her patients to regain their independence and lead active lives once again.

I will forever be grateful to Ashley for her dedication and relentless support during my recovery journey. She was the one who helped me get out of a wheelchair and start walking again. Her encouragement and expertise have been instrumental in my progress, and I am truly blessed to have her by my side.

I still remember the first time I met Ashley. I remember our first conversation like it was yesterday. She said to me, "You are my first stroke patient."

I said, "Well, this is going to work out great because this is my first stroke."

I will always remember teaching her how to speak Portuguese, and with her strong southern accent it made it very interesting. Here is an example: "*Meu nome e* Ashley, y'all." Our interactions were filled with laughter and warmth, and I will always cherish the moments we spent together. I thank God for putting her in my healing life. Amen!

Through Ashley's guidance and support, I have learned that change and healing are possible, no matter how challenging the circumstances may be. She has been a constant source of inspiration and motivation, demonstrating that I was capable of anything I put my mind to.

To showcase the progress I have made in my recovery journey, I have recorded a video this week using chords A minor and F major. I am working on landing the scale on the beat, and I hope you enjoy listening to my musical endeavors.

In conclusion, these ambitious times have been a rollercoaster of emotions, challenges, and victories. Through it all, Ashley has been a pillar of strength and support, guiding me toward a path of healing and recovery. I am forever grateful for her presence in my life, and I thank God for bringing her into my journey. Here's to celebrating another year of survival and warriorship. Amen!

RECOVERY WEEK 88
Celebrating Progress and Faith

"But I will restore you to health and heal your wounds,"
declares the LORD.

—Jeremiah 30:17

https://youtu.be/Xl1hqagfw1g

In my journey, I have experienced the power of faith, determination, and the support of amazing therapy professionals like Jonathan Andrus, the physical therapist manager at Choice Therapy Services in Madison, Alabama. His dedication, expertise, and compassion have been instrumental in my progress toward a positive recovery. This week, I am filled with gratitude for the blessings of health and healing, as I continue to strive toward my goal of playing the guitar again.

Jonathan Andrus embodies the qualities of a true therapy hero. His deep commitment to patient advocacy, effective communication, and operational excellence set him apart as a leader in the field. Under his guidance, the therapy team at Choice Therapy Services provides comprehensive care and support, ensuring that each patient receives personalized treatment tailored to their specific needs. Jonathan's profound knowledge and expertise create a nurturing environment where patients like me feel empowered to overcome obstacles and achieve new milestones in recovery.

Meeting Jonathan for the first time when I was in a wheelchair, I could never have imagined the progress I had made today. His encouragement, faith, and belief in my potential have been a source of inspiration and motivation throughout my recovery journey. With his guidance and support, I have regained strength, independence, and hope for a brighter future. I am truly grateful for the role he has played in my healing process.

As I continue to work toward my goal of playing the guitar again, I am reminded of the importance of patience and positivity. Each week, I strive to challenge myself, push past limitations, and celebrate small victories along the way. My weekly guitar video documents the progress I have made and the determination I carry within me. By exploring new chords, melodies, and techniques, I am not only honing my musical skills but also strengthening my mind–body connection and resilience.

I welcome feedback and input from others who have been following my recovery journey. Your support, encouragement, and constructive criticism help me grow, learn, and improve each day. Feel free to share your thoughts on my guitar video, "Think of Phrases as Hand Choreography," and offer suggestions for future musical explorations. Together, we can inspire and uplift one another on the path toward healing and wholeness.

In conclusion, the road to stroke recovery is filled with challenges, setbacks, and triumphs. With faith, perseverance, and the support of dedicated professionals like Jonathan Andrus, we can overcome obstacles, embrace new possibilities, and redefine our sense of self and purpose. As I continue on this journey of healing and growth, I am grateful for every step forward, every lesson learned, and every moment of grace that guides me along the way. Thank you for being a part of my story, and may we continue to walk this path together with courage, hope, and determination.

RECOVERY WEEK 89
Celebrating Three Years of Hope and Rehabilitation

There is a time for everything, and a season for every activity under the heavens.

—Ecclesiastes 3:1

https://youtu.be/6DC6UHpSjxM

I am so blessed to be celebrating another victorious year of stroke recovery. I have learned that there is life and hope after a stroke—Amen! Rehabilitation has provided me with the strength, capability, and confidence to overcome the challenges that come with recovery. Strokes may seem overwhelming, but with the right support and determination, they can be beatable and the damage reduced.

Rehabilitation is one of the keys to achieving and celebrating all the small victories along our way to recovery. It helps us regain our strength, courage, and independence, making the journey toward recovery more manageable and successful. With the right rehabilitation program, individuals can see significant improvements in their physical and cognitive abilities, leading to a better quality of life.

I want to take a moment to recognize a truly amazing individual who has been instrumental in my stroke recovery journey, Ms. Cami Munn Peters, the physical therapist office manager at Choice Therapy, Madison, Alabama. With the largest smile I have ever seen, she goes above and beyond to ensure that patients are taken care of with compassion and dedication. From checking patients in and out of the office to scheduling appointments and assisting with billing and insurance, Ms. Peters plays a vital role in the rehabilitation process.

Behind all the administrative duties, Ms. Peters greets patients with a warm and welcoming demeanor, offering a listening ear and answering any questions they may have about their care and treatments. She is not just an office manager but a friend who provides encouragement, support, and valuable advice throughout the recovery journey. Thank you, Ms. Peters, for your unwavering dedication and kindness.

Alongside rehabilitation and the support of dedicated professionals like Ms. Peters, faith plays a crucial role in the recovery process. Having a strong belief in a higher power can provide individuals with the strength and courage they need to face the challenges of stroke recovery. Through prayer, faith, and determination, individuals can find hope and inspiration to keep pushing forward toward healing and restoration.

As a symbol of my journey toward recovery, I have included a guitar video showcasing my progress. I call this guitar jam the "Yes" because it signifies not giving up and continuing to build upon a simple, original musical idea. Just like in recovery, once you have a good foundation, you can come back to it and add to it, creating something beautiful and meaningful.

In conclusion, stroke recovery is a challenging journey that requires strength, willpower, and the support of dedicated professionals like Ms. Cami Munn Peters. With the right rehabilitation program, faith, and perseverance, individuals can overcome the obstacles that come with recovery and celebrate the small victories along the way. Remember, there is life and hope after a stroke, and with the right mindset and support, you can achieve your goals.

Recovery Week 90
A Triumph of Progress

*Let us not become weary in doing good, for at the proper
time we will reap a harvest if we do not give up.*

—Galatians 6:9

https://youtu.be/VJpHSKhf9vw

In Week 90 I received some incredibly good news during my visit with
Dr. Theodros Mengesha, a highly esteemed neurologist in Huntsville,
Alabama. He was pleased with my progress, telling me that I am winning
the battle against the challenges I have faced. This positive reinforcement
from Dr. Mengesha has been a tremendous source of motivation for me
as I continue to work hard toward regaining my ability to play the guitar.

Physical therapists play a crucial role in guiding individuals through the
recovery process following injuries and illnesses. They utilize mobility
exercises and customized treatment plans to help patients regain their
strength and function. One particular physical therapist, Ms. Destiny
Wood, stands out for her exceptional skills and dedication to her patients.

Ms. Wood possesses a diverse skill set that sets her apart in her field. Her
effective communication skills ensure that patients and their families are
well-informed and supported throughout their rehabilitation journey.
She demonstrates exceptional dexterity and stamina as she leads patients
through various exercises, always encouraging them to push through

challenges.

Destiny's strong interpersonal skills allow her to build trust with her patients, creating a supportive environment for their recovery. She is detail-oriented, maintaining comprehensive notes on each patient's condition, treatment plan, and progress. This meticulous approach ensures that each therapy session is tailored to the individual needs of the patient, maximizing their potential for improvement.

Ms. Wood's dedication to her profession goes beyond the standard expectations. She continually seeks out new techniques and approaches to physical therapy, eager to explore innovative methods that could benefit her patients. Her passion for learning and willingness to try new strategies have been instrumental in my own recovery journey.

I am immensely grateful for the support and guidance provided by Ms. Destiny Wood throughout my recovery as a Stroke Warrior. Her genuine commitment to her patients and her willingness to go above and beyond in seeking out new treatment methods have been invaluable to me. I thank her every day for her dedication and expertise.

As a token of gratitude and appreciation, I have shared a jam video that reflects the push and pull motif of my recovery journey. The rhythmic interplay of challenges and triumphs is echoed in the music, serving as a reminder of the resilience and determination required to overcome obstacles.

In conclusion, the progress made in Week 90 of my guitar stroke recovery journey is a testament to the power of perseverance, dedication, and the unwavering support of individuals like Ms. Destiny Wood. With each milestone reached, I am reminded of the importance of surrounding oneself with skilled professionals who can inspire, motivate, and guide us toward our goals. As I continue on this journey, I am filled with hope and optimism for the future, knowing that with the right support and determination, anything is possible.

RECOVERY WEEK 91
A Journey of Healing and Resilience

May the God of hope fill you with all joy and peace as you trust in Him, so that you may overflow with hope by the power of the Holy Spirit.

—Romans 15:13

https://youtu.be/9DcK_lcw-6Y

Yesterday morning, as I was playing my guitar in church with the praise band, I couldn't help but feel overwhelmed with gratitude and pride. The members of the church were standing, grooving, and singing along with the music, their beaming smiles and excited energy filling the room. It was a powerful experience, and I felt truly blessed to be able to share my gift of music with others. This journey of guitar stroke recovery has been a long and challenging one, but it has also been filled with moments of triumph, growth, and healing.

After suffering a stroke, I went through a period of emotional turmoil and uncertainty. It took me over a year before I could bring myself to pick up my guitar again, and even longer before I felt confident enough to play lead guitar in church. Playing the guitar has always been a form of self-expression for me, a way to share my innermost thoughts and feelings with the world. It is through music that I have been able to heal and find my voice again after the stroke.

Self-expression is a vital part of the human experience, allowing us to connect with our inner selves and share our emotions with others. Whether through music, dance, writing, or art, finding a way to express ourselves is essential for our emotional well-being. After my stroke, I realized just how important it was for me to reclaim this part of myself and not let the stroke take away my ability to share my music. It has been a journey of rediscovery and resilience, but one that has ultimately brought me closer to my true self.

Research shows that music has a profound impact on our brains, activating the reward system and releasing dopamine when we listen to music we love. This explains why the church members were so joyful and engaged while we played music together. Music has a way of bringing people together, creating a sense of unity and joy that is truly unique. While the science behind musical emotions is fascinating, for me, the true magic lies in the connection we share with each other and with the divine through music.

I have documented my guitar stroke recovery journey through videos, sharing my progress and my passion for music with others. In my latest video, I demonstrate a simple sequencing technique that has helped me break through the challenges of my guitar stroke recovery. It is a reminder that no matter how difficult the journey may be, there is always hope and resilience waiting on the other side. I believe that through music and self-expression, we can find the strength to overcome any obstacle that comes our way.

As I continue on my journey of guitar stroke recovery, I am reminded of the power of music to heal, inspire, and connect us with each other. It is through music that I have found my voice again, rediscovered my passion, and overcome the challenges of stroke recovery. I encourage my fellow Stroke Warriors to never give up on their dreams and to find solace in the healing power of music. Remember, you are stronger than you think, and with faith, perseverance, and a little bit of music, the sky's the limit.

RECOVERY WEEK 92
The Meaning of Recovery

Trust in God, my friends, our great healer.
"Therefore I tell you, whatever you ask in prayer, believe that
you have received it, and it will be yours."

—Mark 11:24

https://youtu.be/d6WSdBcUdjg

What a wonderful day in church, so much rejoicing, so much prayer was offered to people attending church this morning. Thank you, God, for letting me be a part of and witnessing these glorious moments. Amen!

This experience reminded me that there is so much recovery needed in our lives. Recovery from afflictions such as illness, sickness, suffering, operations, strokes, depression, financial stress, or simply the need to be understood and loved. Recovery means a return to a normal state of health, mind, or strength, as well as the action or process of regaining possession or control of something stolen or lost.

After experiencing a stroke, the journey toward recovery can be challenging. The brain, being the most complex part of the human body, continuously seeks to heal itself in miraculous ways. Through the grace and glory of God, recovery is possible. Personally, I experience this every day, especially as I learn to play the guitar again.

Research has shown that spirituality may help patients cope with illness, including stroke. While there are not many studies examining the impact of spirituality on stroke survivors, one study by Gianluca Pucciarelli, Ph.D., from the University of Rome, revealed interesting findings. The study concluded that there is a strong relationship between spirituality and quality of life for stroke survivors. Those with a higher level of spirituality tended to have a higher quality of life and were less prone to depression.

It is important to recognize the role of spirituality in the recovery process of stroke survivors. The Bible also offers words of comfort and strength for those on the journey of recovery. In Isaiah 41:10, we are reminded, "Fear not, for I am with you; be not dismayed, for I am your God; I will strengthen you, I will help you, I will uphold you with my righteous right hand." And in Psalm 41:3, it is written, "The Lord sustains him on his sickbed; in his illness, You restore him to full health." Amen!

I have added a guitar stroke recovery video of my latest practice and jam session. This week, my focus was on "speaking in sentences" on the guitar, aiming to finish thoughts before moving on to new phrases or ideas. Practice and dedication are key to progress in stroke recovery, just as in relearning to play the guitar.

In conclusion, the journey of stroke recovery is one that requires patience, faith, and perseverance. With the support of spirituality, prayer, and dedicated practice, stroke survivors can experience healing and restoration in mind, body, and spirit. Remember, recovery is possible with the grace of God and the determination to keep moving forward, one strum at a time. Amen!

Recovery Week 93
How Learning to Play Guitar Can Aid in Stroke Rehabilitation

Behold, I will bring to it health and healing, and I will heal them and reveal to them abundance of prosperity and security.

—Jeremiah 33:6

https://youtu.be/AgQdxcra5-I

Welcome to Week 93! Today, I want to share with you the incredible blessing I experienced while playing lead guitar in church. It truly is a testament to the healing power of music and the grace of the Lord Jesus. As I continue to learn to play guitar again, I am amazed at the progress I have made and the positive impact it has had on my stroke rehabilitation.

One of the most fascinating aspects of my journey has been the effect that learning to play guitar has had on my stroke rehabilitation. I have noticed significant improvements in my motor function, particularly in my right picking and strumming hand. The act of learning to play with a pick and using my fingers again has been challenging but ultimately beneficial for my recovery. It has forced me to focus on strengthening the affected areas, leading to faster progress in my rehabilitation.

As I encountered various challenges along the way, I turned to music as a form of therapy and motivation. One of the challenges I faced was memory loss due to my stroke. To combat this, I broke down the music I was learning into smaller, more manageable chunks. This approach not only helped me retain information better but also improved my overall cognitive function. By engaging in musical activities, I was able to stimulate my brain's plasticity and enhance my synaptic connections, leading to better memory retention and overall mental acuity.

While I am still on the journey to full recovery, I am confident in the effectiveness of learning to play guitar as a form of stroke rehabilitation. Playing a musical instrument not only provides a creative outlet but also offers a unique way to exercise and strengthen the brain. By challenging myself to learn new songs, scales, and musical ideas, I am constantly pushing the boundaries of my abilities and expanding my cognitive skills.

In conclusion, my experience with guitar stroke recovery has been nothing short of transformative. Through the act of learning to play guitar again, I have not only improved my motor function and memory but also gained a renewed sense of purpose and passion for life. I am excited to continue this journey of healing and discovery, and I invite you to join me in exploring the profound impact that music can have on stroke rehabilitation. Let's embrace the healing power of music together!

Recovery Week 94
Reflecting on My Changed Behaviors

Finally, be strong in the Lord and in his mighty power.
—Ephesians 6:10

https://youtu.be/438ZB2TnIck

Are you struggling with behavior changes following a stroke? Do you feel like a different person after experiencing this major health event? During my recovery journey, I experienced significant behavior changes that left me feeling confused and uncertain about the future. The first year was especially tough, and I found myself struggling to manage my emotions and thoughts effectively. Everything seemed cloudy, and I questioned whether I would ever be able to play guitar again, my old friend.

It is important to remember that a stroke is a major health event that can impact both physical and psychological well-being. The frustration, fear, and wide range of emotions that come with the aftereffects of a stroke can lead to unexpected behavior changes. I didn't realize at first that my stroke had caused these changes in me, but as I became more aware, I recognized that my behaviors were aimed at those closest to me.

If you have experienced behavior changes after a stroke, it's essential to be gentle with yourself. You have gone through a significant and life-altering event, and not all changes are negative. By reframing your thinking and accepting some changes as a new normal, you can begin to adjust to your post-stroke reality.

Through my journey of recovery, I have found comfort in my faith and in music. Playing guitar and expressing myself through music has been a therapeutic outlet, allowing me to process my emotions and navigate my behavior changes. Trusting in God and embracing the healing power of music have been instrumental in my recovery process.

Recovering from a stroke can be a challenging and emotional journey, but you are not alone in your experience. By acknowledging and accepting your behavior changes, seeking support from loved ones, and finding solace in your faith and hobbies, you can navigate this difficult time with resilience and hope.

So, are you ready to approach your behavior changes with compassion and understanding? Remember, recovery is a process, and each step you take is a victory on your path to healing. Trust in the journey and have faith that better days are ahead.

Recovery Week 95
Reclaiming My Passion and Healing Through Music

Music is the language of the spirit. It opens the secret of life bringing peace, abolishing strife.

—Kahlil Gibran

https://youtu.be/bsMUL_nxYvM

As I document my reflections on week 95, I feel a profound sense of gratitude for the progress achieved to date. Playing the guitar in church this morning highlighted the healing power of music and faith. This week, I will journal about recovering from a stroke, brain plasticity, and how music aids my rehabilitation.

The immediate aftermath of the stroke left me paralyzed on the right side of my body, a result of oxygen deprivation to the brain due to high blood pressure. The realization of the extent of brain damage was a difficult pill to swallow, but it also ignited a spark of determination within me to fight for my recovery.

The million-dollar question that haunted me and my family was whether the brain could heal itself after a stroke. Through hours of research and consultations with healthcare professionals, the answer became clear—yes, the brain has the capacity to recover after acute trauma like a stroke. This remarkable ability is attributed to neuroplasticity, the brain's innate capability to reorganize neural networks for information storage and retrieval.

To facilitate my brain's healing process, I have embraced various activities that keep my cognitive functions active and engaged. From writing weekly video vlogs to recording guitar practices and creating music videos, I have employed a range of brain-stimulating tasks to promote recovery. Learning new church songs each week has been particularly rewarding, as it prepares me for my role as a lead guitarist during Sunday services.

Stroke rehabilitation is a challenging and time-consuming process, requiring unwavering commitment and faith in the healing power of both medicine and spirituality. With a strong support system in place and a deep-rooted belief in God as the ultimate healer, the journey toward recovery becomes more manageable. Research indicates that recovery can occur even years after a stroke, underscoring the importance of perseverance and consistency in the healing process.

In my 95th week of recovery, I decided to experiment with a jazzy 8-bar blues composition, a departure from my usual repertoire. This creative endeavor not only challenged me musically but also provided a refreshing outlet for self-expression and growth. As I continue to explore new musical avenues, I am reminded of the limitless possibilities for healing and transformation through music.

As I reflect on my journey of guitar stroke recovery, I am filled with a sense of gratitude for the progress I have made and the lessons I have learned along the way. Through the power of music, faith, and perseverance, I have regained a sense of purpose and hope for the future. While the road to recovery may be long and arduous, I am confident that with dedication and a positive mindset, healing is not only possible but inevitable.

Recovery Week 96
Honoring Veterans and Finding Support

But thanks be to God! He gives us the victory through our Lord Jesus Christ.

—1 Corinthians 15:57

https://youtu.be/v4L7OPcy4nM

As I reflect on my recovery journey in Week 96 after a stroke, I recognize the importance of a strong support system and valuable resources. Today, I want to acknowledge the bravery of our veteran Stroke Warriors and the essential role of the VA community in providing top care and support.

According to data from the Centers for Disease Control and Prevention, a stroke occurs every forty seconds in the United States, affecting millions of individuals. The impact of a stroke can be life-altering, leading to long-term symptoms and consequences. I am grateful for the caregivers who have been by my side, helping me navigate the challenges of stroke recovery and preventing further health complications.

As a retired US Air Force Chief Master Sergeant, I understand the sacrifices veterans have made for our country. I want to take a moment to honor all veteran Stroke Warriors who have bravely faced the challenges of stroke recovery. Their resilience and courage inspire us all to persevere in the face of adversity.

The US Department of Veterans Affairs offers a valuable resource called RESCUE, which provides evidence-based best practices for stroke caregivers. This information is designed to empower caregivers and promote the best possible outcomes for stroke survivors. By accessing these resources, caregivers can better support their loved ones on their journey to recovery.

With over 15,000 veterans hospitalized for strokes each year, it is crucial to enhance awareness and access to resources within the VA community. By sharing knowledge and best practices, we can ensure that every veteran receives the support they need to achieve optimal outcomes in their stroke recovery journey. Together, we can build a stronger and more resilient VA community.

I want to express my gratitude to all veterans for their service and sacrifice. Your dedication to our country has not gone unnoticed, and I thank you for your bravery and commitment. As I continue my own journey of stroke recovery, I am humbled by the support and care I have received. Let us come together to uplift and empower all Stroke Warriors, both veterans and civilians alike.

I have added a jam video of my progress to date. I attempted to play a slow and mellow (old Western sounding) lead using the lower (bass) strings and dual guitars. I hope you enjoy.

In conclusion, stroke recovery is a challenging and ongoing process, but with the right support and resources, individuals can achieve positive outcomes. By honoring our veteran Stroke Warriors and engaging with the VA community, we can create a network of care and empowerment for all stroke survivors. Thank you for joining me on this journey of recovery and resilience. Let us continue to uplift and support one another as we navigate the road to healing.

RECOVERY WEEK 97
Why Playing Guitar Is Beneficial for Your Mental Health

Devote yourselves to prayer, being watchful and thankful.
—Colossians 4:2

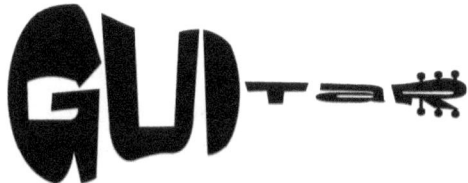

https://youtu.be/AiRa1fGDy7A

Celebrating Guitar Stroke Recovery Week 97! Do you ever feel like you need a creative outlet to unwind from the stresses of daily life? Playing guitar may be the perfect solution for you! In my research this week, I examined the reasons why people enjoy playing guitar and the mental health benefits it can provide. Let's explore some of the key findings that make guitar playing such a therapeutic and enjoyable activity.

1.   Playing Guitar Is a Form of Therapy

Have you ever noticed how playing music on a guitar can have a calming effect on your mind and body? Many individuals, including myself, find that strumming a few chords or playing a melody can reset their emotional state and bring a sense of peace. Clark Vogeler of The Toadies expressed it best when he said, "Playing music on a guitar resets me to zero, calms me down, and puts me in a place where I'm ready to deal with almost anything."

2.   Guitar Playing Is Good for Your Heart

Did you know that playing guitar can actually benefit your cardiovascular health? Studies have shown that individuals who practice guitar for over one hundred minutes a day experience a significant drop in blood pressure and a lower heart rate. This surprising finding highlights the positive impact that music can have on our physical well-being.

3.   Guitar Playing Enhances Creativity

Have you ever felt a surge of creativity while playing guitar and improvising melodies? The guitar is a unique instrument that allows for endless possibilities in terms of musical expression. By picking up a guitar and creating your own music, you can tap into your innate creativity and unleash your artistic potential.

4.   Playing Guitar Can Future-Proof Your Brain

Are you looking for a way to keep your brain sharp and agile as you age? Learning to play the guitar can actually lead to an increase in grey matter volume in various regions of the brain, strengthening the connections between them. This "future-proofing" effect can help improve your coordination, concentration, and memory over time. Finally, playing guitar can provide you with a sense of accomplishment and satisfaction. It's a great hobby to pick up and one you can enjoy for years to come—embrace the 1983 hit song by John Mellencamp, "Play Guitar"!

I recorded a short guitar video this week that most guitar players would describe as an easy tune. For me, in the midst of my recovery, I found it very challenging. My querida Lisa said, "This is something you would hear at the Grand Ole Opry, wow!" I'm just trying to make my leads more melodic sounding. Enjoy!

In conclusion, playing guitar is not only a fun and fulfilling hobby, but it also offers a myriad of mental health benefits. Whether you're a seasoned musician or a beginner looking to pick up a new skill, playing guitar can provide you with a sense of accomplishment, creativity, and relaxation. So why not pick up a guitar today and start strumming your way to better mental health? Remember, music has the power to heal the mind and soothe the soul. So, grab your guitar, play a few notes, and immerse yourself in the joy of creating beautiful music. Your mental health will thank you for it!

Recovery Week 98
Coping With Anger and Frustration Through Faith

Come to me, all who labor and are heavy laden, and I will give you rest. Take my yoke upon you, and learn from me, for I am gentle and lowly in heart, and you will find rest for your souls. For my yoke is easy, and my burden is light.

—Matthew 11:28–30

https://youtu.be/Q_qU1EiBdhg

When I first had my stroke three years ago, I faced many changes in my life. One of the hardest things to deal with was the difficulty in managing anger and frustration. Here, I will share my experiences and insights into coping with these emotions as a stroke survivor.

As a stroke survivor, I found it challenging to control my emotions, especially anger. Family members often bore the brunt of my frustration, which was not fair to them. Through prayer and faith in Jesus Christ, I have been able to manage my anger more effectively over time. However, it is essential to recognize that a stroke survivor may struggle with emotional responses due to brain damage. Seeking help and support from loved ones and professionals can make a significant difference in managing anger.

Frustration is another common emotion experienced by stroke survivors. Realizing the limitations and changes in capabilities can be disheartening, leading to feelings of frustration. Stroke Warriors may struggle to participate in activities they once enjoyed, causing a sense of loss of control. It is crucial for family members and friends to understand the challenges faced by stroke survivors and provide patience and support during their recovery journey.

Stroke survivors may exhibit anger and frustration in various ways, such as irritability, hostility, cursing, or yelling. These emotional outbursts are often attempts to regain a sense of control over their lives. It is important for loved ones to have empathy and understanding toward Stroke Warriors as they navigate through the changes brought about by their condition. Seeking professional help and leaning on faith can also aid in managing these overwhelming emotions.

Turning to our Savior Jesus Christ for guidance and comfort can provide solace during difficult times. The love and forgiveness of Jesus Christ can offer strength and reassurance to individuals struggling with anger and frustration. It is essential to trust in the healing power of faith and lean on the support of a higher power to find peace and resilience in the face of adversity.

In conclusion, coping with anger and frustration as a stroke survivor can be challenging, but with patience, understanding, and faith, it is possible to overcome these emotions. Seeking help from loved ones and professionals, as well as leaning on the support of our Savior Jesus Christ, can make a significant difference in managing emotional responses. As we navigate the ups and downs of recovery, remember that you are not alone, and there is always hope for a brighter tomorrow. Stay strong, have faith, and reach out for help when needed. Together, we can overcome the challenges brought about by stroke and find peace and healing along the way.

Recovery Week 99
Strumming Back to Life

Rejoice in hope, be patient in tribulation, be constant in prayer.

—Romans 12:12

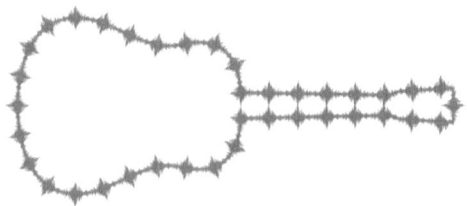

https://youtu.be/2GsNw_WW_jU

Recovering guitar skills after a stroke can be difficult, but it is achievable with determination and the right approach. In this vlog, I will share tips from my own experience in guitar stroke recovery to help you on your musical journey.

One of the key aspects of relearning to play the guitar after a stroke is to approach it step by step. Start by focusing on basic hand and finger exercises to regain strength and dexterity. Your healthcare team or a certified occupational therapist can provide you with specific exercises designed to target the muscles and movements necessary for guitar playing.

For example, practicing with a guitar pick and using resistive putty can be a great way to improve your strumming and picking techniques. Resistive putty is a therapeutic tool commonly used in occupational therapy to strengthen muscles and improve fine motor skills. By incorporating these exercises into your daily routine, you can gradually rebuild the muscle memory needed to play the guitar.

In addition to physical exercises, mental exercises can also play a crucial role in regaining your guitar skills. Practicing visualization techniques can help reestablish the connection between your brain and the muscles involved in playing the instrument. Close your eyes and imagine yourself playing the guitar, focusing on the movements and sensations. This can help stimulate the neural pathways and facilitate the relearning process.

By engaging both your mind and body in the process of relearning to play the guitar, you can accelerate your progress and improve your overall performance. Remember to stay patient and consistent with your practice, as progress may take time but will be worth it in the end.

My final and most important tip for guitar stroke recovery is to trust in God throughout the process. His guidance and strength can provide comfort and motivation, especially during times of frustration and uncertainty. By embracing the journey with faith, you can find solace in knowing that you are not alone and that there is hope for a fulfilling musical recovery.

In conclusion, learning to play the guitar again after a stroke may be challenging, but it is definitely possible with the right mindset and approach. By incorporating physical and mental exercises into your daily routine and trusting in God for guidance and strength, you can overcome the obstacles and regain your ability to play guitar with proficiency and joy. Stay positive, stay motivated, and keep strumming back to life. Keep practicing, keep believing, and never give up on your musical dreams. Your guitar stroke recovery journey may have its ups and downs, but with God by your side, you can overcome any obstacle and make beautiful music once again. Amen!

RECOVERY WEEK 100
Celebrating the Journey of Relearning to Play Guitar

May the God of hope fill you with all joy and peace as you trust in him, so that you may overflow with hope by the power of the Holy Spirit.

—Romans 15:13

https://youtu.be/S6617SFEfOI

Have you ever had a setback that made you reevaluate your passions and abilities? Dealing with a stroke can be a challenging and life-changing experience, especially for a guitar player. However, through patience, perseverance, and a positive mindset, it is possible to embark on a journey of recovery and rediscovery of your love for playing guitar. In this journey vlog, I will explore the process of relearning to play guitar after a stroke, celebrating the 100th week of a video vlog documenting this journey, and sharing insights and tips for fellow musicians facing similar challenges.

When faced with the aftermath of a stroke, it is crucial to seek guidance from healthcare professionals who specialize in stroke recovery, such as physical therapists and occupational therapists. These experts can assess your condition, tailor exercises to aid in your recovery, and provide invaluable support and guidance along the way. Additionally, having a strong support system of loved ones and fellow musicians can offer encouragement and motivation during the challenging moments of your recovery process.

Rebuilding your guitar-playing abilities after a stroke requires dedication to regular practice sessions. Starting with short practice sessions and gradually increasing the duration as your skills improve is essential. Focusing on basic finger movements, chord progressions, and strumming patterns can help rebuild muscle memory and regain confidence in your playing. Consistency, patience, and a positive mindset are key factors in gradually regaining your guitar-playing abilities.

Playing guitar is not just a physical activity; it is a form of self-expression and a source of joy. Choosing songs and writing melodies that you love can make your practice sessions more enjoyable and engaging. Connecting with other musicians who have gone through similar experiences and sharing your progress can provide a sense of community and support. Remember to nurture your mental and emotional well-being throughout your recovery journey, as it is essential for your overall progress and well-being.

As you progress in your recovery journey, it is important to celebrate milestones and achievements along the way. The 100th Charlie's Guitar Stroke Recovery Video Vlog is a testament to dedication, perseverance, and resilience in relearning to play guitar after a stroke. This milestone is a reminder of how far you can come and a celebration of your ongoing progress and growth. Keep moving forward with confidence and determination, knowing that each small step brings you closer to your goals.

In conclusion, learning to play guitar again after a stroke is a challenging yet rewarding endeavor. By seeking professional guidance, practicing consistently, nurturing your mental and emotional well-being, and receiving support from loved ones and fellow musicians, you can overcome the challenges and obstacles on your recovery journey. Remember to celebrate every milestone, no matter how small, and keep moving forward with faith and determination. The journey may be long and challenging, but the pleasure of playing guitar once again will be worth every moment. Keep strumming, keep playing, and keep believing in yourself.

RECOVERY WEEK 101
The Healing Power of Music

Peace I leave with you; my peace I give to you. I do not give to you as the world gives. Do not let your hearts be troubled, and do not let them be afraid.

—John 14:27

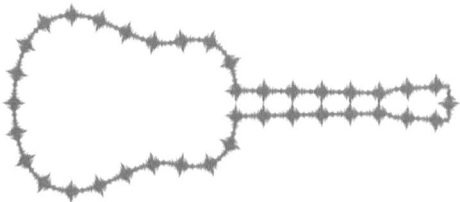

https://youtu.be/vkfsGoNawrM

Playing the guitar can be an effective way to express oneself and experience joy. Learning to play the guitar has been beneficial for many, including individuals recovering from medical conditions such as a stroke. This week, the focus was on the concept of relearning to play the guitar and exploring its potential benefits for overall well-being.

Playing the guitar is not just about creating music; it is a therapeutic outlet that can alleviate stress, tension, and anxiety. When you strum the strings and produce melodious tunes, it has a calming influence on the mind, allowing you to express your creativity and establish a deep connection with your emotions. Whether you are enjoying a solo session or jamming with fellow musicians, the harmonies generated by the guitar foster unity and connectivity, ultimately enhancing your state of being. So, why not let the guitar be your joyful voice, speaking volumes in the language of music?

One of the most valuable aspects of playing the guitar is its ability to restore and strengthen faith in God. As you strum a few chords or play intricate melodies, the act of creating music can be a deeply spiritual and uplifting experience. Music has the power to touch hearts and souls, and when combined with your faith, it can be a truly transformative experience. Through the guitar, you can express your devotion, find solace, joy, and a deeper connection to your spiritual beliefs. So, have you considered using the guitar as a tool to strengthen your faith in God?

The guitar serves as a powerful tool for expressing oneself, channeling emotions, and connecting with the soul. Its versatility as an instrument allows individuals to communicate their deepest thoughts, feelings, and beliefs through the language of music. Whether you are strumming chords or plucking melodies, the guitar enables you to convey your innermost emotions and draw closer to the spiritual realm. For many, the guitar is not just an instrument but a gateway to self-expression, soulful connection, and sharing the faith we hold in God.

Don't forget to check out this week's video, where I played a classic Christmas melody with a bluesy twist. It may not be perfect, but I hope you enjoy the tune and find inspiration in the healing power of music!

In conclusion, playing the guitar during my stroke recovery has been a journey of healing, self-discovery, and spiritual connection. It has allowed me to express myself blissfully, while also strengthening my faith and fostering unity with others through the power of music. So, if you are seeking to nurture your soul and explore the healing power of music, consider picking up a guitar and letting its melodies guide you on your own journey of self-expression and faith.

RECOVERY WEEK 102
A Real-Life Success Story
(Merry Christmas)

She will give birth to a son, and you are to name him Jesus,
because he will save his people from their sins.

—Matthew 1:21

https://youtu.be/JykC24t2COo

I have come a long way after my stroke, and I have to value how blessed I am that God has so much mercy and love. The lord has lifted me up from zero movement on the right side of my body to be able to drive to church, walk in church, and play lead guitar in church. So, I cry out to you, the most wonderful Hebrew liturgical expression "Hallclujah" ("Praise the Lord").

For this week, I would like to share a summarized real-life success story, highlighting the incredible healing power of music. Music has been known to have a profound impact on our emotions, mental well-being, and physical health. In this journey vlog, we will delve into the inspiring journey of Maria, a professional musician who overcame a devastating setback with the help of music therapy. We will also explore the magic of the Christmas season and the message of hope it brings.

Maria, a professional musician, faced a life-altering setback when she suffered a stroke that left her with significant motor and speech difficulties. Determined to regain her musical abilities, Maria turned to guitar playing as a way to reconnect with her passion for music. With the guidance of a music therapist, she embarked on a rehabilitation program that incorporated guitar playing exercises and techniques to help her recover. Through consistent practice and unwavering determination, Maria's fine motor skills gradually improved, enabling her to play complex melodies once again. The process not only contributed to her physical recovery but also reignited her love for music and rejuvenated her sense of purpose. Music became a powerful tool in her healing journey, providing comfort, motivation, and a sense of accomplishment.

As we celebrate the Christmas season, it is important to hold onto hope. Hope is what drives us to continue striving for a better tomorrow, despite the adversities we may face. It fuels our drive to reach new milestones and achieve our dreams, no matter how taxing the circumstances may be. Together, we can overcome life's obstacles and embrace the joy and magic that the holiday season brings.

During this Christmas season, let us show our support and uplift stroke survivors and their families. Let us celebrate their resolute spirits. Stroke survivors inspire us to never give up, to cherish the gift of life, and to embrace the magic of the holiday season. As we gather with our loved ones, let us remember and honor their courage and strength. Stroke survivors are true heroes, and their messages of love and hope resonate deeply within our hearts.

Reflecting on childhood experiences during the Christmas season, I was inspired to create a heartfelt melody on my guitar. Growing up in Rhode Island, the festive lights, Newport Mansions, Christmas parades, and cherished family traditions filled every moment with joy and excitement. These memories created a sense of nostalgia and gratitude that will last a lifetime. This holiday season let's take a moment to reflect on the magic and beauty that surrounds us and embrace the spirit of Christmas with the same wonder and joy we had as children.

In conclusion, the healing power of music is a remarkable force that can transform lives, inspire hope, and bring happiness even in the face of adversity. As we celebrate the Christmas season, let us remember the strength of stroke survivors and cherish the magic and beauty that surrounds us. Let music be a source of comfort, healing, and renewed purpose in our lives.

Recovery Week 103
Robust Hope for the New Year 2024

*"For I know the plans I have for you," declares the Lord,
"plans to prosper you and not to harm you, plans to give you
hope and a future."*

—Jeremiah 29:11

https://youtu.be/KnWEuW5rnTo

I believe we stroke survivors must have robust hope for the New Year. As we welcome in the New Year, (can you believe 2024) we stroke survivors around the world need to be filled with hope and determination. A stroke can be a life-altering event, affecting a person's physical and mental abilities. However, with the right support and mindset, we stroke survivors can overcome challenges and build a new life for ourselves. Our hopeful future is what changes how we live as we await Jesus's making all things new. This reminds me of 2 Corinthians 5:17, I believe this is one of the most important Bible verses about new beginnings, "Therefore if any man be in Christ, he is a new creature: old things are passed away; behold, all things are become new." It's a scripture that reminds me that embracing

Jesus and living a life like him can enable us to become a "new creation." Our old self is gone, and a new self emerges.

As determined stroke survivors, we are embarking on our journey of recovery in the New Year, it is also essential to embrace faith and positivity. Please ensure every small achievement and milestone is celebrated vigorously, as it signifies progress and our continued determination.

Setting realistic goals is crucial in our stroke recovery. Whether it's regaining the ability to walk independently or relearning a favorite hobby (like playing guitar), breaking down goals into smaller, achievable steps can provide a sense of accomplishment and motivation along the way.

Focusing on self-care plays a significant role in our stroke recovery. Taking care of one's physical, emotional, and mental well-being is essential for long-term success. Simple activities like getting enough sleep and practicing relaxation techniques can contribute to overall well-being and aid in the recovery process.

This week's video is an interesting mix of voicings, enjoy. ♫♫

Final Thoughts, Yes, us stroke survivors need to have robust hope, celebrated positivity, and faith in our Lord and Savior Jesus Christ for the New Year. With the right support, mindset, and determination, we can overcome challenges and rebuild our lives. Embracing hope, setting realistic goals, and taking care of oneself are key aspects of the recovery journey. Let's support all our stroke survivor friends in their pursuit of a fulfilling life in the New Year and beyond. Amen!

Recovery Week 104
I've Always Been Drawn to Music

Be strong and courageous. Do not fear or be in dread of them, for it is the Lord your God who goes with you. He will not leave you or forsake you.

—Deuteronomy 31:6

https://youtu.be/ugXlfwND7H0

Guitar is an instrument that has captured the hearts of millions of people around the world. From its melodic tones to its versatility, it has become a popular choice for both professional musicians and hobbyists alike. This week I would like to reveal just a few reasons, before my stroke, why I became interested in guitar in the first place, highlighting the journey that led me to this beautiful instrument.

I remember the initial spark that ignited my passion for music like it was yesterday. Growing up, I spent endless hours mesmerized by my parents' vinyl records, spinning on the record player, filling our home with their favorite tunes. However, it was during my early teenage years when I encountered the true catalyst that drove me to pick up the guitar. Living next to a professional guitar player was like having a front-row seat to magic. On those enchanting Rhode Island summer evenings, he would serenade the neighborhood from his porch, effortlessly coaxing mesmerizing melodies out of his electric guitar. I was spellbound, captivated by the beautiful sounds that resonated through the air. The emotions stirred within me were profound, unlike anything I had ever felt. That pivotal moment under the starlit sky made me realize that I needed to learn the guitar, to create my own enchanting music and embark on an adventurous journey through the harmonious realm of music. What's your story?

Another reason why I became interested in the guitar was its incredible versatility. Unlike some other instruments, the guitar can be played in a variety of genres, ranging from classical and jazz to rock and blues. This versatility meant I could explore different styles of music and truly express myself through the instrument.

Another aspect of the guitar that attracted me was its ability to unleash creativity and self-expression. Through its strings, I discovered a means to convey my emotions, thoughts, and experiences in a way that words alone could not. The guitar became my outlet, allowing me to share my innermost feelings with the world, even when words failed me.

Learning to play the guitar again because of a stroke has been and still is a difficult journey. This has required dedication, patience, countless hours of practice, and a strong faith in our Savior Jesus Christ. Yet, despite the challenges, the sense of accomplishment I felt with each note I mastered was unparalleled. Today, the guitar is still a teacher, shaping my discipline and persistence, while also rewarding me with the joy of progress. Amen!

For my guitar video this week I explored the iconic chord progression of F, C, A minor, and G, widely used in many hit songs from the 2000s and earlier. Not perfect, just having fun, I hope you enjoy it.

***

Final Thoughts: My interest in guitar was sparked by a profound experience that left an indelible mark on my soul. The guitar's versatility, its ability to foster self-expression and creativity, and the journey of relearning have deepened my love for this instrument. Playing the guitar has not only brought immense joy into my life but has also shaped me as a person. The guitar holds a special place in my heart, and I am grateful for the day I decided to embark on this musical journey.

RECOVERY WEEK 105
Remembering our Beloved Dog Dixie Do

Every creature which is in heaven and on the earth and under the earth and such as are in the sea, and all that are in them, saying, "Blessing and honor and glory and power be unto him that sitteth upon the throne and unto the Lamb forever and ever."

—Revelation 5:13

https://youtu.be/P4Gru1Ym3zM

Friday, January 12, 2024, marked the day we said goodbye to our little beautiful dog named Dixie Do. Born on February 8, 2008, Dixie Do graced our lives for sixteen years before her health started to deteriorate rapidly. With two strokes and a seizure, Dixie Do's journey on earth came to an end, and she crossed over the "Rainbow Bridge." In this week's heartfelt vlog post, I will share the emotional rollercoaster of losing our treasured companion and the impact she had on our lives.

Dixie Do was not just a dog; she was a cherished member of our family. Her wagging tail, bright eyes, and unconditional love brought immense joy into our lives. Losing her has created a void that cannot be filled. Our bond with Dixie Do went beyond that of a pet; she was a loyal companion who touched our hearts in ways words cannot convey.

Dixie Do's playful nature and boundless energy brought laughter and happiness wherever she went. Whether chasing squirrels in the backyard, cuddling on the couch, or listening to music in the music room, Dixie Do was always by our side, offering comfort and companionship. The memories we shared with her will forever be etched in our hearts.

The loss of Dixie Do has been overwhelming, and grief has consumed us. It is important to allow oneself to feel and process the emotions that come with such a significant loss. We believe it is okay to cry, mourn, and seek support from loved ones during this difficult time. Everyone handles grief differently, and there is no right or wrong way to mourn the loss of a beloved companion.

Although Dixie Do is no longer physically with us, her memory will live on in our hearts. We will honor her memory by cherishing the moments we shared and keeping her spirit alive in our home. While coping with the loss of a beloved pet takes time and patience, we find solace in the love and happiness Dixie Do added to our lives.

Losing Dixie Do has left a void in our hearts, but we take comfort in knowing that her memory will forever be cherished and celebrated. As we navigate the grieving process, we will hold onto the love and joy Dixie Do brought into our lives. This week's recorded music is dedicated to our little Dixie Do, a tune filled with mystery and unconventional melodies that we hope you enjoy.

> **Little Dixie she is gone, Her joy now flown away**
> **She brought smiles that linger on, In my heart she'll stay**
> **Every step echoes her paws, Silent rooms feel so bare**
> **Among shadows she'd so pause, Now just memories there**
> **Oh Dixie where'd you go, Your light my sorrow's foe**
> **Through the good and the woe, I'm missing you so**

As we bid farewell to Dixie Do, we held onto the love and memories she brought into our lives. Cherishing her memory, we find solace in the bond we shared and the joy she brought us. Dixie Do will forever hold a special place in our hearts, and her spirit will be celebrated always.

Recovery Week 106
Pushing the Envelope of Faith as a Stroke Survivor

And whatever you ask in prayer, you will receive, if you have faith.

—Matthew 21:22

https://youtu.be/xI0ayO0YC1Y

In studying the Gospel of Mark, we can learn valuable lessons from the faith of the people of that time. They believed in Jesus as the Son of God, a savior who performed miracles and healed the sick. They pushed the envelope of faith by believing in their hearts that he was the Messiah. Similarly, as stroke survivors, we can push the envelope of our own faith by challenging and expanding our beliefs, seeking a deeper understanding of spirituality, and growing closer to Jesus Christ in the face of adversity.

My good friend John, a stroke survivor, found strength and solace in his faith throughout his recovery journey. Despite facing physical and cognitive challenges, John's unwavering belief in God's plan has enabled him to push the envelope of his faith. Through prayer, counseling, and the support of his faith community, John has found hope and inspiration in the midst of difficulties. His story serves as a testament to the power of faith in overcoming adversity.

Dr. Emily Williams, a renowned neurologist and spiritual counselor, emphasizes the importance of self-compassion and patience in pushing the envelope of faith as a stroke survivor. She advises survivors to prioritize self-care, utilize positive affirmations, engage in meaningful activities, and practice gratitude to nurture both the body and the spirit. By following these practices, stroke survivors can find strength, renewed purpose, and a deepened faith on their journey to recovery.

1. Push the envelope of faith by challenging and expanding beliefs.

2. Find strength and inspiration in faith during recovery.

3. Prioritize self-care, positive affirmations, and gratitude.

4. Embrace challenges and seek support on the journey to recovery.

Hey there, fellow music explorer! Get ready for an electrifying journey in this week's video as I dive into the thrilling world of drop D tuning on my guitar. Brace yourself for a rollercoaster of creativity and innovation as we uncover fascinating ways to push the boundaries of this unique tuning. Join me on this audacious musical escapade, and let's embark on a wild ride together. So, grab your guitar, buckle up, and get ready to rock out in ways you've never imagined before! Adventure awaits, let's dive in and explore the endless possibilities of drop D tuning!

Pushing the envelope of faith as a stroke survivor is a deeply personal and transformative journey. It requires resilience, self-reflection, and a willingness to embrace challenges. By seeking support, engaging in practices that nurture the body and spirit, and holding onto faith, stroke survivors can find inspiration and healing in their recovery process. Remember, faith has the power to guide us toward a meaningful and fulfilling life, even in the face of adversity.

PS...I miss my special little Dixie Do very much.

RECOVERY WEEK 107
Finding Hope Through Faith

Rejoice in hope, be patient in tribulation, be constant in prayer.

—Romans 12:12

https://youtu.be/6ZHB0TaITzE

Hope produces courage (Romans 5:4–5), salvation (Romans 8:24), patience (Romans 8:25), joy (Romans 12:12), stability (Colossians 1:23), assurance (Hebrews 6:18–19), and purity (1 John 3:3). The Bible says that we're not ashamed to have hope because God's love has been poured into our hearts by the Holy Spirit (Romans 5:5).

At first, I felt overwhelmed by fear and uncertainty, questioning the purpose of my existence. However, as I sought solace in the comforting words of the Bible, I discovered a newfound understanding of hope. According to the Scriptures, hope is not just a mere wish or desire, but a firm belief in God's promises and His unwavering love for us. It is an anchor for the soul during trying times, providing the strength to persevere and the assurance that there is a greater plan unfolding.

This understanding has empowered me to not only overcome the physical challenges brought about by my stroke but also to embrace each day with renewed enthusiasm and gratitude. Through faith and hope, I have found peace in knowing that even amidst life's unexpected setbacks, there is always a glimmer of light guiding me toward a brighter future.

One of the most significant milestones on this path has been learning to play the guitar again. As I strum those familiar chords, it's not just about the music; it's a celebration of growth and accomplishment. There were moments when doubts crept in, and my fingers seemed to betray me, but I refused to give up. With each note I relearned, my confidence grew, and I realized that my stroke was not the end of my musical journey but merely a detour.

Now, when I lose myself in the rhythm of the strings, I not only see the progress I've made on my guitar, but I also see how far I've come in my own personal healing. It's a sweet reminder that no matter what challenges we face, we can still find pleasure and fulfillment in the things we are passionate about.

Reflecting on my life after a stroke has been a profound and transformative journey. From the initial shock and uncertainty to finding resilience, purpose, and hope, the process is one filled with both challenges and triumphs. By embracing our strength, seeking support, and redefining success, we can navigate the aftermath of a stroke with grace and determination. Together, let us find hope and inspire others as we rebuild our lives brick by brick.

PS: Thank you, David and Joyce, our wonderful neighbors and cherished friends, for the very thoughtful gift; we miss our little Dixie Do every day.

RECOVERY WEEK 108
Unleash the Power of Your Heart

Blessed are the pure in heart, for they will see God.

—Matthew 5:8

https://youtu.be/xUMrVNVKBLM

Are you ready to join a powerful team dedicated to fighting against strokes and supporting those affected by them? God believes in you and wants you to show your heart and share the valuable lessons you have learned along the way. Being a Stroke Warrior means embracing your inner warrior spirit, spreading love, hope, and healing, and making a positive impact on the lives of stroke survivors and their families.

Faith plays a crucial role in the lives of Stroke Warriors. By placing our trust in God, we can find relief and draw strength during the most difficult moments of our journey. Our faith enables us to find meaning and purpose in our circumstances, allowing us to persevere with unwavering determination. So, are you ready to trust in God and unleash the power of your heart as a Stroke Warrior?

Every small act of kindness or gesture of support can bring a ray of light into someone's life. Whether it's volunteering your time, organizing awareness campaigns, or simply offering a listening ear, your passion and empathy can create a positive impact. Joining the Stroke Warriors team means actively fighting against strokes, raising awareness, and supporting those affected by this condition. Will you join us in spreading love and hope to those who need it the most?

By hiding our hearts, we shut ourselves off from meaningful connections and hinder our personal and emotional growth. Embracing vulnerability can empower us, fostering deeper connections with others, empathy, compassion, personal growth, and self-acceptance. Let your heart guide you on this journey and inspire others to join the army of Stroke Warriors. Together, we can make a powerful difference and bring hope to those in need. So, please, *não esconda seu coração*—do not hide your heart!

In this week's video journal, I took on the challenge of playing some old-timey blues on the guitar, channeling the iconic B. B. King. Embracing the adventurous spirit, I pushed the boundaries of my right-hand picking control, striving to emulate the masterful style of the blues legend. The journey was not without its hurdles, but with each strum and bend of the strings, I felt a sense of growth and accomplishment. Grateful for the guidance and inspiration, I can't help but feel thankful for the progress made on this musical expedition. Thank you, God, for the opportunity to embark on this soulful musical adventure.

In conclusion, as Stroke Warriors, it is crucial to show our hearts, share our experiences, and support those in need. By embracing vulnerability and fostering deeper connections, we can make a positive impact on the lives of others. Let your heart guide you on this journey and be a beacon of hope and healing for those affected by strokes. Join the Stroke Warriors team today and make a difference in the world.

Recovery Week 109
Embracing Accountability and Faith

So then each of us will give an account to God.

—Romans 14:12

https://youtu.be/fxzFy9aDQ7E

All this week I have been exploring and pondering the pestering idea of taking accountability for myself, I will do my best to get these hounding ideas out my head and onto paper. In the beginning, living with the aftermath of a stroke was overwhelming (still battling small bouts of emotions); however, I realized it doesn't mean my life is over. We stroke survivors have the ability to take control of our destiny and regain independence. By embracing personal responsibility and having belief in oneself and faith in our Lord and Savior Jesus Christ, we can embark on a transformational journey toward empowerment and reclaiming our lives. What in the cat hair am I getting at? We Stroke Warriors need to explore the importance of accountability, the role of faith in the recovery process, and practical steps to cultivate a sense of empowerment.

Taking accountability for oneself is the first step toward regaining control and embracing personal responsibility. Instead of dwelling in the past or blaming external factors for our unfortunate condition, Stroke Warriors have the power to focus on the present and future. By acknowledging our role in the recovery process, we can actively participate in rehabilitation programs, make healthier lifestyle choices, and seek support from health-care professionals, caregivers, and support groups.

Here are some ways to stay on target:

1. Setting realistic goals for recovery
2. Implementing the SMART goals method
3. Overcoming setbacks and cultivating resilience
4. Using faith as a guiding light

Faith plays a significant role in anyone's recovery journey. Believing in a higher power or having a strong spiritual connection can provide comfort, strength, and hope during challenging times. Faith can serve as a guiding light during uncertainties and moments of doubt, allowing us Stroke Warriors to draw upon our inner resilience and tap into God's perfect spiritual resources.

Other ways to support yourself include:

1. Finding support in faith communities
2. The Church of Jesus Christ of Latter-day Saints' view on faith
3. The comfort and strength of fellow believers
4. Resources for stroke survivors on social media
5. Using music therapy for rehabilitation

During my thirty-year military career, I learned that accountability goes hand in hand with setting realistic goals. The military taught me to apply valuable accountability lessons by defining clear and attainable objectives. We Stroke Warriors can create a roadmap for our recovery journey. Whether it is improving mobility, regaining speech, or managing emotions, setting achievable goals helps us maintain a sense of direction and motivation.

For this week's video journal, I embarked on an exploration of the blues theme, taking another exciting leap forward in my musical journey. Delving into the nuances of my picking hand, I embraced the challenge of refining my strumming and picking techniques with a newfound sense of adventurous curiosity. By focusing on cultivating a lighter touch and mastering controlled timing with my right hand, I am venturing into uncharted territories of skill and artistry, driven by a relentless passion for growth and experimentation in my music.

Living life to the fullest after a stroke is possible by embracing accountability, having faith, and taking practical steps toward empowerment. Stroke survivors have the strength and resilience to overcome challenges and reclaim their lives. By setting realistic goals, cultivating a resilient mindset, and finding support in faith communities, we can navigate the journey toward recovery with confidence. So, let's take that leap of faith and embark on a transformational journey toward empowerment.

Recovery Week 110
Trusting in God and Embracing the Healing Power of Music

Hear this, you kings! Listen, you rulers! I, even I, will sing to the LORD; I will praise the LORD, the God of Israel, in song.

—Judges 5:3

https://youtu.be/3aHiaXTz5Pc

Growing up, I had always been interested in playing the guitar, but it wasn't until after my stroke that I truly appreciated the therapeutic benefits of music. Learning to play the guitar or relearning to play guitar, as I have been saying for months, can be a transformative experience for stroke survivors. This journey has not only improved my cognitive functions but has also provided me with a creative outlet and enhanced my overall well-being.

As stroke survivors embark on the journey of learning to play the guitar, it is essential to have trust in God. Trusting in a higher power can provide comfort, strength, and resilience during challenging times. By surrendering to God's will and believing in His plan, stroke survivors can find peace as they navigate the ups and downs of their recovery journey. The verse from Proverbs 3:5–6 reminds us to "Trust in the LORD with all your heart and lean not on your understanding; in all your ways submit to Him, and He will make your paths straight."

When learning a new skill or relearning a skill, such as playing the guitar, it is crucial to approach the process with objectivity. This means setting realistic goals, practicing patience, and being open to feedback and guidance. Stroke survivors may face physical and cognitive challenges along the way, but by taking a step back and looking at the progress objectively, we can stay motivated and continue to improve.

Learning to play the guitar is not just about mastering a musical instrument; it is about the journey of self-discovery, growth, and healing. As a stroke survivor, I have found joy and fulfillment in expressing myself through music, connecting with other stroke survivors, and achieving personal milestones in relearning to play the guitar. By staying positive, patient, and trusting in God, stroke survivors can experience the healing power of music in their recovery process.

Also, learning to play the guitar can be a transformative experience for stroke survivors. By approaching this journey with trust in God, objectivity, and a positive mindset, stroke survivors can reap the benefits of music therapy and enjoy the healing power of music. As we overcome challenges, celebrate victories, and find joy in the journey, we can discover new ways to express ourselves and connect with others through the universal language of music.

For my guitar video this week, I took on the challenge of playing swing. While it may not be perfect, the challenge was worth the effort and discovery. My son Chad, who is an excellent drummer and toured throughout the US with the Spirit Drum Core, explained playing swing as being able to play on the beat, behind the beat, or ahead of the beat. Playing swing is like playing all three, and the experience of tackling this challenge was truly rewarding.

In conclusion, the journey of relearning to play the guitar as a stroke survivor has been both challenging and rewarding. Through trust in God, objectivity, and a positive mindset, stroke survivors can harness the healing power of music to enhance their recovery process. Embracing the challenges, celebrating victories, and finding joy in the journey are all part of the transformative experience of music therapy in stroke rehabilitation.

Recovery Week 111
The Acorn Parable Reminder

But I will sing of your strength, in the morning I will sing of your love; for you are my fortress, my refuge in times of trouble.

—Psalm 59:16

https://youtu.be/5gaFkweFbdg

Have you ever come across a story that sticks with you for years, even if you can't quite remember all the details? I've been reflecting on a tale I read many years ago called *The Journey of an Acorn*. Although the specifics elude me, the essence of the parable has stayed with me, especially during this Recovery Week 111. The acorn parable beautifully illustrates the potential for growth and transformation found in even the smallest of things. Stroke survivors, like the acorn, face immense challenges but possess the innate power to not only survive but thrive. Just as the acorn must weather storms to become a towering oak, stroke survivors navigate their own tumultuous journeys with unwavering determination and courage. Embracing the essence of the acorn parable is a choice to assert resilience and believe in the boundless possibilities that lie ahead. It serves as a reminder that hope and renewal are always within reach, urging stroke survivors to tap into their inner strength and unyielding spirit.

Imagine a tiny acorn, seemingly insignificant yet containing the potential for greatness within its small shell. Similarly, faith in something greater than ourselves, like faith in God, allows for miraculous transformations. Just as the acorn trusts in the unseen process that turns it into a mighty oak, embracing faith in God helps us weather life's storms with resilience. With unwavering faith, we can surpass our limitations and reach heights we never thought possible. Trusting in divine purpose and wisdom guides us through challenges, knowing that our roots run deep, and our future is secure.

This week's video journal brought about my biggest challenge yet, creating motifs using major and minor scales to craft a slow, melodic jazz lead in my video recording. Despite the hurdles, I dove in with determination to push my musical boundaries and create something truly engaging. I hope you enjoy the fruits of my labor as I continue to push myself in my recovery journey.

In conclusion, the acorn parable serves as a powerful reminder of the resilience and potential for growth within all of us, especially in the face of adversity. Just as the acorn transforms into a mighty oak, stroke survivors have the capacity to rise, bloom, and flourish against all odds. Embrace your inner strength, have faith in the process, and trust in the journey ahead, the possibilities are endless.

RECOVERY WEEK 112
Trusting in God and Embracing Music

*Have I not commanded you? Be strong and courageous. Do
not be frightened, and do not be dismayed, for the LORD
your God is with you wherever you go.*

—Joshua 1:9

https://youtu.be/f_0N9967TCI

As a Stroke Warrior, I am incredibly blessed to have the opportunity to
play lead guitar in church every Sunday. This role is not only a passion of
mine but also a way for me to express my trust in God through music. I
am so grateful for the strength and resilience that has allowed me to continue pursuing my passion despite the challenges I have faced. With each
strum of the guitar and each note I played, I sense the grace and mercy of
God in my life. I hope to demonstrate my dedication of my craft, and I
am so willing to share God's gift of music with the congregation, which
is a true reflection of my deep-rooted faith. Through music, I hope to
spread a message of hope, love, and perseverance, proving that with God

by your side, anything is possible.

Trust in God isn't just about saying it; it's about truly living it out. By placing your trust in God, you are embracing a source of hope, strength, and resilience in the face of adversity. Imagine God as your divine GPS, guiding you through life's chaotic traffic with a calm voice saying, "Turn left on Faith Street, proceed straight on Perseverance Avenue, and you will reach Blessings Boulevard." It's not always easy, but with a sprinkle of faith, a dash of determination, and a pinch of humor, you'll find that your belief in God can become the compass that steers you through the stormiest seas of life. So, dear Stroke Warriors, hold onto that trust in God like it's the last piece of chocolate in a room full of stressed-out adults, savor it, enjoy it, and let it carry you through the highs and lows with a wink and a smile!

I am doing something different for my video this week. A good friend of mine, Todd Hartwell, has written a beautiful song and asked me to add some guitar. Todd has been so encouraging since the beginning of my stroke recovery—I mean every step along the way. We talk every Sunday evening on MS Teams. You see, many years ago Todd and I went on a world tour together. I have to add that Todd is the best keyboard/piano player I ever had the chance to perform with. I have so many fond memories, like when I was stationed in the United Kingdom. We played so many English pubs together—the most enjoyable were the Three Horses Shoes and The Punch Bowl. Todd is an excellent musician in the Seattle area, and he has played with some greats. Todd is also an excellent music producer and has his own recording studio. I hope and pray I do his song justice!

In Week 112 of my guitar stroke recovery, my journey continues on a path of faith, resilience, and musical collaboration with my good friend Todd Hartwell. Despite the challenges faced along the way, I truly remain steadfast in my trust in God, using music as a form of expression and hopefully inspiration for others. Through my experiences, I am reminded of the power of perseverance and the beauty of blessings in my life and hopefully in your life. Stroke Warriors, let's work together to overcome obstacles and shine a light of hope through music.

RECOVERY WEEK 113
Understanding Velocity and Alignment

In the same way, let your light shine before others, so that
they may see your good works and give glory to your Father
who is in heaven.

—Matthew 5:16

https://youtu.be/xRS0yrLqX_M

In this week's vlog post, we will delve into the importance of velocity and alignment in the recovery journey of a Stroke Warrior. Velocity and alignment refer to the speed and direction in which we operate in our daily lives. Some individuals may thrive in a fast-paced environment, while others may prefer a more methodical approach. However, it is essential to recognize our own unique velocities and alignments to avoid feeling stressed, overwhelmed, or unbalanced. By aligning ourselves with our natural rhythm, we can enhance our overall well-being and achieve a greater sense of fulfillment.

As Stroke Warriors, maintaining a life balance is paramount in our recovery journey. This balance encompasses our physical, emotional, and spiritual well-being, all of which play a crucial role in our strength and resilience. By prioritizing self-care and nurturing all aspects of our being, we can overcome challenges more effectively and build a solid foundation for our healing journey. It is vital to listen to our bodies, minds, and spirits, and honor our unique needs to achieve a harmonious balance in life.

Music is a powerful form of worship that allows us to express our praises, love, and gratitude to God. Through music, we can enhance our worship experience, uplift and encourage one another, or find solace and peace in times of need. Playing the guitar, in particular, can be a therapeutic and spiritual practice that enables us to connect with our innermost thoughts and emotions. As I relearn how to play the guitar, I find joy in expressing myself through music, knowing that it is a form of worship that brings me closer to God.

In this week's guitar video, I attempted to play some rock blues in the key of A7 using a call-and-response approach. Through music, I aim to share my journey of resilience and faith as a Stroke Warrior, demonstrating the power of velocity and alignment in driving my recovery progress. I hope you enjoy this musical rendition and find inspiration in embracing your own journey of healing and restoration.

As Stroke Warriors, it is crucial for us to find our own velocity and alignment in life. By aligning ourselves with our natural rhythms and honoring our unique needs, we can achieve a sense of balance, harmony, and well-being. Through music, worship, and self-care practices, we can cultivate a deep connection to our inner selves and to God, finding strength, peace, and resilience in the face of adversity. Let us strive to embody velocity and alignment in our recovery journey, knowing that with faith and determination, we can overcome any challenge that comes our way. Amen!

RECOVERY WEEK 114
Trusting in God: Finding Strength and Purpose as Stroke Warriors

Blessed is the man who trusts in the LORD, whose trust is the LORD. He is like a tree planted by water.

—Jeremiah 17:7–8

https://youtu.be/IEA4dduas6M

In the Creed of the US Junior Chamber of Commerce, William Brownfield penned the powerful words, "Faith in God gives meaning and purpose to human life." These words resonate deeply with those who face adversity, such as Stroke Warriors, who rely on unwavering trust in God to navigate life's challenges. In this week's vlog journal, let's explore how faith in God empowers us to find strength, purpose, and resilience in the face of adversity.

As Stroke Warriors, we face unique challenges that test our physical, emotional, and spiritual resilience. It is during these difficult times that our faith in God serves as a guiding light, shining through the darkness and providing us with hope and comfort. By entrusting our struggles and triumphs to a higher power, we are able to draw strength from our faith and find purpose in our journey.

When we anchor our sense of purpose in our faith, we are able to find meaning in even the most chaotic and uncertain circumstances. Trusting in God transforms our struggles into opportunities for growth, our pain into avenues for healing, and our journey into a profound testament of faith. By embracing our role as Stroke Warriors with unwavering trust in God, we are able to navigate life's challenges with grace and dignity.

With each passing week of my recovery, I am presented with new opportunities to challenge myself and embrace growth and healing. By pushing myself to relearn guitar chords and melodies, I am not only improving my physical abilities but also reaffirming my trust in God's plan. Through perseverance and dedication, we all are able to discover the gold in ourselves and others, rather than focusing on the coal.

Ultimately, faith in God allows us to experience the joy of His unconditional love and presence in our lives. It is through this profound trust in His plan that we are able to find strength in moments of weakness, courage in moments of fear, and hope in the face of uncertainty. By embracing our role as Stroke Warriors with faith as our foundation, we are able to walk confidently through life's challenges, knowing that we are never alone.

As we continue on our journey as Stroke Warriors, let us remember the profound impact that faith in God can have on our lives. By trusting in His plan and embracing our role with unwavering belief, we are able to find strength, purpose, and resilience in the face of adversity. Let us continue to challenge ourselves, grow, and heal, knowing that God's love and guidance are ever-present. Trusting in God truly gives meaning and purpose to our human lives.

RECOVERY WEEK 115
Embracing the Power of Friendship in Recovery

A friend loves at all times, and a brother is born for a time of adversity.

—Proverbs 17:17

https://youtu.be/x9iOjsgLxko

This week, my curious mind was working overtime, wondering how many friend categories are out there in the world and how us Stroke Warriors can count on and need these friend types. I believe the differences in these classifications lie in the amount of intimacy and how much you are willing to share about yourself to others. With best friends, your commitment is deep, while with casual friends, your intimacy level is lower, indicating less commitment.

Types of Friends Based on intimacy levels:

1. Best Friends: These are the friends with whom you share a deep bond and can confide in without hesitation.

2. Casual Friends: These friends are more surface-level but provide companionship and support in times of need.

3. Work Friends: Colleagues who offer a different perspective and can provide a sense of normalcy during recovery.

4. Church Friends: Spiritual companions who uplift your spirit and provide comfort and guidance.

5. Neighbor Friends: Those who are close by and can offer practical help and support during your recovery journey.

Stroke Warriors, it is essential for us to surround ourselves with all types of friends to enhance our recovery journey. From compassionate listeners to motivating cheerleaders, each friend plays a unique role in our path toward healing. These friends offer emotional, physical, and mental support that are crucial during our recovery process. It is also vital to highlight the importance of having friends who help strengthen our trust in God, uplifting our spirits and reminding us that we are never alone in our struggles.

By fostering a assorted network of friends, we create a robust support system that empowers us to overcome the challenges of stroke recovery and emerge stronger on the other side. Let us embrace the power of friendship in all its forms and lean on the generosity of companionship to aid us in our journey toward recovery.

In conclusion, Stroke Warriors, remember that having a variety of friends in your life is beneficial for your recovery. Different friends offer different forms of support, all of which are essential in your journey toward healing. Surround yourself with a supportive network, and you will find the strength to overcome any obstacle that comes your way.

RECOVERY WEEK 116
A Source of Comfort and Guidance

In Psalm 91, the psalmist says, "For he commands his angels with regard to you, to guard you wherever you go. With their hands they shall support you, lest you strike your foot against a stone."

https://youtu.be/0Rf8QUbRAqM

Have you ever found yourself in unexplained situations that seem to have a guiding force behind them? Many stroke buddies have shared remarkable stories of inexplicable events that have taken place during their journey of recovery. From sudden bursts of clarity in the midst of confusion to experiencing a soothing presence during moments of distress, these occurrences often leave us pondering the existence of guardian angels. Despite the skeptics, these stories can't be easily dismissed as mere coincidence or hallucination. There's a compelling sense of divine intervention at play when you reflect on the sheer complexity of surviving and thriving after a stroke. Maybe, just maybe, these guardian angels are working behind the scenes, watching over us, and offering a helping hand in our times of need.

Believing in the presence of guardian angels is a deep personal conviction, and for many, it serves as a source of comfort and guidance in times of need. The idea that these celestial beings could have played a role in helping me to rediscover my passion for playing the guitar is indeed a compelling and heartwarming notion. Whether through subtle nudges, a stroke of inspiration, or a sense of calm that envelops me during practice, the belief in guardian angels provided me the motivation and encouragement needed to persevere through challenges. Embracing this belief not only gives me a renewed sense of purpose but also serves as a reminder that support and guidance may come from unexpected sources.

So, Stroke Warriors, as you navigate through the challenges and victories of your recovery, consider the possibility of guardian angels being by your side, guiding you through unexplainable situations with a reassuring presence. After all, in a world filled with uncertainties, having faith in these unseen forces can provide an extra layer of comfort and assurance as you continue to defy the odds and forge ahead on your journey of healing.

Unfortunately, I did not record a video this week; I have been under the weather all week long. However, I put together a reflecting video beginning with the first time I picked up my guitar after my stroke. Reflecting on where you have been and where you are now is crucial for personal growth and development. This self-reflection not only helps you understand yourself better but also empowers you to set new goals and make informed decisions for your future. So, give yourself the gift of reflection, and watch how it transforms your life in positive ways.

In conclusion, believing in guardian angels can provide a sense of comfort, guidance, and reassurance in times of need. Whether it's through subtle signs or a comforting presence, these celestial beings may be working behind the scenes to help us navigate through life's challenges. So, embrace the possibility of divine intervention, trust in the unseen forces that may be guiding you, and allow yourself to reflect on the journey of healing and growth. After all, having faith in guardian angels can be a powerful source of strength and inspiration as you continue to overcome obstacles and thrive in the face of adversity.

Recovery Week 117
Finding Strength in the Right People at the Right Time

You saw me before I was born. Every day of my life was recorded in your book. Every moment was laid out before a single day had passed.

—Psalm 139:16

https://youtu.be/MbDbI7ba_ag

As I continue my journey of recovery from a stroke and rediscover the joy of playing the guitar, I am constantly reminded of the incredible individuals who have crossed my path at just the right moment. From friends and family to healthcare professionals and even strangers, each person has played a crucial role in providing me with the support and strength I need to overcome this challenging time in my life.

In the midst of adversity, it is easy to feel isolated and alone. However, I have come to realize that God has a way of orchestrating the people we meet and the relationships we form in order to bring us the support and encouragement we need to persevere. "There are no coincidences when it comes to the people God placed and planned to be in our lives," said a staff writer on the Deep Spirituality editorial team. This belief has been a source of great comfort and inspiration for me throughout my recovery journey.

As a Stroke Warrior, I have been blessed to be surrounded by individuals who not only offer their unwavering support but also provide me with the courage and determination to face each day with resilience. Whether it is the healthcare professionals who guide me through rehabilitation, the friends and family who stand by my side, or even the kind strangers who offer a helping hand, each person has become a pillar of strength in my life.

In times of hardship, it is often the people around us who give us the strength to carry on. The words of encouragement, acts of kindness, and ongoing faith in our ability to overcome obstacles serve as a constant reminder that we are never truly alone. As Stroke Warriors, we are part of a community that understands the challenges we face and is there to lift us up when we stumble. I am endlessly grateful for the incredible individuals who have come into my life during this challenging time. Their presence has been a constant source of comfort and inspiration, and I know I would not be where I am today without their support.

I invite you to watch a short guitar video I posted this week, where I explore string bending to create a bluesy-rock feel. I hope you enjoy this jam and feel the love and support that surrounds me on this journey. Together, we are stronger.

Remember, we are never alone in our struggles. God has a way of putting the right people in our lives at the right time to help us overcome even the toughest challenges. So, embrace the support around you, lean on your community, and together, we can conquer anything that comes our way. Stay strong, Stroke Warriors!

Recovery Week 118
A Story of Faith and Resilience

The Scriptures teach, "God is love" (1 John 4:8). You can feel that love as you speak daily with Him through prayer, seeking His guidance in your life.

https://youtu.be/IXURKKHETlA

The past week has been quite a challenging yet rewarding experience for me as I traveled up north to Maine to help my older brother during his time of need. Despite the difficulties and uncertainties we faced, prayer served as a guiding force that helped us navigate through the obstacles with strength and resilience. In this week's vlog, I will share with you the valuable lessons I learned from this experience and how the power of faith can truly make a difference in the face of adversity.

When my older brother's health deteriorated to the point where he could no longer live on his own, my *querida gracioso* and I turned to prayer for guidance on how to best support him. Through our faith and unwavering belief in God's plan, we were able to devise a solid plan of action that alleviated a great deal of stress and worry from my brother's life. The sheer act of seeking divine guidance through prayer brought us clarity, peace, and a sense of direction in the midst of uncertainty.

As Stroke Soldiers, individuals facing the challenges of a stroke and its aftermath often find themselves in difficult and trying situations. In times like these, the power of prayer can offer a profound sense of comfort, hope, and resilience. By turning to God and seeking His guidance, we can tap into a deep well of inner strength and motivation that enables us to face adversity with courage and determination. It is a testament to the remarkable ability of faith to uplift and empower individuals in their darkest moments.

For those of us who have older brothers in need of support and care, prayer can be a powerful tool in providing comfort and assistance. By relying on our faith and trusting in God's plan, we can offer our loved ones a sense of reassurance and strength that helps them navigate through life's challenges. The act of praying for our older brothers not only brings us closer to them but also enables us to be a source of comfort and inspiration in their time of need.

As I reflect on the events of this past week, I am reminded of the remarkable power of faith and prayer in guiding us through life's toughest challenges. By placing our trust in God and seeking His guidance, we can find solace, hope, and resilience in the face of adversity. Remember, we are never alone in our journey and with faith as our guiding light, we can overcome any obstacle that comes our way.

In conclusion, the journey of Charlie's Guitar Stroke Recovery Week 118 has been a testament to the transformative power of faith and prayer in navigating life's most difficult challenges. Through our unwavering belief in God's plan, we were able to support my older brother with love, compassion, and strength. As I return home from Maine, I am grateful for the lessons learned and the resilience gained through this experience. Amen! And now, enjoy this older video from Week 36 of guitar recovery. Let's continue to walk this path of faith and resilience together, knowing that with God's grace, all things are possible. Amen!

Recovery Week 119
Embracing Change Through Faith

Have I not commanded you? Be strong and courageous. Do not be afraid; do not be discouraged, for the LORD your God will be with you wherever you go.

—Joshua 1:9

https://youtu.be/tcvpNNQ5zFc

Are you ready to embrace change and trust in the process of recovery? Change is a natural part of life, and even though it can be challenging, it is essential for growth and healing. As we navigate through the chapters of our lives, there will be unexpected changes that we must face with courage and resilience. In this week's journal, let's explore how trust in God can help us embrace change with a positive mindset, especially during difficult times like stroke recovery.

How do we navigate through life's unexpected changes, especially when they are as significant as a life-changing event like having a stroke? It can be overwhelming and daunting to face the uncertainties that come with such a transition. However, by trusting in God and believing in His plan for us, we can find the strength and guidance we need to move forward.

When we place our trust in a higher power, we can find comfort in knowing that we are not alone in our journey toward recovery. By leaning on our faith, we can gain a sense of peace and assurance that everything will work out for the best. Trusting in God allows us to surrender our fears and worries, knowing that He is in control of our lives.

Every obstacle we face, including the challenges of stroke recovery, is meant to shape us into stronger individuals. By embracing change with a positive mindset and complete trust in God, we can adapt to new circumstances with grace and resilience. With faith as our guide, we can navigate through the waves of change and come out stronger on the other side.

This week, I made a short recovery video showcasing my progress in applying the harmonic minor scale over the chords of Am, E7, and E. I hope you enjoy it and witness the journey of growth and healing through music. As I continue on this path of recovery, I challenge you to guess the last chord I used at the end of the tune. Stay tuned for more updates on my guitar stroke recovery journey!

In conclusion, embracing change through trust in God is essential for our growth and healing, especially during challenging times like stroke recovery. By surrendering our fears and worries to a higher power, we can navigate through life's transitions with grace and resilience. Trust in the process, believe in the journey, and know that every obstacle we face is meant to shape us into stronger individuals. Let your faith be your anchor as you embrace the changes that come your way.

Recovery Week 120
Embracing the Process and Purpose

The steadfast love of the Lord never ceases; his mercies never come to an end.

—Lamentations 3:22

https://youtu.be/oeWFjVG0KgU

Have you ever stopped to consider whether you are driven by the process or the purpose behind your actions? This week, a good friend and work-mate reminded me of the importance of understanding the deeper meaning behind our endeavors. He exemplified how being purpose-driven can significantly impact our journey toward success. So, let's delve into the concept of embracing the process and purpose, especially as Stroke Warriors relearning how to play musical instruments such as the guitar.

Are you someone who finds joy in the intricate details of the process, or are you more focused on the why behind what you are doing? Some individuals thrive on the steps, the skills, and the nuances of the journey. For them, the process itself is just as rewarding as the end result. On the other hand, purpose-driven individuals are motivated by the impact, the end goal, and the greater meaning of their actions. They are driven by a deeper sense of fulfillment and meaning in their endeavors.

For me, I personally resonate more with being purpose driven. I find that understanding the why behind my actions gives me a sense of direction and drive. What about you? Take a moment to reflect on what truly inspires you and gives your efforts meaning.

As Stroke Warriors, we are on a unique journey of recovery and rediscovery. We are constantly challenged to relearn skills and overcome obstacles. The process of rehabilitation provides us with structure and guidance, but it is the deeper purpose behind our journey that fuels our passion and determination. Trusting in a higher power, such as God, gives us strength and courage to face each challenge with confidence.

By embracing both the process and purpose, we can find a balance that propels us forward. The process gives us the tools and resources we need, while the purpose ignites our inner fire and motivates us to keep pushing forward. Together, we stand united in our journey as Stroke Warriors, with a shared purpose driving us toward our goals.

This week's guitar recovery video showcases a new chord progression and musical scale that I am exploring. By experimenting with different musical elements, such as the hexatonic minor scale, I am not only improving my guitar skills but also engaging in a form of music therapy. Music has the power to heal, inspire, and uplift us, making it a valuable tool in our journey of recovery and rediscovery. Music therapy can help us express emotions, enhance cognitive skills, and improve physical coordination. By incorporating music into our rehabilitation journey, we can tap into a powerful form of therapy that supports our overall well-being.

In conclusion, whether you are driven by the process itself or the deeper purpose behind your actions, it is essential to find a balance that resonates with your values and goals. As Stroke Warriors, we can embrace both the process and purpose, allowing us to navigate our journey with courage, passion, and resilience. Let's continue to explore new horizons, push boundaries, and strive for growth as we walk this extraordinary path of recovery.

RECOVERY WEEK 121
Harnessing the Power of Human Values in Stroke Recovery

*Finally, brothers, whatever is true, whatever is honorable,
whatever is just, whatever is pure, whatever is lovely,
whatever is commendable, if there is any excellence, if there
is anything worthy of praise, think about these things.*

—Philippians 4:8

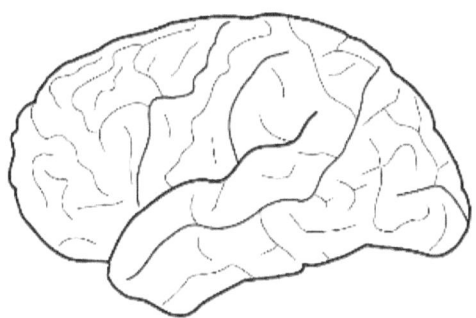

https://youtu.be/-27-WbCUJi0s

Just how important are our human values in the road to recovery after a stroke? This week, I delved into the topic, drawing on my experience as a former military instructor and present Army Civilian career manager. Join me as we explore the profound impact our values can have on the healing process.

Our values, whether learned or natural, form the core of who we are as individuals. Shaped by our upbringing, culture, and personal beliefs, they guide our actions and decisions every day. When faced with a challenging journey like stroke recovery, our values become even more crucial. They give us the resilience, determination, and positive mindset needed to overcome obstacles and keep pushing forward.

So, how can we leverage our values to bolster our recovery as stroke survivors? By embracing compassion, empathy, and gratitude, we create a nurturing environment that supports our healing process. Trusting in a higher power can also provide comfort, strength, and hope during difficult times. Together, we can lean on our values, support each other with kindness, and trust in the journey toward full recovery.

Each of us is on a unique journey toward healing and recovery. It's a challenging path, but one that can be illuminated by the light of our values. By reflecting on our experiences, contemplating what truly matters to us, and refining our values, we deepen our understanding of ourselves and the world around us. This introspection can be a powerful tool in our recovery, helping us stay focused on what's truly important as we navigate the ups and downs of the healing process.

In this week's guitar recovery video, I experimented with chord voicings of E, F#m, and B to create greater freedom on the fretboard. By incorporating intervals and other expressive elements into my playing, I challenged myself to explore new ways to connect with the music. As a Stroke Warrior, the journey toward full recovery is not always easy, but it's incredibly rewarding. I hope you enjoy the musical journey as much as I have. Keep shining bright, warriors, and remember to lean on your values, support each other with kindness, and trust in the healing power of music and community. Together, we can overcome any obstacle that comes our way.

As we continue on our journey of stroke recovery, let's remember the power of our human values to guide us through. With resilience, determination, and a positive mindset, we can overcome any challenge that comes our way. So, keep strumming those chords, keep pushing forward, and keep shining bright, warriors. We're in this together.

RECOVERY WEEK 122
A Journey of Gratitude and Faith

*Gracious words are a honeycomb, sweet to the soul and
healing to the bones.*

—Proverbs 16:24

https://youtu.be/z4RCeAEx7Tk

As I reflect on the month of May, which is recognized as American Stroke Month, I am filled with gratitude for the progress I have made in my recovery journey. Stroke, the second leading cause of death worldwide, has impacted millions of lives, including my own. The statistics are staggering, with an estimated seventeen million strokes occurring globally each year and someone suffering a stroke every forty seconds in the United States. It is a sobering reality that requires awareness and action.

In 1989, President George H. W. Bush signed Presidential Proclamation 5975, officially designating May as National Stroke Awareness Month. This initiative brought much-needed attention to the prevention and treatment of stroke, highlighting the urgency of recognizing symptoms and seeking immediate medical help. Organizations like The American Stroke Association play a crucial role in educating the public and providing lifesaving programs to those at risk.

It is essential to be aware of the common symptoms of stroke, which can be remembered as "BE FAST":

1. Balance: Sudden loss of balance.
2. Eyes: Sudden blurry or loss of vision.
3. Face: Sudden numbness or one side drooping.
4. Arms: Sudden weakness in arms, inability to raise arm(s).
5. Speech: Slurred or mumbling speech, severe headache.
6. Time: Time to call 911 and seek emergency medical attention.

Responding quickly to these symptoms can make a significant difference in the outcome of a stroke. It is crucial to act fast and call for help, as time is of the essence when it comes to stroke treatment.

As a stroke survivor, I have faced moments of doubt and despair during my recovery journey. However, it is through my unwavering faith and inner strength that I have found the courage to overcome challenges that once seemed insurmountable. God's presence and love have been a constant source of grace and mercy, guiding me through the complexities of life with resilience and hope.

In my guitar recovery video for Week 122, I chose a soulful backing track to showcase the progress I have made with my pick hand. This performance served as a culmination of all the hard work and dedication I have put into my recovery journey. It was a testament to my perseverance and determination to overcome adversity.

In closing, I am grateful for the blessings and protection that have been bestowed upon me throughout my recovery. God's guidance and endless love have carried me through the darkest moments, filling my heart with hope and gratitude. As I continue on this journey, I am reminded of the power of faith and inner strength to overcome any challenge that comes my way.

Recovery Week 123
Embracing the Power of Music and Faith

Have mercy on me, Lord, for I am faint; heal me, Lord, for my bones are in agony.

—Psalm 6:2

https://youtu.be/JdHjUIPjPVs

As Stroke Warriors, harnessing the power of musical intelligence can significantly enhance our recovery journey. Music possesses a unique ability to engage various parts of the brain simultaneously, potentially aiding in cognitive, emotional, and physical rehabilitation post-stroke. By immersing ourselves in melodies and rhythms, we stimulate neural pathways, promote relaxation, and elevate mood, all of which are crucial elements in the healing process. Additionally, music can serve as a form of self-expression and a source of motivation, driving us toward setting and achieving rehabilitation goals.

In addition to the therapeutic benefits of musical intelligence, we cannot overlook the importance of faith in our God. During challenging times like stroke recovery, turning to God can provide strength, hope, and resilience that go beyond what music or any other form of therapy can offer. Integrating musical intelligence with spiritual support can create a holistic approach to recovery, nurturing both the mind and soul on our path to healing. Let us embrace the power of music and the guidance of God as Stroke Warriors, forging ahead with determination and faith toward our journey of recovery.

In this week's video, the primary focus was on using a pick and fingers, a very challenging technique. Pushing forward with determination, there was also an attempt to increase speed in solo playing, which proved to be extremely challenging. The chords (voicings) used in the beginning were: Dmaj7, D7, Gmaj7, GmMaj7, F#m11, Bm11, Em9, and G/A. As Stroke Warriors, it's important to keep challenging ourselves and pushing beyond our comfort zones to progress in our recovery journey. By incorporating music, faith, and determination, we can enhance our cognitive and emotional rehabilitation post-stroke, leading to a more holistic and fulfilling recovery experience.

In conclusion, developing our musical intelligence and leaning on our faith as Stroke Warriors can greatly aid in our recovery efforts. By immersing ourselves in music, we can stimulate neural pathways, promote relaxation, and elevate mood, all crucial elements in the healing process. Integrating musical intelligence with spiritual support creates a holistic approach to recovery, nurturing both the mind and soul. Let's embrace the power of music and the guidance of God as we forge ahead with determination and faith on our journey of recovery.

RECOVERY WEEK 124
Faith, Music, and Resilience on the Journey to Healing

So do not fear, for I am with you; do not be dismayed, for I am your God.

—Isaiah 41:10

https://youtu.be/GexBYEKuqHU

It feels like just yesterday when my first neurologist delivered the crushing news that I may never be able to pick up my beloved instrument again. His words felt like a heavy weight on my shoulders, but little did he know that his discouragement would only fuel my determination to prove him wrong.

Despite the initial setback, I refused to let the prognosis dictate my future. Instead, I embraced the challenge head-on and turned it into an opportunity for growth and self-discovery. The road to recovery was long and arduous, filled with moments of frustration and doubt. However, with each passing day, I found strength in my faith and determination to defy the odds.

One of the key pillars that supported me throughout my recovery journey was my unshakable trust in a higher power. By surrendering my struggles to God and seeking solace in His promises of restoration and renewal, I found the courage to press on even when faced with seemingly insurmountable obstacles. My faith became the guiding light that illuminated the path toward healing and wholeness, reminding me that I was never alone in my battle.

I discovered a newfound sense of purpose and passion for music. The melodies and rhythms that once brought me joy now served as a source of motivation and inspiration, propelling me forward in my quest to reclaim my identity as a guitar player. With each strum of the strings and each chord progression, I felt a renewed sense of purpose and fulfillment.

In this week's guitar video, I decided to challenge myself by experimenting with new rhythms and melodies. I pushed the boundaries of my comfort zone, discovering new ways to express myself through music. While the road ahead may still be long and challenging, I am filled with hope and optimism for the future. With faith as my compass and music as my muse, I am confident I will continue to make progress toward my goal of fully recovering my guitar-playing abilities.

As I look back on how far I've come since that fateful day when my world was turned upside down, I am filled with gratitude for the lessons learned and the strength gained through adversity. The journey toward recovery is not just about regaining physical abilities; it is also a spiritual and emotional metamorphosis that has reshaped me into a stronger, more resilient individual. With each note played and each hurdle overcome, I am reminded of the power of faith, perseverance, and the unwavering belief that anything is possible if we set our minds to it. So, as I continue to document my progress in these weekly videos, I invite you to join me on this extraordinary journey of resilience, hope, and the triumph of the human spirit. Together, we can inspire and uplift each other through the power of music and faith, proving that with determination and a positive mindset, anything is within our reach.

As I wrap up another week I am filled with a sense of pride and accomplishment. Despite the challenges and setbacks along the way, I have remained steadfast in my belief that nothing is impossible with faith and perseverance. So, until next week, keep strumming, keep believing, and never lose sight of the incredible potential that lies within you. Remember, it's not about the destination but the journey that shapes us into the people we are meant to be. Stay tuned for more updates and progress in the coming weeks. Let's rock on!

Recovery Week 125
Embracing a Mindset

For the spirit God gave us does not make us timid, but gives us power, love, and self-discipline.

—2 Timothy 1:7

https://youtu.be/84lpdcY2ZQI

This week I was embracing how control of my mindset has been a tremendous tool for my recovery. If you start your day with optimism, you start the day with much needed valuable energy and you can possibly create new directions or new paths. Of course, starting your day with the opposite of hopefulness is just a waste of time and energy.

Stroke Champions, embracing a mindset of control is an essential tool for our recovery journey. By taking charge of your thoughts and emotions, we can empower ourselves to navigate the challenges of stroke recovery with resilience and determination. Maintaining a positive attitude and focusing on our strengths can significantly impact our progress. Visualizing our goals and believing in our ability to achieve them can motivate us to push past limitations and reach new milestones in our recovery. Remember, our mindset is a powerful force that can shape our reality, so choose to cultivate a mindset of strength, perseverance, and hope as we continue on our path to healing. Embrace the control you have over your mindset, and let it be a guiding light in your journey toward recovery.

Most importantly, controlling our mindset can significantly boost our trust in God. By consciously directing our thoughts toward faith, gratitude, and positivity, we can cultivate a stronger connection with our beliefs. Trusting in God becomes more natural when we choose to focus on His guidance, blessings, and promises rather than getting bogged down by doubts or fears. Embracing a mindset of unwavering faith allows us to surrender control of our lives to a higher power, leading to a sense of peace, comfort, and reassurance in the face of challenges and uncertainties. When we proactively shape our mindset to align with trust in God's plan, we open ourselves up to experiencing His presence and guidance more profoundly in our daily lives, ultimately deepening our faith and belief in His divine power.

In this week's video, I attempted to create some interesting rhythm parts that are experiential at best. I believe it is so much fun to use experiential learning, which is the process of learning through experience and observation. I used the following chord voicings: E Maj, F#m, and D#/B. I hope you enjoyed my musical ideas.

Stroke Champions, keep strumming for life! Amen!

RECOVERY WEEK 126
Trusting in God's Plan for Relearning to Play Guitar

"For I know the plans I have for you," declares the Lord,
"plans to prosper you and not to harm you, plans to give you
hope and a future."

—Jeremiah 29:11

https://youtu.be/Nj51-huTRm8

When I suffered a stroke that left me paralyzed on the right side of my body, my passion for playing the guitar seemed like a distant dream. The road to recovery seemed long and uncertain, but I knew that with God by my side, anything was possible. "With God all things are possible," as Matthew 19:26 reminds us. I turned to my faith for strength and guidance, putting my trust in God's plan for my recovery. Through prayer, diligence, and the support of my loved ones, I began to see small victories in my journey toward regaining mobility in my wrist and fingers.

As I started relearning to play guitar, I knew that patience and practice would be key. With God as my inspiration, I embraced each chord and note as a testament to the power of faith and resilience. "Trust in the

Lord forever, for the Lord himself is the Rock eternal," as Isaiah 26:3–4 reminds us. While the road has not been easy, I have never lost faith in God's plan for me. Each day, I am grateful for the progress I have made and continue to rely on my faith as I face new challenges. Playing guitar again has been a transformative experience, teaching me the importance of patience, perseverance, and unwavering trust in God's plan.

In this week's guitar recovery video, I am exploring new ways of playing guitar using chords, modes, motifs, and scales in the key of D minor. As I continue on this musical journey, I am reminded that learning to play guitar again is not just a physical challenge but a spiritual one as well.

My final thought is simple yet profound: with God, all things are possible. My faith has been a source of strength and hope throughout this journey, guiding me through moments of frustration and doubt. As I look back on how far I have come, I am filled with gratitude for the road that led me to this point. Stay tuned for more updates on my guitar recovery journey and remember, with faith and perseverance, anything is possible.

RECOVERY WEEK 127
Cherishing Moments with Jesus, Querida, and Special Friends

Do not be anxious about anything, but in everything, by prayer and supplication with thanksgiving, let your requests be made known to God.

—Philippians 4:6

https://youtu.be/vwP6YYABAqM

Last night, me and my querida had an early dinner with a group of very important cherished friends. It had been a few years since we had all gathered together, as we had grown accustomed to the convenience of virtual communication. However, the reunion was a magical moment that reminded us of the value of face-to-face interactions.

As a stroke survivor, the overwhelming emotions of the evening began to take a toll on me. The flood of conversations and laughter triggered a sense of panic within me. Despite trying to mask my internal struggle, the intensity of the moment became too much to bear. It was in that moment of distress that I turned to prayer for solace and guidance. Pausing to thank Jesus for the blessing of being surrounded by loved ones,

I felt a wave of peace wash over me. The power of prayer and gratitude helped me shift my perspective and appreciate the precious time spent with my querida and friends. In that moment, I realized the importance of cherishing these connections and finding strength in faith.

Moments like these offer a sense of comfort and support that is invaluable in the journey of stroke recovery. By embracing the love and compassion shared with others, we find comfort in the knowledge that we are not alone in our struggles. Together, we can weather any storm with faith and resilience, knowing that our bonds will carry us through the toughest of times.

In this week's guitar stroke recovery video, I delved into the realm of melodic movement within chord progressions. By targeting specific intervals and exploring different chord variations, I aimed to create a harmonious flow of music that resonates with the soul. The progression of chords—F, A7, Bb, G7/B, C, Dm, Dm7, Dm6, Gm7—allowed for a creative exploration of sound and harmony.

Music has always been a source of solace and inspiration for me on my way to recovery. The act of strumming the strings and creating melodies serves as a form of therapy that soothes the mind and uplifts the spirit. Through music, I find a sense of peace and tranquility that transcends the physical limitations imposed by my stroke. As a Stroke Warrior, I have come to appreciate the value of cherishing moments of prayer with Jesus, my querida, and special friends. These interactions not only provide comfort and support but also remind me of the power of faith and resilience. Each strum of the guitar and each prayer uttered is a testament to the strength that lies within me, guiding me on the path to recovery.

In conclusion, the journey of stroke recovery is a challenging yet transformative experience that calls for faith, gratitude, and resilience. By embracing moments of prayer, music, and connection with loved ones, we find the courage to face our struggles head-on and emerge stronger than ever before. The power of faith and the support of those around us are the pillars that uphold us in times of adversity, reminding us that we are never alone in our journey toward healing and wholeness.

Recovery Week 128
Pushing Forward with Courage and Determination

Fear not, for I am with you; be not dismayed, for I am your God; I will strengthen you, I will help you, I will uphold you with my righteous right hand.

—Isaiah 41:10

https://youtu.be/FuqqGw9lK40

Have you ever felt like you were embarking on a thrilling adventure into the unknown? As a stroke survivor, every day is a new challenge, a new opportunity to push yourself beyond your limits. In this week's guitar recovery journey, I am attempting to incorporate the interval of a sixth into a mid-tempo rhythm part, using the chord progression: E Maj, F#m, and B Maj. It's a small step, but a significant one in my quest to reclaim my strength and resilience.

As a Stroke Warrior, it's essential to ask yourself the right questions to understand your recovery. Have you been asking yourself the right questions? There are two basic types of questioning methods: closed questions that require a short direct answer and open-ended questions that allow for more elaboration. Are you engaging in self-reflection to ensure you are on the right path toward healing? Trusting in God adds faith and hope to your journey, guiding you through the challenges with unwavering support.

Navigating the twists and turns of recovery can be daunting, but rediscovering the joy of learning to play the guitar serves as a reminder of your determination and perseverance. Every step you take, every question you ask, is a bold stride toward conquering any obstacles in your path. So, keep asking those important questions, keep seeking answers, and keep moving forward with the spirit of an adventurous warrior.

Recovering from a stroke is not an easy journey, but it's one that can be filled with growth and triumph. Embrace the challenge, push yourself beyond your limits, and never lose sight of your ultimate goal: to reclaim your strength and resilience. With each chord you strum, each note you play, you are reaffirming your commitment to your recovery and your passion for music.

In Psalm 34:8, it is written, "Oh, taste and see that the Lord is good! Blessed is the man who takes refuge in him!" Let these words be a source of inspiration and strength as you continue on your path to recovery. With faith, determination, and a love for music, you can overcome any obstacles that stand in your way.

Remember, the journey of recovery is not just about physical healing, it's about emotional and spiritual growth as well. Embrace the challenge, trust in the process, and never lose sight of the warrior within you. So, keep pushing forward, keep asking the right questions, and keep strumming those chords with courage and determination. The best is yet to come.

Recovery Week 129
Conduct, Connections, and Faith

We remember before our God and Father your work produced by faith, your labor prompted by love, and your endurance inspired by hope in our Lord Jesus Christ.

—1 Thessalonians 1:3

https://youtu.be/3-g2HXf-2OY

In my lifetime, I have come across numerous books and articles on change and leadership. As an Air Force instructor and now a civilian Army employee, I have had the privilege of teaching these subjects to many individuals. One saying that has always piqued my interest is, "If you keep doing what you have always done, you will keep getting what you have always gotten." This thought constantly reminds me that our behavior and the people around us play a crucial role in shaping our future.

To reach the future you desire, it is important to start by getting clear on your goals. In my case, as I strive to relearn to play the guitar after a stroke, I must exhibit dogged determination and maintain an unshakable moral compass. Conducting yourself with integrity and perseverance is key to overcoming obstacles and achieving your dreams.

Surrounding yourself with individuals who have genuine intentions is vital on the path to recovery. Family, friends, and even church members should have the ability to understand your needs and support you wholeheartedly. By homing in on your intuition and listening to your instincts, you can identify those who truly have your best interests at heart. Trusting in God's guidance can also help you discern the intentions of others and build deeper connections with sincere individuals.

Faith plays a crucial role in shaping the future you desire. By placing your trust in God and channeling your inner warrior spirit, you can find the strength and resilience to overcome any obstacles. Foster a deeper connection with your faith and allow divine guidance to lead you on your journey toward recovery. By strengthening your belief in God's plan for you, you can navigate challenges with confidence and determination.

In this week's guitar recovery video, I experimented with a simple Dorian-flavored progression of Dm, C, Dm, G. Focusing on creating a supportive and atmospheric texture, I aimed to let the space and tone shine rather than complex playing. This style of progression was popular in early Pink Floyd music, and it served as a reminder of the power of simplicity and mood in music.

As I continue my journey toward guitar recovery after a stroke, I am reminded of the importance of conducting myself with unwavering determination, surrounding myself with genuine individuals, and strengthening my faith for a brighter future. By staying true to my goals and beliefs, I am confident I will overcome any challenges that come my way. As Ephesians 4:32 reminds us, "Be kind to one another, tenderhearted, forgiving one another, as God in Christ forgave you." Keep rocking, my friends, and let faith guide you on your path to recovery!

RECOVERY WEEK 130
A Journey of Hope and Inspiration

May the God of hope fill you with all joy and peace as you trust in him, so that you may overflow with hope by the power of the Holy Spirit.

—Romans 15:13

IMPOSSIBLE

https://youtu.be/EnGvGQ8_4us

As I reflect on my journey of stroke recovery and relearning to play the guitar, I am reminded of the importance of being optimistic and maintaining hope through difficult times. It has been a challenging road, but with each strum of the guitar, I am reminded of the progress I have made and the resilience that has carried me through. In this week's journal, I will share my experiences and insights from Week 130 of my recovery, highlighting the power of hope, motivation, and faith in God.

During my first year of stroke recovery, I was filled with wishes and passive desires to pick up my guitar again. However, it wasn't until my second year that I mustered the hope and motivation to take action. The formula of hope + being optimistic + creating motivation + taking action has been the key to my success thus far. Through unwavering determination and trust in God, I have been able to overcome setbacks and make progress in my journey of relearning to play the guitar.

For Stroke Warriors like me, having faith in God has been a source of comfort and strength throughout the recovery process. The trust in a higher power has guided us through difficult times and provided us with the resilience needed to push through obstacles. It's important to remember that progress may not always be linear, but with persistence and faith, we can continue on our path of rediscovering our passion for music.

In my most recent guitar video, I challenged myself by playing against a unique rhythm in the key of D minor. It served as an exercise in fingering, picking, and strumming techniques, but I also took the opportunity to create an interesting tune. While it may not have been perfect, the experience was both fun and rewarding. As I continue to practice and improve, I am reminded of the words from Psalm 94:18–19, "Your steadfast love, O LORD, helped me up… Your consolations cheer my soul."

As we navigate through the ups and downs of stroke recovery and musical relearning, it's important to stay positive and maintain a sense of hope. Each strum of the guitar is a step forward, no matter how small or imperfect. With the support of our faith, the encouragement of our fellow warriors, and the dedication to our craft, we can continue to make progress and inspire others along the way.

In conclusion, Week 130 has been filled with moments of hope, inspiration, and progress. By embracing the power of optimism, motivation, and faith, I have been able to push through challenges and continue on the path to recovery. I encourage my fellow warriors to keep strumming, keep believing, and keep trusting in God as we navigate this actionable journey together.

RECOVERY WEEK 131
The Power of Optimism and Faith

Have I not commanded you? Be strong and courageous. Do not be frightened, and do not be dismayed, for the Lord your God is with you wherever you go.

—Joshua 1:9

https://youtu.be/archHI6D428

In Week 131 of my stroke recovery journey, I had a powerful reminder of the role that optimism and faith play in the healing process. It was a visit from my dear friend Roger that sparked this realization and reignited my determination to keep pushing forward.

Roger, a friend who feels more like a brother, stopped by to deliver his famous homegrown tomatoes from his garden. As we caught up, he remarked on the progress he's seen in my recovery journey since the beginning. His words struck a chord with me, emphasizing the importance of maintaining a positive outlook in the face of adversity. As we chatted, I couldn't help but reflect on the impact that optimism has had on my recovery. Roger's reminder that a healthy dose of positivity can fuel our progress resonated deeply with me, serving as a much-needed boost to my spirits.

Embracing optimism in our recovery journey is not just a choice; it's a powerful tool that can propel us toward regaining our abilities. By believing in our potential to overcome challenges and achieve our goals, we set the stage for our minds and bodies to work together in harmony. Maintaining a strong trust in God can also provide comfort and guidance during the toughest moments of our rehabilitation. By surrendering to a higher power and placing our faith in a divine plan, we can find the strength needed to face any obstacle head-on.

I am reminded of the words from Joshua 1:9: "Have I not commanded you? Be strong and courageous. Do not be frightened, and do not be dismayed, for the Lord your God is with you wherever you go." These words serve as a beacon of hope and a reminder that we are never alone in our journey. Through the power of optimism, faith, and trust in God, we can pave the way to a triumphant recovery. It is through true belief in ourselves and a higher power that we can overcome any challenge that comes our way.

This week, I tried something different in my practice routine. While the tune may have been a bit sloppy, it was filled with energy and funk. Playing in Db minor, I embraced the imperfections that gave the song character and charm. With each strum of the guitar, I found joy in the process of creating music and pushing myself beyond my comfort zone. It was a reminder that progress is not always linear, but rather a journey filled with highs and lows.

Through the power of optimism, faith, and trust in God, I am reminded that anything is possible with determination. Let us continue to believe in the extraordinary possibilities that lie ahead and march forward with unwavering conviction. Together, as Stroke Warriors, we can conquer any obstacle that stands in our way. Amen!

RECOVERY WEEK 132
Facing Adversity with Courage

When I am afraid, I put my trust in you. In God, whose word I praise—in God, I trust and am not afraid. What can mere mortals do to me?

—Psalm 56:3–4

https://youtu.be/Lz1rGsWX9xE

In this week's guitar stroke recovery video, I have been inspired by the powerful song "Courageous" by Casting Crowns. The lyrics speak to the bravery and boldness that define the journey of Stroke Warriors like me. As we face the challenges of recovery, we embody the strength and resilience that set us apart as courageous warriors. Let's dive into this week's guitar jam and explore the theme of courage in our journey to healing.

Stroke Warriors, our essence is wrapped in bravery, daring, and boldness. We embrace the label of courage with a capital C in every step of our recovery journey. Each challenge we face, each obstacle we conquer, we do so with unwavering determination and fearlessness. Our resolve is fortified by an unshakeable trust in God, knowing that with faith as our armor, we are destined to emerge triumphant. We choose to embody the strength and resilience that define us as Stroke Warriors, facing each day with a relentless spirit that refuses to be subdued.

What does courage mean in the journey of stroke recovery? Courage in stroke recovery means having the quality of being ready and willing to face negative situations like having a stroke. It involves facing challenges despite fear and showing bravery in the face of adversity. As Stroke Warriors, we march forward with the boldness of a warrior charging into battle, ready to claim victory over our adversities.

How can we cultivate courage in our recovery journey? Cultivating courage in our recovery journey involves embracing the challenges we face, harnessing the power within us, and refusing to be held captive by the limit's others may impose. We must have unwavering determination, fearlessness, and trust in God to guide us through the difficult times. By embodying bravery, daring, and boldness, we can conquer obstacles and emerge stronger than ever.

This week, I played against a fun chord progression of E, A, B, A, Cm, D, A. This almost sounds like an Eric Clapton-inspired lead, using just a few notes from the major pentatonic scale in one position. The recording may not be perfect, but it was a joy to play, and I hope you enjoy this short jam.

As Stroke Warriors, we navigate the path to recovery with courage as our compass. We face each day with a boldness and determination that define us as warriors. Let us continue to play the chords of courage, resilience, and faith in our journey toward healing. Keep strumming for life!

Recovery Week 133
Embracing the WIN Principle

After you have suffered a little while, the God of all grace...
will himself restore, confirm, strengthen, and establish you.

—1 Peter 5:10

https://youtu.be/FLRukbqCLeM

This week, I delved into an article highlighting the wisdom of legendary coach Lou Holtz and his leadership principles. One concept that particularly resonated with me as a stroke survivor was the WIN principle—short for "What's Important Now?" This principle serves as a guiding light for me in my recovery journey, constantly reminding me to focus on the present moment and prioritize what truly matters in my pursuit of regaining my abilities.

When confronted with the aftermath of a stroke, the past may be filled with struggles and the future may seem uncertain. However, the key to progress lies in grasping the essence of the WIN principle and adapting it to our own journeys. Instead of dwelling on what has already transpired, we must shift our focus to the now and ask ourselves, "What's Important Now?" This mindset shift enables us to channel our energy toward productive actions that can propel us toward our goals.

As Stroke Warriors, it is essential to maintain a bold and resilient attitude in the face of adversity. By homing in on what truly matters at each moment, we can navigate the challenges of recovery with a sense of purpose and determination. This unwavering faith in the power of progression and the resilience of the human spirit drives us toward our shared goals, fostering a community of support and encouragement along the way.

Central to the process of stroke recovery is the cultivation of a positive mindset. Believing in our own capabilities and fostering a sense of self-assurance can pave the way for significant strides in our journey. Drawing strength from faith and a higher power can serve as a beacon of hope during dark times, providing the motivation needed to push forward. As I always say, I trust in God that I will play guitar again; affirming our belief in eventual success can fuel our determination and perseverance.

While the road to recovery may be arduous, by adhering to the WIN principle and affirming our priorities, we can set ourselves up for success. Through a combination of positivity, perseverance, and self-care, we can overcome the obstacles that lie ahead and triumph in our journey toward full recovery. Remember to celebrate small victories, lean on your support system, and trust in the process—for with dedication and a clear focus on the present moment, anything is possible.

For this week's Charlie's Guitar Stroke Recovery video, I explored the intricacies of improvising a blues lead over a minor key. As I navigated the chord progression of Am, Dm, Am, F maj7, Em, Am, E7#9, I was reminded of the beauty in thoughtful musical expression. While speed may dazzle, it is the emotional depth and melodic richness that truly lingers in the soul. In the words of the legendary George Benson, "When Charlie Parker played, you could always hear that melody. The song never left you." As we navigate the challenges of stroke recovery, let us embrace the power of melody, the capacity of the human spirit, and the faith that restoration is within reach.

In conclusion, by focusing on *what's important now*, maintaining a positive mindset, and trusting in the process, we Stroke Warriors can overcome any obstacle and prevail in our pursuit of recovery. Let us continue to press forward with determination, faith, and an unwavering focus on the present moment.

Recovery Week 134
I'm Okay, You Are Okay.

Do not conform to the pattern of this world but be transformed by the renewing of your mind. Then you will be able to test and approve what God's will is—his good, pleasing, and perfect will.

—Romans 12:2

https://youtu.be/BLK-H9dUybI

Many moons ago when I was serving in the United States Air Force, I achieved the rank of Master Sergeant and was placed in charge of the Mobility/War Readiness Spare Kits. During that experience, I had a very interesting Airman placed under my supervision; let's call him Airman Izzy. The first thing I noticed about Airman Izzy was his very apparent negativity. His language was filled with phrases like "I can't," "they won't," "it couldn't," "I am not good enough," and other pessimistic proclamations. His life position was clear: "I'm not okay, and you are okay." What bothered me the most, and the most concerning for Izzy, was that his self-talk was keeping him small and unsuccessful. So, Izzy and I started working together on changing his self-talk. We built trust, mutual respect, and safety. The following year, Airman Izzy earned "Airman of the Year" for the squadron. Izzy changed his self-talk to positive dialogues with his words and his mind, and his life position changed to "I'm okay, you are okay." Airman Izzy changed how he viewed himself and the world around him. Stroke Warriors changing our self-talk and how we view ourselves and the world around us, especially when we are relearning to play those musical instruments we love, can reduce or even eliminate our own analogous pessimistic proclamations. Amen!

Embracing the identity of Stroke Warriors is a powerful step toward reshaping our self-talk and altering our perspective on the world as we navigate the journey of relearning beloved musical instruments, like the guitar. By channeling a bold tone of voice and declaring affirmations such as "I trust in God that I will play my instrument again," we can witness a profound shift in our mindset. These empowering beliefs have the potential to dismantle pessimistic notions that may hinder our progress. As Stroke Warriors, we acknowledge the challenges we face, but with unwavering faith and determination, we can overcome them. The act of relearning a skill we cherish serves as a testament to our resilience and powerful spirit, proving that with the right mindset, we are capable of achieving the seemingly impossible. Thank You, God!

This week's guitar stroke recovery was very fun to play and very challenging for my right picking hand. The chord progression I used was: Dm, Bb, Dm, Bb, G, Dm, very nice sounding guitar voicings. Some of my scale and melody ideas reminded me of Christopher Cross and maybe Mark Knopfler, you decide. I had a fun guitar recovery week. Thank you, Jesus!

As Stroke Warriors, we face unique challenges in relearning how to play the musical instruments we love. It requires determination, faith, and a shift in mindset to overcome obstacles and achieve our goals. By changing our self-talk and embracing our identity as Stroke Warriors, we can pave the way for success and growth in our musical journey. With each stroke of the guitar strings, we are not only relearning a skill but also proving to ourselves that we are capable of greatness. Let us continue to trust in God, believe in ourselves, and march forward as Stroke Warriors, conquering every challenge that comes our way.

RECOVERY WEEK 135
Relearning to Play Guitar

"Let the word of Christ dwell in you richly, teaching and admonishing one another in all wisdom, singing Psalm and hymns and spiritual songs, with thankfulness in your hearts to God."

—Colossians 3:16

https://youtu.be/Qg_ovZndaFM

In the 135th week of recovering from a stroke, the focus has been on relearning how to play the guitar. This process has presented challenges but also provided rewarding experiences. Through this journey, there has been an understanding of the significance of perseverance and the importance of maintaining recovery goals. Making these healing objectives visible to others is essential for progress.

One of the most crucial aspects of stroke recovery is setting clear and visible healing goals. By making these goals known to others, we not only hold ourselves accountable, but we also inspire those around us. This external motivation can be incredibly powerful in pushing us to keep going, even when the road ahead seems daunting. Setting visible healing goals also helps us track our progress and celebrate our achievements. By breaking down our recovery journey into smaller, manageable goals, we can measure our success along the way. Each milestone reached is a cause for celebration and a reminder of how far we have come. This sense of progress is essential for maintaining motivation and staying on course toward full recovery.

As a Stroke Warrior, I have come to understand the importance of warrior courage in the journey of recovery. This inner strength and determination are what drive us to push through the challenges and obstacles that may arise. Warrior courage is not about being fearless but about facing our fears head-on and refusing to let them hold us back. It is about having the resilience to keep going, even when the odds are stacked against us. The path to recovery is not always easy, but with warrior courage, we can face each day with determination and a positive mindset. It is this courage that propels us forward, giving us the strength to overcome setbacks and continue moving toward our goals. As Stroke Warriors, we must tap into our inner warrior courage every day, knowing that we have the resilience and determination to conquer any obstacle in our way.

For me, relearning how to play the guitar has been a powerful way to reconnect with my love for music. Music has always been a source of comfort and inspiration for me, and being able to play the guitar again has brought me immense joy. Through this process, I have discovered new depths of creativity and expression, using music as a form of therapy and healing. Playing the guitar has not only improved my physical dexterity and coordination but has also helped me regain a sense of normalcy and routine in my life. The act of strumming the strings and creating beautiful melodies has been a cathartic experience, allowing me to express myself in ways words cannot. Music has the power to heal the soul, and for me, playing the guitar has been a vital part of my recovery journey.

In conclusion, the journey of recovery after a stroke is a challenging but ultimately rewarding experience. By setting visible healing goals, tapping into our warrior courage, and reconnecting with activities we love, such as playing the guitar, we can find strength and resilience in the face of adversity. As Stroke Warriors, we must never give up and always strive to show the world our determination to heal. With faith, perseverance, and a positive mindset, we can overcome any obstacle and continue on the path toward full recovery.

Recovery Week 136
Make Our Healing Goals Visible

He gives strength to the weary and increases the power of the weak.

—Isaiah 40:29

https://youtu.be/iA0iWqzVKKA

This process has been demanding but also highly rewarding. I have gained a greater understanding of myself and my beliefs through this experience. The recovery journey has highlighted the importance of persistence. For those recovering from a stroke, it is important to make our healing goals clear to others.

One of the most crucial aspects of stroke recovery is setting clear and visible healing goals. By making these goals known to others, we not only hold ourselves accountable, but we also inspire those around us. When people see us working toward our goals, they are encouraged to support us and cheer us on. This external motivation can be incredibly powerful in pushing us to keep going, even when the road ahead seems daunting. Setting visible healing goals also helps us track our progress and celebrate our achievements. By breaking down our recovery journey into smaller, manageable goals, we can measure our success along the way. Each milestone reached is a cause for celebration and a reminder of how far we have come. This sense of progress is essential for maintaining motivation and staying on course toward full recovery.

I have come to understand the importance of warrior courage in the journey of recovery. This inner strength is what drives us to push through the obstacles that may arise. Warrior courage is not about being fearless but about facing our fears head-on and refusing to let them hold us back. It is about having the resilience to keep going, even when the odds are stacked against us. The path to recovery is not always easy, but with warrior courage, we can face each day with determination and a positive mindset. It is this courage that propels us forward, giving us the strength to overcome setbacks and continue moving toward our goals. As Stroke Warriors, we must tap into our inner warrior courage every day, knowing that we can conquer any obstacle in our way.

Relearning to play the guitar has reconnected me with my love for music, providing comfort and inspiration. This journey has enhanced my creativity, acting as therapy and aiding in recovery. Playing the guitar has improved my dexterity, routine, and allowed me to express emotions beyond words. Music's healing power has been essential in my life.

RECOVERY WEEK 137
Blaze New Pathways to Musical Recovery

For the Lord your God is he who goes with you to fight for you against your enemies, to give you the victory.

—Deuteronomy 20:4

https://youtu.be/5YH6pGCQuro

I would like to share my insights on utilizing music as a therapeutic tool for recovery, as well as the profound satisfaction gained from reacquainting oneself with the art of playing musical instruments.

Music has long been known to have therapeutic benefits for stroke survivors. Not only does it provide a creative outlet for emotional expression, but it also helps improve motor skills, cognitive function, and overall well-being. For me, picking up the guitar again after my stroke was a way to reconnect with a part of myself that I thought I had lost.

Relearning to play the guitar was no easy feat. It required patience, dedication, and a willingness to embrace the challenges that came with it. At first, my fingers felt stiff and clumsy, and the sound of the strings seemed distant and unfamiliar. However, with each practice session, I could feel my muscles loosening up and my confidence growing.

Every small step forward in my guitar-playing journey felt like a monumental victory. Whether it was mastering a new chord or playing a familiar tune with more ease, each achievement brought a sense of accomplishment and pride. As Stroke Warriors, we must celebrate these victories and recognize the progress we are making, no matter how small.

Throughout this journey, my faith in God has been a guiding light. It has given me the strength and courage to persevere through the tough days and setbacks. As I continue to blaze new pathways in my recovery, I hold onto the belief that a brighter future awaits, filled with music, joy, and endless possibilities.

In this week's recovery video, I challenged myself to play some rock blues on the guitar. The unique sound and emotion in the music captivated me, pushing me to explore new horizons in my playing. I experimented with a variety of guitar chords and patterns, including Am, Dm7, Am7, F maj7, and E7, creating a tapestry of melodies and rhythms that spoke to my soul.

Playing the guitar after a stroke is not just about regaining physical strength; it is also about rebuilding neural connections and creating new memories. Each strum of the strings, each change of chord, is a step toward reclaiming what was lost and embracing what is yet to come. The process of learning and playing music has become a source of gladness and inspiration in my recovery journey.

While I still have a long way to go in my guitar-playing journey, I am filled with hope and determination. I know that with each practice session, each new song learned, I am moving closer to my goal of playing music with confidence and passion once again. As Stroke Warriors, we have the power to shape our own destinies and create a future filled with music, laughter, and endless possibilities. Relearning to play the guitar after a stroke has been a transformative experience, filled with challenges, victories, and moments of pure joy. Music has been my guiding light, my source of strength, and my constant companion on this journey of recovery. As I continue to blaze new pathways and explore the depths of my musical potential, I am reminded of the spirit that defines us as Stroke Warriors. So, pick up your instrument, play that first chord, and let the music carry you forward on a journey of healing and hope.

Recovery Week 138
Stroke Warrior, Faith, Perseverance, Support, Invisible Effects, Love, Compassion!

Rejoice in the Lord always; again I will say, rejoice.
—Philippians 4:4

https://youtu.be/AUzUABtRFF0

Just a couple of days ago, on August 30, 2024, I celebrated entering my fourth year of stroke survival and being a Stroke Warrior. Through prayer and unwavering faith, I have been guided toward relearning to play guitar. The journey has not been easy, but as Psalm 46 beautifully expresses, "God (alone) is the refuge of His people; He is the One who helps us in trouble." I am reminded that with God, all things are possible, as stated in Matthew 19:26.

When my first neurologist told me I would never play guitar again, I refused to accept defeat. I held onto my passion and identity as a musician, believing in the healing power of prayer and the support of my loved ones. Psalm 34:18 reassures me that "The Lord is close to the brokenhearted; He rescues those whose spirits are crushed." With each small victory in my recovery journey, I am reminded of the strength and resilience that lies within me.

One of the greatest challenges I have faced is the lack of understanding from others regarding the invisible effects of a stroke. While the physical implications are apparent, the psychological and physiological impact on behavior, emotions, and thinking are often overlooked. Through professional therapy and self-education, I have come to recognize the importance of raising awareness and fostering empathy toward those dealing with the aftermath of a stroke.

During these past three years, I have learned the true value of friendship and compassion. As I navigate the ups and downs of recovery, I have witnessed the ongoing support of my friends and family, who have stood by me through it all. I am reminded of Corinthians 13: "Finally, brothers, rejoice. Aim for restoration, comfort one another, agree with one another, live in peace; and the God of love and peace will be with you." It is through love and understanding that we can truly make a difference in the lives of others.

In conclusion, my journey to recovery after a stroke has been filled with challenges, victories, and valuable lessons. Through faith, perseverance, and the support of loved ones, I have been able to overcome obstacles and move toward a brighter future. As I continue on this path, I am grateful for the strength and resilience that has carried me through the darkest moments.

RECOVERY WEEK 139
Experience Neurofatigue:
The Brain Fog Challenge

So do not fear, for I am with you; do not be dismayed, for I am your God.

—Isaiah 41:10

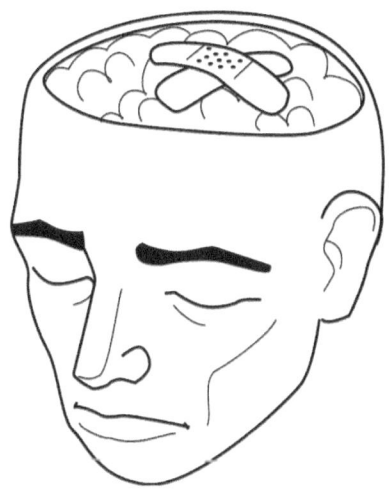

https://youtu.be/JTqeEX573us

Have you ever experienced difficulty concentrating, forgetfulness, or feeling mentally exhausted for no clear reason? As I am still on this adventurous path to learning to play guitar again, one challenge I have is what I call brain fog. What do you call Stroke Warriors? I decided to explore further and do some research. What I have learned from Tamar Rodney, PhD, PMHNP-BC, CNE, mental health nurse practitioner, is a new term for brain fog, which is "neurofatigue." I am no expert; however, I experience this every day.

Neurofatigue, also known as neurological fatigue or mental fatigue, is a decrease in concentration, focus, memory, recall, and word retrieval. This fatigue or tiredness is not the same as exhaustion due to physical exertion, insufficient sleep, or overworking. Neurofatigue may also be referred to as brain fog; it is the brain not working as well as it can normally.

According to Dr. Rodney, individuals experiencing neurofatigue may encounter various challenges, such as difficulty thinking clearly, feeling confused or disoriented, difficulty concentrating, and having a short attention span. Additionally, neurofatigue can lead to feelings of irritability, stress, and being overwhelmed. Does any of this sound familiar to you?

It's essential to recognize the symptoms of neurofatigue early on, as everyone's experience may differ. Dr. Rodney emphasizes that pushing through neurofatigue rarely yields positive results. So, how can we effectively manage neurofatigue in our daily life? Here are some practical suggestions from Dr. Rodney to help us cope with neurofatigue effectively:

1. Get quality sleep
2. Try to pace yourself
3. Manage your fatigue
4. Split tasks into manageable chunks
5. Schedule activities based on your energy levels throughout the day
6. Avoid pushing yourself beyond your limits
7. Maintain a healthy diet
8. Incorporate regular exercise into your routine
9. Stay hydrated
10. Practice active relaxation techniques
11. Prioritize self-care activities

So, I have learned this week by implementing these strategies, you can improve your cognitive function, reduce mental fatigue, and enhance overall well-being. Remember, self-care is crucial when it comes to combating neurofatigue.

In this week's video vlog adventure, I decided to dive into the realm of blues rock on my guitar. Embracing an adventurous spirit, I experimented with an up and down motion using my right hand, focusing on enhancing my wrist movement to elevate my playing skills. With determination and excitement, I practiced a lively rock guitar chord progression in the key of B, infusing each strum with enthusiasm and creativity. The journey of exploring new techniques and pushing boundaries allowed me to immerse myself in the world of music and to relearn guitar, pushing me to grow as a musician while having a blast along the way.

In conclusion, neurofatigue, or brain fog, can significantly impact your daily life, making simple tasks seem more challenging than usual. By understanding the symptoms and adopting healthy coping mechanisms, you can effectively manage neurofatigue and regain control over your cognitive abilities. Don't let brain fog hinder your progress; I am planning to take proactive steps to combat neurofatigue and hopefully we can do this together to live our best lives.

Recovery Week 140
What Does Success Really Mean?

*Commit to the LORD whatever you do, and he will
establish your plans.*

—Proverbs 16:3

https://youtu.be/7-5Wkth1Qx4

Are you wondering if it's about achieving exactly what we set out for, or is it more about the journey and the decisions we make along the way? Success can be a subjective concept, and for Stroke Warriors like me, it can take on a whole new meaning.

Success, to me, is not just about the end result but also about the process and the values that guide us. It's about controlling our actions, dedicating ourselves to what truly matters, and living a life that we can look back on with pride, regardless of the outcomes. I love the following "big ideas" from Joshua Becker, in his book *The Seven Laws of Success*. He highlights some key principles that can help us redefine success on our own terms. Choosing our own values, aligning resources with those values, committing to continuous growth, and living for others are just a few of the core principles that can shape our definition of success. It's essential to measure success based on our own values and not by society's standards. Success should be about pursuing what truly matters to us and having the courage to do the next right thing, the best way we know how.

As a Stroke Warrior, I know the importance of pushing beyond limitations and not letting setbacks define us. In my journey to stroke recovery and with this week's video journal, I challenged myself to play a guitar solo over a C9 chord progression, refusing to let my condition hold me back. Success, for me, is about putting myself in the hustle, muscling through, and never giving up on my passions.

Success is a personal journey, shaped by our values, actions, and dedication to what matters most. By redefining success on our terms and embracing challenges with determination, we can truly measure our lives by the impact we make and the fulfillment we experience along the way.

Don't let setbacks define you. Keep pushing yourself beyond limitations and embracing challenges with determination. Success is not just about the end result but also about the values that guide you and the journey you take. So put yourself in the hustle, muscle through, and never let anything hold you back. Success is within reach, for those who are willing to chase after it with courage and passion.

Embarking on this week's musical journey, I delved into the quintessential blues format of a 12-bar progression with enthusiasm and a twinge of daring. As my fingers traced the familiar path of three sets of 4 bars each, I couldn't help but revel in the quirky boogie-woogie essence woven into the music. The challenge was not just in mastering the notes but in the sheer adventure of coaxing melodies from my right hand, still on the mending road post-stroke. The sense of accomplishment that washed over me as the music flowed was nothing short of exhilarating, a testament to both practice and perseverance. Grateful for the progress and the opportunity to immerse myself in this cherished style, I couldn't help but whisper a heartfelt "thank you" to our Savior Jesus Christ, Amen!

RECOVERY WEEK 141
Stimulate Your Guitar
Learning Journey

When the Holy Spirit lives within us, our natural behaviors will be love, joy, peace, patience, kindness, goodness, faithfulness, gentleness, and self-control.

—Galatians 5:22–23

https://youtu.be/TcBPjxiK8kI

Are you trying to achieve a goal that is incredibly important to you? One key aspect of achieving any goal is to surround yourself with stimuli that incite action, quicken thought, and fuel your determination. But how can you use stimuli to enhance your guitar learning journey after a stroke? Let's explore some ideas and strategies to help you stay motivated and on track.

Stimuli can be defined as something that incites action, feeling, or thought. When it comes to behavior change goals such as losing weight, exercising more, or relearning to play guitar, stimuli play a crucial role in influencing our behaviors and decisions. Many people fail to achieve their goals because they do not effectively utilize methods of stimulus control. By surrounding yourself with the right stimuli, you can increase your chances of success in your guitar learning journey.

Stimulus Control Strategies for Relearning Guitar:

1. Posters and Inspiration: Surround yourself with posters of your favorite guitar players and guitar brands to stay motivated and inspired.

2. Reward System: Create a reward system for yourself every time you make progress, no matter how small. Celebrate your achievements along the way.

3. Success Stories: Read about guitarists who have overcome injuries and challenges to inspire you to keep pushing forward.

4. Immerse Yourself in Music: Attend live music events, listen to various music styles, and constantly challenge yourself to learn new songs.

5. Learn and Practice: Break down songs into smaller parts, learn about your favorite guitarists' stories, and set up a dedicated practice space with a consistent schedule.

In addition to stimuli, the people you surround yourself with can also have a significant impact on your journey. Surround yourself with individuals who support and encourage your guitar learning goals. Whether it's friends, family, or a guitar teacher, having the right support system can make a world of difference in your progress.

In my recent video vlog, I attempted to play an old-school ballad that reminded me of the classic song "Sleep Walk" by Santo & Johnny. The song's intricate sections and guitar chords presented a challenge, but I embraced the opportunity to explore new styles of music. Songs have different sections, so for "A" section I use these guitar voicings of, D, Bm, F#m, D7, G, A, D, C-G, D; for the "B" section I used these guitar voicings, G,

Gm, D, B7, Em, Gm, A; give those guitar chords a try and let the music guide you on your recovery journey! The timing and style of this tune was very challenging, but I am so happy I gave this style of music a try. By incorporating different stimuli and techniques into my practice sessions, I was able to enhance my guitar learning experience after my stroke.

Relearning to play the guitar after a stroke is a challenging yet rewarding journey. By surrounding yourself with the right stimuli, setting achievable goals, and immersing yourself in the world of music, you can make significant progress in your guitar learning goals. Remember, success is a combination of passion, dedication, and the right stimuli to keep you inspired and motivated along the way.

RECOVERY WEEK 142
A Journey of Liberation

Stand fast therefore in the liberty wherewith Christ hath made us free.

—Galatians 5:1

https://youtu.be/nyltNtFKXU8

Have you ever experienced a moment in your life where you had to make a bold decision to break free from your limitations? That moment when you declared independence from your fears, doubts, and insecurities? This is exactly what I did on the day I decided to pick up my old friend, my guitar, and embark on a journey of recovery after a stroke. It was a day filled with courage, determination, and a sense of liberation. You see, I waited a whole year to accomplish this after my stroke for many reasons. This was also the day I decided to write about and video my "Guitar Stroke Recovery Journey," to document and vlog my progress to hopefully inspire other musicians affected by any ailment to give it a try and join me on this journey. So, what the cat hair does a "declaration of independence" mean to us Stroke Warriors?

The concept of a "declaration of independence" may seem familiar, as it mirrors the historical event where the thirteen American colonies broke free from Great Britain. In my case, it symbolized my decision to liberate myself from the shackles of fear, doubt, and self-pity. It was a proclamation to myself that I was capable of overcoming my physical limitations and reclaiming my passion for music.

As a stroke survivor, I understand the challenges and struggles that come with such a life-altering event. According to the National Library of Medicine, millions of stroke survivors face physical, cognitive, and emotional difficulties post-stroke. However, it is crucial for us Stroke Warriors to take charge of our lives and start building a path toward recovery and healing.

In my weekly video vlog journals, I document my progress in reclaiming my love for music, guitar playing, and, most importantly, trusting in God. This week, I took a step back to basics by revisiting a classic guitar chord progression—G major, B minor, C major, and D major. By exploring different triad positions on the guitar fretboard, I aimed to create captivating motifs, and I hope you enjoy listening, most significantly to inspire others to never give up on their passions.

It is essential to keep strumming for life, as music has the power to heal, uplift, and motivate us during our darkest moments. As the famous verse from Galatians 5:1 state, "Stand fast therefore in the liberty wherewith Christ hath made us free." This serves as a reminder to embrace the freedom and joy that music brings into our lives.

Through my guitar stroke recovery journey, I have learned the importance of faith, resilience, and perseverance. Each strum of the guitar strings represents a step toward recovery and a celebration of life's beauty. It is a testimony to the human spirit's ability to overcome adversity and find solace in art, creativity, and music.

As I continue on this journey of liberation, I invite fellow musicians and stroke survivors to join me in embracing the power of music as a healing force. Let us break free from our limitations, doubts, and fears, and immerse ourselves in the joy of creating melodies that resonate with our souls. Together, we can inspire others to strive for greatness and never give up on their dreams.

My final thought is this, the road to recovery after a stroke may be challenging, but with faith, determination, and a passion for music, we can overcome any obstacle that comes our way. Let us declare independence from our limitations and embrace the freedom that music brings into our lives. Keep strumming, keep playing, and never lose sight of the healing power that music holds. Embrace the journey, embrace the music, and let your soul soar to new heights. Amen!

RECOVERY WEEK 143
Inspiring Tips for Stroke Warriors

Be on your guard; stand firm in the faith; be courageous; be strong. Do everything in love.

—1 Corinthians 16:13–14

https://youtu.be/_NfDFmKol8M

What inspired you to continue persevering? This week, while diligently working on my weekly guitar practice with the goal of relearning the instrument after experiencing a stroke, I began to reflect on the source of my motivation. I considered how I could effectively share this motivation with other individuals recovering from strokes who are also pursuing musical goals.

Big Ideas for Stroke Warriors:

1. Have Faith and Trust in God: Sometimes, when facing a daunting challenge, it is essential to have faith and trust that there is a higher power guiding us through difficult times.

2. Practice Consistently: Consistent practice is key for all musicians, especially those on the road to recovery. By staying dedicated to your craft, you can make gradual progress each day.

3. Set Goals: Having specific goals in mind can give you something to strive for and keep you motivated along the way.

4. Learn New Things: Challenge yourself by trying out a new style, tuning, or song. Learning new things can reignite your passion for music.

5. Play with Others: Collaborating with other musicians can bring fresh perspectives and ideas to your playing. It can also help you improve your skills and expand your musical horizons.

6. Take a Break: It's important to give yourself time to recharge and refresh. Taking a break can help prevent burnout and keep your motivation levels high.

7. Explore Songwriting: Get creative by writing your own songs or composing music. This can be a fulfilling way to express yourself and experiment with different sounds.

8. Try a Different Instrument: If you feel stuck in a rut with your guitar playing, consider picking up another instrument. It can invigorate your creativity and broaden your musical abilities.

9. Practice Something Difficult: Challenge yourself by tackling something that pushes you out of your comfort zone. Overcoming difficulties can boost your confidence and skill level.

10. Relax and Have Fun: Remember to enjoy the process of playing music. It's a gift to be able to express yourself through your instrument, so don't forget to have fun along the way.

For this week's video vlogging journey, I decided to go back to basics and explore some blues in the delightful guitar key of A seventh. I believe that creating different atmospheres in your solos is a crucial aspect of musical expression, allowing you to craft unique motifs and melodies.

Philippians 4:13 says, "I can do all things through Christ, who gives me strength." This verse serves as a reminder that with faith and perseverance, anything is possible.

As you navigate your own journey of recovery and rediscovery with the guitar, remember the importance of balance, patience, and consistency. These qualities will serve you well as you continue to hone your skills and embrace the joy of making music. In conclusion, don't be afraid to take risks, try new things, and keep pushing yourself to new heights. With dedication and a positive mindset, you can achieve remarkable progress on your musical journey. Stay motivated and inspired and let the healing power of music guide you toward a brighter future. Remember, the path to recovery may be long and challenging, but with perseverance and a positive mindset, you can overcome any obstacle that comes your way. Keep strumming those strings and let the music be your guide on this incredible journey of healing and growth.

RECOVERY WEEK 144
Reflecting on Lessons Learned

Show me your ways, Lord, teach me your paths.
—Psalm 25:4

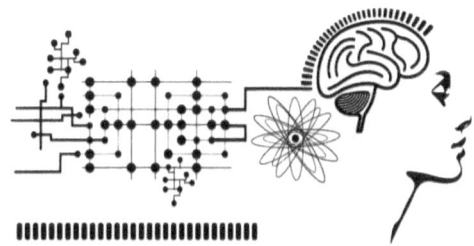

https://youtu.be/UTuB1mD1m-M

Throughout the past 144 weeks, I have learned valuable lessons that have not only helped me regain my strength but have also enriched my soul in ways I never thought possible. In this journaling vlog, I will reflect on the enduring attributes I have gained during my "breathe" and "stop to think" moments, as well as share some insights from my latest video vlog.

In my journey as an educator in the US Air Force to my current role as an Army Civilian, I have always held onto the belief that genuine learning flourishes through reflection and keeping a journal. As I immerse myself in the process of relearning how to play the guitar, I find solace and strength in looking back at my progress, honoring every milestone achieved. Stepping forward, I make it a practice to pause, breathe, and allow moments of self-discovery to unfold. Through these moments of quiet contemplation, I have unearthed everlasting attributes that continue to guide me. And in this beautiful journey, I gratefully acknowledge the steadfast presence of God by my side. Amen!

Having a Stroke Taught Me:

1.   Strength: Having a stroke taught me that I am stronger than I think. It challenged me to face adversity head-on and move forward with resilience.

2.   Life's Preciousness: This experience taught me the true value of life, prompting me to cherish every moment and embrace the beauty of existence.

3.   Gratitude: My stroke taught me to appreciate the love and support of those who truly care for me while also urging me to pray for those who may not understand or appreciate me.

4.   Faith: Through this journey, I have learned to trust in God's plan and guidance, finding solace in the knowledge that He is always by my side.

5.   Appreciation: The stroke taught me to find joy in the little things in life, celebrating even the smallest achievements and milestones.

6.   Imperfection: I learned to let go of the quest for perfection, understanding that relearning to play the guitar takes time, patience, and dedication.

7.   Patience: This experience has taught me the importance of patience, both in my own recovery process and in navigating the ups and downs of life.

8.   Compassion: My stroke has made me more compassionate and empathetic toward others, encouraging me to connect with and support those who are facing similar challenges.

9.   Work-Life Balance: Last but not least, this journey has taught me that health should always come first, reminding me not to sacrifice my well-being for the sake of work or other obligations.

For this week's guitar recovery video vlog, I wanted to do something different. I chose a soothing track in the key of C major and focused on using the guitar and chords of G major and D minor seventh. I showcased simple motifs using the D Dorian scale, which consists of the notes D, E, F, G, A, B, and C. The D Dorian mode is particularly interesting to me because of its relative relationship to C major. The notes of the D

Dorian scale are reflections of those in the C major scale, providing a unique and enjoyable challenge for guitar players. By exploring this scale and incorporating it into my playing, I have found new ways to express myself musically and to further my recovery journey.

As I reflect on the lessons learned and the progress made during my guitar stroke recovery journey, I am reminded of the words of Psalm 27:1, "The Lord is my light and my salvation, whom shall I fear? The Lord is the stronghold of my life, of whom shall I be afraid?" These words serve as a reminder to trust in God's plan and to have faith that He will guide me through any challenge that comes my way. Closing my eyes, taking a deep breath, and strumming the chords of G major and D minor seventh, I feel a sense of peace and contentment wash over me. The music fills the room, surrounding me with its gentle melody and soothing tones. As I continue on this journey of recovery and self-discovery, I am grateful for the lessons learned, the strength gained, and the unwavering presence of God by my side.

So, to all my fellow Stroke Warriors out there, remember that you are not alone. Embrace the lessons learned, celebrate the victories achieved, and trust in the path that lies ahead. And above all, never forget to pause, breathe, and take a moment to reflect on the beauty and value of the world around you.

RECOVERY WEEK 145
Reflecting on "Never Blame"

God expects people to take responsibility for their actions,
and he helps those who do.

—Proverbs 28:13

https://youtu.be/4791I6bKZLI

One important lesson I have learned throughout my recovery journey is the concept of "never blame." When I first had my stroke, I found myself pointing fingers at everything around me. However, I soon realized that it wasn't the circumstances that were holding me back, but rather my own mindset and perspective. It was my own thinking that was limiting my ability to understand what had happened and take action to move forward.

Blaming everything around me only served as a distraction from taking accountability for my own role in the stroke. By constantly blaming external factors, I was pushing away the responsibility to take action and make positive changes in my life. I had to come to terms with the fact that I was the only one who could truly make a difference in my own recovery journey. It was essential for me to stop creating excuses and start focusing on developing solutions.

Blaming is often a defense mechanism known as projection. This involves denying one's own negative characteristics and attributing them to others instead. It is a way for individuals to protect themselves from feeling guilty or ashamed of their own actions. I may not be an expert in this field, but I have experienced firsthand the negative impact of constantly blaming everything around me.

What I have learned is that when dealing with negative emotions, individuals with poor emotion regulation tend to blame external circumstances for their own choices. Blaming everything around you can temporarily reduce one's negative emotions such as anger, guilt, or shame. Individuals who struggle with managing their emotions often find it easier to point fingers rather than take responsibility for their actions; I am guilty of every bit of this.

In my video vlog this week, I decided to challenge myself by creating minor chord magic on the guitar. I experimented with playing minor chords on top of major chords, using various shapes and combinations. Despite the challenges I faced with my right-hand post-stroke, I was able to regain control and confidence in my playing. It was a rewarding experience that reminded me of the progress I have made in my recovery journey.

As I continue on my guitar stroke recovery journey, I am reminded of the importance of taking accountability for my actions and refraining from blaming external factors. It is essential for me to focus on developing solutions and moving forward with a positive mindset. With the support of God and my unwavering determination, I am confident I will overcome any obstacles that come my way. I am truly grateful for the progress I have made and look forward to the continued growth ahead.

In conclusion, it is essential to acknowledge the importance of taking responsibility for our actions, especially in times of adversity. By refraining from blaming external factors and focusing on developing solutions, we can overcome challenges and move forward with a positive mindset. With determination and faith, anything is possible.

RECOVERY WEEK 146
Savoring Life and Thanking God

I will give thanks to you, Lord, with all my heart; I will tell of all your wonderful deeds.

—Psalm 9:1

https://youtu.be/kpjNbsts8KY

What's that old phrase, "Stop and smell the roses"? And if you really physically smell the roses, take time to savor every moment. To me, this means to relax, take time to enjoy the beauty of life, intentionally slow down, lift your eyes, and pay attention. Ecclesiastes 3:11 says: "He has made everything beautiful in its time. He has also set eternity in the human heart, yet no one can fathom what God has done from beginning to end."

This thought takes me back to when I was six to seven years old, going to South Portland, Maine, to spend summer vacation with my cousins. The ride from Rhode Island felt like a lifetime, but the memories made at 12 Webster Street were priceless. Imagine eleven kids of various ages, four adults, and a house full of never-to-be-forgotten memories. Our biggest adventure was creating an army to make a trek to Willard Beach, where we swam in freezing water, played in the sand, and dug clams in the mud flats at low tide. So please picture all the kids' pushing strollers and pulling wagons full of beach supplies, with my Aunt Salem and my dear mother leading the way. How in the cat hair did they pull this off so successfully? We were ready to take the hill. The walk back to 12 Webster Street was the most memorable, stopping halfway at the corner store for the best ice cream cones, all of us kids would line up and order our cones, my favorite was chocolate. I remember sitting on the stoop, savoring my chocolate cone and feeling like all was right in the world. So even at my young age of six to seven years old, I savored this moment by taking time to enjoy the beauty of life, intentionally slowing down, lifting my eyes, and paying attention, and I still do today.

"Time Machine Dreams," a song by Charles Webber

Wish I had a time machine for laughter's golden days
Moments flash like sparklers under summer's moonlit rays
Echoes of our voices in the corners of the park
Dancing in the shadows until the night's turned dark

Memories like photographs inside a weathered book
Each page a whisper of the love and chance we took
Wishing I could pause the world at every gentle glance
Capture every heartbeat in our timeless dance

Take me back to moments when the world was young and free
When the hours stretched like oceans longing for their sea
Hold my hand through ages lost and places we have seen
If only I could live it with my time machine

Wishing on the distant stars that guide our fated paths
Longing for the laughter that time forever hath
Glimpses through a telescope of days that once were bright
Traveling the universe of memories tonight

Sing the song of yesterday with notes that never fade
Show me every sunrise in the dreams we've made
Guide me through the constellations of your sweet embrace
Time machine, take me to that magic place

Take me back to moments when the world was young and free
When the hours stretched like oceans longing for their sea
Hold my hand through ages lost and places we have seen
If only I could live it with my time machine dream

For this week's video vlog, I used an interesting but straightforward guitar chord progression of C major, B flat major, and F major. I couldn't resist incorporating the G Mixolydian scale to create motifs and melodies. The G Mixolydian scale is a mode of the C major scale, containing the same notes but starting on a different one. With notes G A B C D E F and a key signature of 0 flats or sharps, it adds a unique touch to the music. Though the recording may not be perfect, I am gaining more control in my right wrist. Let's keep rocking, Stroke Warriors, thank God for our blessings, and savor the moment.

In conclusion, cherishing the simple moments in life and expressing gratitude for the blessings we have is essential for our overall well-being. Whether it's savoring the taste of a delicious ice cream cone or working on a guitar chord progression, taking the time to appreciate these experiences can bring joy and fulfillment to our lives. Let's continue to rock on and appreciate all that life has to offer.

RECOVERY WEEK 147
Reflect on My Musical Journey

Do not be misled: "Bad company corrupts good character."

—1 Corinthians 15:33

https://youtu.be/Lgwvz-7mwX4

One of the best church praise bands I had the pleasure and opportunity to play guitar for was at Maxwell AFB, Chapel 2, Montgomery, Alabama, led by Colonel Mike Martin. When I think back to those days, that was family. Thank you, retired Colonel Mike Martin, for making the praise band a wonderful learning experience and fun.

It's beautiful how blessings from God can fuel our passions and guide us toward growth and joy. Expressing appreciation for this gift can be done through heartfelt prayer, dedicating your music practice to divine inspiration, or simply taking a moment to reflect on the life-enriching experience of playing the guitar again. May your journey be filled with melodies of gratitude and harmony.

When embarking on a musical journey to rediscover the joy of playing the guitar, it's essential to acknowledge the role of faith in guiding and blessing your path. Expressing gratitude toward God for His divine intervention can bring a sense of peace, fulfillment, and inspiration to your practice sessions. Let's explore together the various ways to thank God for blessing us Stroke Warriors on our musical journey to learning to play the guitar again or any other musical instrument.

One of the most heartfelt ways to thank God for His blessings on our musical journey is through prayer. Take a moment each day to express your gratitude, offer thanks, and seek His guidance and inspiration as you practice and hone your guitar skills. By connecting with God through prayer, you can cultivate a deeper sense of faith and purpose in your music-making endeavors.

Take time to reflect on the many ways in which God has blessed you on your musical journey. From the opportunity to rediscover your love for playing music or guitar to the progress you have made in mastering new chords and melodies; there are countless blessings to be grateful for. Keeping a gratitude journal can help you stay mindful of God's presence and love in your life.

Another way to thank God for blessing you on your musical journey is by sharing your talent with others. Whether it's performing for family and friends, volunteering to play at church events, or joining a community music group, using your gift of music to uplift and inspire others can be a powerful way to express gratitude toward God. Remember that your musical journey is not just for your benefit but also for the enjoyment and cdification of those around you.

Stay humble and patient while relearning guitar to achieve musical excellence. Recognize that God's blessings are meant to be shared and used for the greater good. Stay open to feedback, embrace challenges as opportunities for growth, and trust in God's plan for your musical journey. By staying humble and patient, you can honor God's blessings and continue to progress in your guitar playing.

For this week's guitar stroke recovery video, I played against an interesting backing track using guitar chords A minor, G major, F major back to G major. I used the A Aeolian (minor—A B C D E F G A) scale to create some interesting phrasing and guitar voicings. It's not perfect, but I am trying to increase my pick hand speed. I hope you enjoy it.

***

In conclusion, learning to play the guitar again is a rewarding and fulfilling journey that can be enriched by acknowledging and thanking God for His blessings along the way. Through prayer, gratitude, sharing your talent, and maintaining humility and patience, you can honor God's role in guiding and inspiring your musical endeavors. Remember that God is the ultimate healer and source of all blessings, including the gift of music. Embrace each note you play as a token of gratitude and praise for the divine guidance that has brought you back to the joy of playing the guitar.

Recovery Week 148
Humbled by the Progress

But he gives more grace. Therefore, it says, "God opposes the proud but gives grace to the humble."

—James 4:6

https://youtu.be/WAFEi2B60GA

While every stroke is different, there are common emotional aftereffects that many of us face. Through my experiences, I have learned the importance of courage, advocacy, and faith in the recovery process. Join me as I share my insights, struggles, and triumphs along the way.

I reflect on the significance of courage in the face of adversity. As Mary Anne Radmacher beautifully said, "Courage doesn't always roar, sometimes courage is the little voice at the end of the day that says, 'I'll try again tomorrow.'" It is this quiet determination that propels us forward, even on the toughest days.

What should we be advocating for in our journey toward recovery of greatness? How can we stand up for ourselves fearlessly? To me, recovery greatness is about believing in the possibility of healing, shifting our mindset from obligation to privilege, and placing our faith in a higher power, our God. It is about taking small steps toward progress, even when the road ahead seems daunting.

In times of uncertainty and doubt, it is important to lean on our faith and trust in God. The Bible offers us words of encouragement and strength, reminding us that we are never alone. God's presence gives us the courage to face our fears, overcome obstacles, and emerge stronger on the other side. As Philippians 4:13 reminds us, "I can do all things through him who strengthens me."

In my guitar recovery video, I had the pleasure of experimenting with the E Phrygian guitar scale. The E Phrygian scale is the third mode of the C major scale, with notes including E, F, G, A, B, and C. This unique scale offers a fresh perspective on musical expression, showcasing the beauty of complexity and diversity within music. I invite you to listen and explore the richness of the E Phrygian scale in your own musical journey.

I am grateful for the lessons learned, the progress made, and the support received along the way. Each day presents a new opportunity to grow, to heal, and to embrace the journey toward fearlessness and faith. May we all find the courage to keep going, the strength to persevere, and the faith to believe in brighter days ahead. Remember: Fear not, believe, and play on!

RECOVERY WEEK 149
Overcoming Obstacles and Celebrating Wins

For God has not given us a spirit of timidity, but of power and love and discipline.

—2 Timothy 1:7

https://youtu.be/0oH9nk7cM1g

It has been a crazy road filled with setbacks and failures, but I have learned to change my perspective and see these challenges as opportunities to try again. As Stroke Warriors, our role is to keep moving forward, be persistent in the face of adversity, and keep our creativity alive.

One of the most important steps in overcoming obstacles is to acknowledge them. Ask yourself what is getting in the way, what challenges the obstacles are creating, and what you have tried so far. By acknowledging the obstacles, you can start to work toward overcoming them.

Next, prioritize the obstacles. Figure out which ones you can handle, which ones need your immediate attention, and what you can stop doing to prioritize these obstacles. This step is crucial in moving forward and making progress in your recovery journey.

Lastly, celebrate your persistence and small wins along the way. Recognize what is working, what you have learned so far, and what you are most proud of. By celebrating your wins, you can stay motivated and continue pushing forward toward your goals.

In this week's recovery video, I attempted to play some interesting country-style guitar. It was both fun and challenging, especially as I am still recovering the use of my right hand. I focused on creating a guitar lead with lots of open space and some pedal steel licks, using chords such as D, A, and G. I hope you enjoy the tune and can see the progress I have made in my guitar playing journey.

As Romans 5:3–5 says, hardships can produce patient endurance, proven character, hope, and assurance of eternal salvation. This verse serves as a reminder that through our struggles and challenges, we can find strength and grow both personally and spiritually.

In conclusion, overcoming obstacles and celebrating wins are essential elements of the stroke recovery journey. By acknowledging, prioritizing, and celebrating our progress, we can continue to move forward and achieve our goals. As Stroke Warriors, let us not be discouraged by setbacks but see them as opportunities for growth and improvement. Stay strong, stay persistent, and keep moving forward on your recovery journey.

RECOVERY WEEK 150
Immense Changes

Keep your face to the sunshine and you cannot see a shadow.

—Helen Keller

https://youtu.be/X92cbrEM6Xc

From relearning simple daily tasks to attempting to play the guitar again, it has been a rollercoaster of emotions. However, with God's blessings and the guidance of skilled therapists, I have seen remarkable progress, reversing some of the effects of this life-altering event.

As Stroke Warriors, our goals are clear: to increase independence, improve physical functioning, and ultimately gain a satisfying quality of life post-stroke. We strive to make lifestyle changes that will prevent another stroke, recognizing the importance of taking charge of our health and well-being.

Here are some key areas of focus:

1. Activities of Daily Living: From eating and bathing to dressing, mastering these everyday tasks is crucial for reclaiming autonomy.

2. Mobility Skills: Whether it's transferring from bed to chair, walking, or using a wheelchair, mobility is a key component of stroke recovery.

3. Communication Skills: Restoring speech and language abilities is essential for reconnecting with loved ones and expressing oneself.

4. Cognitive Skills: Working on memory, problem-solving, and other cognitive functions is vital for overall mental well-being.

5. Social Skills: Relearning how to interact with others and build meaningful relationships is an integral part of post-stroke rehabilitation.

6. Psychological Functioning: Coping with the emotional impact of a stroke and seeking treatment for depression, if needed, are crucial steps in the recovery process.

In this week's guitar recovery video, I tackled a soulful funky groove in G Mixolydian, pushing myself to regain movement in my right wrist. The journey has been challenging, but I am reminded of the words from 2 Chronicles 15:7, "But as for you, be strong and do not give up, for your work will be rewarded."

As I continue to navigate this path of recovery, I am filled with hope, determination, and gratitude for the support and guidance that have been pivotal in my healing journey. Each day presents new challenges and victories, pushing me closer to my goals and a life that is defined by resilience and perseverance.

In Conclusion, I hope my guitar stroke recovery journey serves as a testament to the power of faith and resilience in the face of adversity. Through unwavering commitment and the support of loved ones, therapists, and fellow Stroke Warriors, we can continue to make strides toward a life filled with independence, joy, and music. The road may be long and arduous, but each strum of the guitar and strumming for life, embodies the spirit of hope and perseverance that defines our remarkable journey. Stroke Warriors never quit!

Recovery Week 151
Overcoming Challenges with Music-Supported Therapy

The righteous cry out, and the Lord hears them; he delivers them from all their troubles. The Lord is close to the brokenhearted and saves those who are crushed in spirit.

—Psalm 34:17–18

https://youtu.be/P9xJWt891Ag

I've seen the great benefits of music-supported therapies for motor function rehab. I've made significant progress and am eager to share my experience in this week's recovery update.

I delved deeper into the world of music-supported therapy and its impact on rebuilding motor skills. Through my research and personal experiences, I have identified key strategies that have helped me on my path to regaining my ability to play the guitar.

One of the most significant revelations I have had during my recovery journey is the unique benefits that music-supported therapies can offer for individuals recovering from a stroke. From improving coordination between rhythmic and discrete movements to strengthening neurological connections, music has been a powerful tool in my rehabilitation process.

Through dedicated practice and perseverance, I have focused on maintaining a constant rhythmic strumming movement to strengthen my elbow and wrist kinematics. By homing in on controlling weak motion points and developing new neurological bridges, I have seen significant improvements in the smoothness of my movements while playing the guitar.

One of the key components of my guitar recovery journey has been understanding and utilizing the ulnar nerve, the largest unprotected nerve in the human body. By focusing on joint coordination patterns that involve the ulnar nerve, such as elbow extension and wrist pronation, I have been able to make progress in relearning to strum the guitar.

In this week's recovery video, I challenged myself to play a soulful lead in the key of F# on the guitar. By incorporating major and minor pentatonic scales and omitting open notes, I aimed to create a bluesy feel to the jam. I hope you enjoy this glimpse into my ongoing recovery journey.

As I continue on my path to relearning how to play the guitar after my stroke, I remain committed to utilizing music-supported therapies and trusted strategies to overcome challenges and make progress. My faith and dedication drive me forward, and I am grateful for the opportunity to share my journey with others. Keep strumming for life!

RECOVERY WEEK 152
A Testimony of Resilience and Faith

Not only that, but we rejoice in our sufferings, knowing that suffering produces endurance, and endurance produces character, and character produces hope.

—Romans 5:3–4

https://youtu.be/fGGT2wubexQ

The guitar has always been more than just an instrument to me; it has been a source of solace and healing during difficult times. From a young age, I found refuge in the strings and chords, allowing me to express myself when words failed. Playing guitar for the United States Air Force was an unexpected honor, and this was one of many moments that solidified my love for music.

Throughout my recovery, faith has been my constant companion. With each strum of the guitar, I am reminded of the unwavering presence of God in my life. The verse from Isaiah 30:21 resonates deeply with me, guiding me on this musical journey with a sense of purpose and direction. In moments of doubt, I hold onto the belief that all things are possible with God by my side (Matthew 19:26).

Relearning to play the guitar after a stroke has come with its own set of challenges, especially in terms of fine motor skills. However, I have learned that consistent practice and rehabilitation can lead to significant improvements. I applied the same age-old adage for all aspects of guitar playing practice, practice, practice. There is no standard level of recovery that any one person can achieve, as every stroke will have very specific impairments, as will any pathological condition resulting from a disease, injury, therapy, or other trauma. I guess it depends on exactly what areas were damaged. The brain's ability to adapt and create new pathways gives hope for continued progress, despite the obstacles along the way. With my therapist's guidance, I am focusing on enhancing my shoulder strength to improve wrist and finger dexterity, a small step toward greater musicality.

Each week, I embrace new challenges and explore different sounds, pushing myself to grow as a guitarist. This week's video features a groovy guitar backing track with a bluesy vibe in A minor, showcasing my efforts to incorporate various scales and techniques into my playing. Through this creative exploration, I am reminded that music is a journey of self-expression and growth.

In conclusion, the journey of relearning to play the guitar after a stroke has been a testament to resilience and faith. By embracing the power of music and staying committed to practice, I continue to make progress on this musical path. As I strum through each week of recovery, I am reminded of the unrelenting support of God and the joy that music brings into my life. Keep strumming for life, fellow Stroke Warriors, and never lose sight of the healing power of music.

RECOVERY WEEK 153
World of Pentatonic Scales

Let us then with confidence draw near to the throne of grace,
that we may receive mercy and find grace to help in time of
need.

—Hebrews 4:16

https://youtu.be/nserNiHv-5o

As I reflect on completing my journey of relearning guitar with Week 153, I am filled with gratitude for God's grace and mercy. Despite the challenges I face in not being able to play as well as I once did, I am reminded of the progress I have made since Week 1. The journey of stroke recovery is a complex and emotional one, but I have learned to trust in God's plan for my healing. Isaiah 41:10 reminds me, "Fear not, for I am with you; be not dismayed, for I am your God; I will strengthen you, I will help you, I will uphold you with my righteous right hand."

One of the most important things I have learned during my recovery process is that the effects of a stroke can vary greatly depending on its severity and the area of the brain affected. This can result in a wide range of challenges, from language and vision issues to physical disabilities like paralysis. However, it is crucial to remember that there is always hope, as stated in Isaiah 40:31, "But those who hope in the LORD will renew their strength."

For this week's guitar journey, I decided to delve into the world of pentatonic scales. These scales are fundamental tools for any guitarist, providing the building blocks for solos and melodies across different genres. A scale is a sequence of notes arranged in ascending or descending order, forming the basis for musical compositions. The pentatonic scale consists of five notes per octave, with the major pentatonic scale being derived from the major scale, and the minor pentatonic scale from the natural minor scale. The structure of these scales is as follows:

Major Pentatonic Scale: Root, 2nd, 3rd, 5th, 6th
Minor Pentatonic Scale: Root, b3rd, 4th, 5th, b7th

Here are examples of the major and minor pentatonic scale diagrams for practicing using guitar tablature (TAB) which is a way of writing music specific to fretted instruments. It's a perfect system for musicians who don't read traditional, standard music notation. A TAB has six horizontal lines that represent the six strings on the guitar. The top line represents the thinnest string, (high E note) and the lowest line represents the thickest string (low E note).

1. Key: C Major Pentatonic Notes: C, D, E, G, A in TAB:

```
e|-------------------0--3--|
B|-----------------1------|
G|-------------0--2------|
D|---------0--2----------|
A|-----0--2--------------|
E|--0--3-----------------|
```

Here is an example in TAB of the A minor pentatonic scale diagram to practice:

2. Key: A Minor Pentatonic Notes: A, C, D, E, G

```
e|-----------------------5--8--|
B|--------------------5--8------|
G|----------------5--7----------|
D|-----------5--7--------------|
A|------5--7------------------|
E|--5--8--------------------|
```

In this week's guitar recovery video, I explored a contemporary backing track using chords Cmaj7, Eb dim, Em7, Cmaj7, B7, Em7. Pay close attention to how I utilized guitar chord voicing for Eb dim, which can serve as an interesting substitute voicing for the B7 chord. I incorporated guitar scales C major, D Dorian, and major/minor pentatonic showcasing the progress I am making in strengthening my rhythm hand.

For my fellow Stroke Warrior guitar players, I hope this information proves helpful in your own relearning endeavors. Remember, progress may not be perfect, but every step forward is a victory worth celebrating. Enjoy the journey and keep strumming toward recovery.

In conclusion, as I navigate through Week 153 of my guitar stroke recovery journey, I am reminded of the power of perseverance and faith. Despite the setbacks and challenges I face, I hold onto the hope that each day brings new opportunities for growth and healing. With dedication and a positive mindset, I am confident that I will continue to make progress in reclaiming my love for music and guitar playing.

RECOVERY WEEK 154
Merry Christmas, Stroke Warriors!

Behold, the Lamb of God, who takes away the sin of the world!

—John 1:29

https://youtu.be/cCyLI4yZ6aw

Christmas is the perfect time to celebrate the love of God and family and to create memories that will last forever. As Joel Osteen beautifully puts it, "Jesus is God's perfect, indescribable gift." This sentiment resonates deeply with me as I reflect on the significance of Christmas and the blessings I have received during this festive season.

Life may present us with challenges, especially in the aftermath of a stroke, but the mere fact that we are breathing is a gift in itself. We must be thankful for the opportunity to overcome adversity and strive for better days ahead.

Without Jesus Christ, there would be no Christmas. His presence in our lives serves as a reminder of hope, love, and salvation. Let us be grateful for the ultimate sacrifice He made for our sins and celebrate His birth with reverence and joy.

Our families provide us with unwavering support and love, especially during trying times. Let us not take their presence for granted and cherish every precious moment spent together during the Christmas season.

Reflecting on a pivotal moment from my past, I vividly recall the thrill of discovering my first guitar beneath the Christmas tree. That morning, nothing else mattered; the anticipation and joy of holding that instrument in my hands eclipsed all other gifts.

The message of the Gospel is the cornerstone of Christmas. Its teachings guide us toward a life filled with faith, love, and compassion. Through music, such as the gospel blues style, we can express our gratitude for the divine grace bestowed upon us.

In this week's stroke recovery video, I embarked on a musical journey using a gospel blues-style backing track in C major. Despite the challenges posed by my affected right picking hand, I navigated through intricate guitar chords and scales with determination and resilience. The unconventional blend of guitar voicings, including C major, E7, Am, F, C, A, and more, created a harmonious symphony that symbolized the spirit of Christmas. Each chord progression resonated with the essence of the holiday season, evoking feelings of joy and gratitude. As I strummed my guitar strings, I felt a sense of empowerment and liberation. The music served as a healing balm for my soul, replenishing my spirit with hope and inspiration. Through my musical journey, I rediscovered the strength within me and embraced the power of resilience.

This Christmas, let us give thanks for the gift of life, the presence of our Savior, the love of our families, and the everlasting message of the Gospel. As Stroke Warriors, we are resilient, courageous, and steadfast in our pursuit of recovery and renewal. May this festive season bring us closer together, inspire us to overcome adversity, and fill our hearts with the melody of hope and joy. Merry Christmas, Stroke Warriors! Let us celebrate the spirit of Christmas with gratitude, love, and music that transcends all boundaries. Strumming for life!

Recovery Week 155
Looking Ahead to 2025

https://youtu.be/13bm6PFzwCU

As we wrap up 2024 and prepare to welcome the new year, many of us are filled with hope and anticipation for what the future holds. For us Stroke Warriors who are also passionate musicians, 2025 brings a sense of excitement and optimism. What are the expectations and hopes of stroke survivors, especially musicians, as we look ahead to the coming year?

What have we learned from 2024? It's clear from the 2024 Heart Disease and Stroke Statistical Update that strokes can affect people of any age, presenting survivors with a tough journey of navigating physical, emotional, and cognitive changes. The data from the American Heart Association highlights the sobering reality that every forty seconds, someone in the US experiences a stroke, underscoring the urgency of the issue. A poignant reminder emerges, as nearly one in four stroke survivors confront the risk of a second stroke, sometimes due to a lack of understanding about the root cause of their initial stroke. Let's stand together in empathy and understanding, supporting those who have endured such challenges on their path to recovery and wellness.

What can we expect in 2025? As we enter the new year, one can't help but wonder what lies ahead for us stroke survivors. Will 2025 bring new breakthroughs in stroke recovery techniques? Could there be advancements in music therapy specifically designed to help musicians to regain their musical abilities? These are just a few questions that swirl around in my mind as we embark on this journey into 2025.

For us Stroke Warriors, I hope and pray for a tremendous year of healing and recovery. For many stroke survivors, 2025 holds this promise. As we continue to navigate the challenges of life after a stroke, we are hopeful that this new year will bring renewed strength and vitality. For stroke recovery musicians, the road to recovery can be particularly challenging, as we strive to regain our ability to play our beloved instruments. However, with determination and support, I believe that 2025 will indeed be a tremendous year for all Stroke Warriors.

As we look to the future, the hopes and dreams of stroke survivors are as diverse as the individuals themselves. Some may hope to regain full mobility and independence, while others may aspire to return to their pre-stroke level of functioning. For musicians like me, I have a strong, self-powering force inside me and a relentless desire to once again play guitar with skill and passion, which I hope is a driving force in your recovery journey as well. In 2025, I hope for continued progress, healing, and empowerment for all stroke survivors.

A look back at my 2024 journey: As I reflect on my guitar stroke recovery journey in Week 155, I proudly see a story of resilience, determination, and hope. Despite the challenges I faced, I remained steadfast in my commitment to overcoming this stroke and reclaiming my music. Through hard work, therapy, and the support of loved ones, I have made remarkable progress in my recovery.

As we all celebrate our achievements and look ahead to the future, I hope we all are inspired with unwavering spirit and dedication. Most of all for 2025, in times of struggle and uncertainty, let us find solace in the boundless support of our faith and the healing power of God. As Stroke Warriors, we face challenges that may seem insurmountable, but with our trust in God's guidance and love, we can find strength in our journey toward recovery. Let your faith be a beacon of hope and a source of comfort as you navigate the ups and downs of this difficult road. Remember, you are not alone, for God walks beside you, offering solace and renewal to your spirit. Let us hold onto our faith and let it illuminate our path to healing and recovery.

Embarking on this week's guitar recovery video was like diving into a musical adventure full of challenges and growth. Attempting a smooth and comforting backtrack in the key of A major, I delved into the world of connecting chords through an A-Bm-F#m-D progression, experimenting with fills along the way. The journey pushed my stroke-effected right rhythm hand to its limits, but I embraced the challenge with determination and perseverance. Moving forward, I am excited to keep testing my musical boundaries and pushing myself even harder. The thrill of this musical exploration is set to continue well into 2025, and I can't wait to see where this adventurous path will lead. So, sit back, relax, and enjoy the ride as I take on new musical horizons and strive for greater heights!

In conclusion, as we stand on the cusp of a new year, the possibilities for Stroke Warriors are endless. With each passing week, we are reminded of the resilience of the human spirit. In 2025, we hope and pray for a year filled with healing, recovery, and joy for all Stroke Warriors, especially our stroke recovery musicians. As we continue to support one another on this journey, we are confident that the best is yet to come. Please remember— keep strumming for life! God Bless!

Recovery Week 156
The Power of Faith: A Source of Strength

My flesh and my heart may fail, but God is the strength of my heart and my portion forever.

—Psalm 73:26

https://youtu.be/U22WtN3c6qU

This week, I focused on practicing over a nice slow 6/8 ballad feel, incorporating 3rds passing tones with guitar articulations of A, Bm, C#m, and E/D. It's been a challenging week as I work toward harmonizing the major scale up the neck and applying it musically in fills. But I'm determined not to give up, even as I face the greatest challenge of relearning how to play with both my guitar pick and fingers again.

As I dive deeper into my mission of strumming for life, I find strength in Psalm 27:14: "Don't give up; don't be impatient; be entwined as one with the Lord." Let's walk through this week's progress together.

This week, I embarked on the task of harmonizing the major scale up the neck. It's a technique that requires precision and practice, but the results are truly rewarding. By exploring new ways to apply this musical concept in my fills, I'm expanding my guitar skills and creative expression. With each challenge I face, I remind myself of the importance of perseverance and determination.

One of the highlights of this week was the opportunity to relearn how to play using both my guitar pick and fingers. This task has proven to be the most difficult aspect of my recovery journey so far. But I refuse to back down. With each strum and pluck, I am reminded of the power of resilience and my unconstrained commitment to my musical passion.

In moments of doubt and frustration, I turn to the wisdom of Psalm 27:14. These words serve as a beacon of light, guiding me through the darkest of times. As I navigate the challenges of my guitar stroke recovery, I find solace in the belief that with faith I will find my way.

Are you facing your own challenges in your musical journey? Remember, you are not alone. Let's embrace each obstacle as an opportunity for growth and transformation. Together, we can overcome any hurdle that comes our way. Let's keep strumming for life, one chord at a time.

As I reflect I am reminded of the power within me brought forth by my faith. Each strum and pluck brings me one step closer to my musical goals, and I am determined to continue this journey with full commitment. Join me as we strum for life, embracing challenges and celebrating victories along the way. Remember, with faith and determination, anything is possible. Let's keep strumming!

RECOVERY WEEK 157
Overcoming Challenges and Finding Inspiration

The steadfast love of the Lord never ceases; his mercies never come to an end; they are new every morning; great is your faithfulness.

—Lamentations 3:22-23

https://youtu.be/Fd3DS3qrgGA

From struggling with the tiring work of rebuilding muscle memory in my hand and fingers to attempting to play unison notes using both a guitar pick and my fingers, the challenges have been plentiful. However, in the midst of the difficulties, I have also found moments of inspiration and growth that have kept me motivated to keep pushing forward.

As I tackled this week's practice session, I found myself faced with the task of using a rhythm track with guitar voicings of C, Am, Dm, and G. Attempting to incorporate neighboring intervals using both 6ths and 3rds from the C major scale added an extra layer of complexity to my practice routine. Despite the initial struggles and frustrations, I quickly realized that pushing through the challenges was essential for my progress.

One of the unexpected joys of this week's practice was discovering how experimenting with neighboring intervals could add a new dimension of color and depth to my playing. By landing on an interval on either side and then resolving it within the chord, I was able to create a musical journey that was both satisfying and fulfilling. This experience reinforced the importance of putting in the work to understand the harmonized major scale up the neck in 3rds and 6ths, as it opened up a world of creative possibilities.

I found reassurance in the words of Isaiah 41:10, "So do not fear, for I am with you; do not be dismayed, for I am your God. I will strengthen you and help you; I will uphold you with my righteous right hand." These words served as a constant reminder that no matter how challenging the journey may be, I am never alone. Drawing inspiration from my faith has been a source of comfort and motivation throughout this process.

I am reminded of the importance of will power in the face of adversity. While the road may be long and the challenges may be daunting, I am committed to staying the course and continuing to grow as a musician. With each strum of the guitar and each note played, I am one step closer to reclaiming my passion for music and overcoming the obstacles that stand in my way.

By embracing the difficulties, discovering new creative possibilities, finding strength in faith, and staying committed to growth, I am confident I will continue to make progress and ultimately achieve my goal. So, to all those facing their own musical challenges, remember to stay strong, stay inspired, and stay committed, the rewards are well worth the effort.

Recovery Week 158
Journey of Determination and Faith

Fear not, for I am with you; be not dismayed, for I am your God; I will strengthen you, I will help you, I will uphold you with my righteous right hand.

—Isaiah 41:10

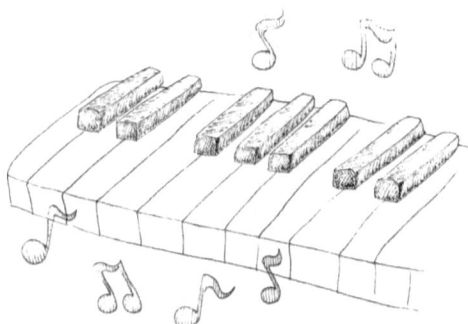

https://youtu.be/A8A6AcX74os

It has been another challenging week on my journey to relearn how to play the guitar after my stroke. But as Thomas Edison famously said, "Our greatest weakness lies in giving up. The most certain way to succeed is always to try just one more time." With this mindset, I am determined to keep pushing myself and not give up on my passion for music.

Before my stroke, playing the guitar came so naturally to me. I could strum the strings and hit the right chords even with my eyes closed. But now, I am faced with the challenge of using my guitar pick and fingers to create music once again. It is not easy, but I am not one to back down from a challenge.

One of the things that keeps me going on this journey is the inspiration I find in music. As I attempted to play harmonies this week, I challenged myself by visualizing chord shapes and playing them on the 2nd and 4th strings. The moment when the bridge transitions to B minor and the harmony notes shift from major to minor is truly magical. It reminds me of the power of music to uplift and inspire us, even in our darkest moments.

In times of difficulty, I turn to my faith for strength and guidance. Psalm 25:4–11 speaks to me in this moment, "Show me the right path, O LORD; point out the road for me to follow. Lead me by your truth and teach me, for you are the God who saves me." I put my hope in the Lord and trust in His compassion and unfailing love to carry me through this challenging time.

As I continue on this journey of recovery and rediscovery, I am filled with hope and determination. I know that the path ahead will be filled with challenges, but I am ready to face them head-on. With each strum of the guitar strings and each chord played, I am one step closer to reclaiming what I thought I had lost. And for that, I am grateful.

In conclusion, the path to recovery is not easy, but with determination, faith, and a love for music, anything is possible. I will continue to strive to improve my guitar playing skills and embrace the challenges that come my way. As I navigate through this journey, I am reminded of the words of Thomas Edison and the power of music to uplift and inspire. And with each note played, I am one step closer to reclaiming my passion for music.

Recovery Week 159
Pushing Through Challenges

For I know the plans I have for you, declares the Lord, plans for welfare and not for evil, to give you a future and a hope.

—Jeremiah 29:11

*live
laugh
love*

https://youtu.be/-WxBfdAFDbo

This week, I decided to take a break from using my guitar pick and fingers, but rest assured, I will be getting back to it very soon. In this week's guitar recovery video, I challenged myself by playing a 12-bar blues progression using the G Mixolydian scale in the key of G7th.

Playing with different scales and keys can be daunting, especially when dealing with a stroke-related challenge. However, I decided to incorporate using G Mixolydian over the I chord, C Mixolydian over the IV chord, and D Mixolydian over the V chord. To add more depth to my playing, I also experimented with incorporating the b3rd of G (Bb) and the blue note.

This week's practice session was extremely challenging, but I believe in pushing myself beyond my comfort zone to gain more control with my affected right hand. It's essential to stay determined and focused on the end goal, despite the obstacles that may come my way. With each passing week, I can feel myself getting closer to reaching my full potential as a guitarist.

Throughout this journey, I have leaned on my faith in God for strength and guidance. Psalm 34:8 reminds us to "Taste and see that the LORD is good; blessed is the one who takes refuge in him." This verse serves as a constant reminder that with faith and perseverance, anything is possible.

As I walk along my path of recovery, I'm truly grateful for the chance to connect with others facing similar challenges. It's a journey filled with ups and downs, but I'm here to share my story and inspire anyone going through a rough patch. Remember, with a positive attitude and unwavering determination, no obstacle is too great to overcome. Keep strumming those strings, stay hopeful, and never stop believing in your dreams. Together, we can find solace in music and strength in resilience.

RECOVERY WEEK 160
A Challenging Journey

Trust in the Lord with all your heart, and do not lean on your own understanding. In all your ways acknowledge him, and he will make straight your paths.

—Proverbs 3:5-6

Be You ♥
♥ Be True
Just Be ♥

https://youtu.be/byfDB04aRd4

I decided to push myself to the limit by attempting to play some of the intricate guitar licks of the great John Mayer. It was a daunting task, especially considering that my right hand, affected by the stroke, has been a major obstacle in my musical journey. However, I was determined to challenge myself and see how far I could push my limits.

As I embarked on this challenging endeavor, I primarily relied on G major pentatonic guitar scales to navigate through the complex melodies. The main rhythm of the piece was accentuated by the use of G major and D/C chords, which added depth and richness to the overall sound. As the composition progressed, I found myself weaving through chords such as Am7, D7, Gm/Bb, and Ebmaj7, each presenting its own unique set of challenges. Despite the difficulties I encountered along the way, I continued to explore alternative ways of playing these chords, pushing myself to think outside the box and experiment with new techniques. While my performance may not have been flawless, I am incredibly proud of the progress I have made and the determination I have shown in tackling this formidable challenge.

As the saying goes, "If you keep doing the same things, you'll end up getting the same results." This simple yet profound statement resonates deeply with me, reminding me of the importance of pushing boundaries and venturing outside my comfort zone. By continually challenging myself and striving for improvement, I am not only enhancing my musical abilities but also fueling my stroke recovery journey.

The word "gravity" holds significant meaning, both in the context of music and spirituality. In the Bible, it is used to convey a sense of seriousness, dignity, and sanctified reverence. The Apostle Paul, in his letter to Pastor Titus, emphasized the importance of embodying "gravity" in one's teachings, highlighting the need for solemnity and respect in all endeavors. Furthermore, the concept of gravity can also be interpreted as the divine power of God. Hebrews 1:3 speaks of Christ upholding all things by the word of his power, underscoring the omnipotence and authority of the divine presence. By embracing the gravity of the situation and acknowledging the higher power at play, we can find strength and inspiration in our darkest moments.

Week 160 has been a testament to fortitude and the power of challenging oneself. By taking on the formidable task of mastering John Mayer's guitar licks, I have not only pushed my musical boundaries but also deepened my understanding of the healing power of music. As I continue to strum toward recovery, I am reminded of the importance of embracing challenges, harnessing the gravity of the situation, and never losing sight of the ultimate goal—to keep strumming for life.

RECOVERY WEEK 161
Finding Inspiration in the Bible

But he answered, "It is written, 'Man shall not live by bread alone, but by every word that comes from the mouth of God.'"

—Matthew 4:4

https://youtu.be/qcBeQM51TvQ

I developed an exercise this week, playing triads on the guitar with scale notes. I incorporated triads and scale tones using notes from B natural minor (B, C#, D, E, F#, G, A) to create a new effect. I also added another idea to move the same triad shapes on the guitar an octave lower to the G and D strings. For the backing track, I used guitar chords Bm, A, G, F# and this repeats for the entire track.

I believe these motifs and guitar ideas are awesome writing tools for composers. By experimenting with different scales and chord progressions, musicians can discover new sounds and ways to express themselves through music. The combination of triads and scale tones opens up a world of possibilities for creating unique melodies and harmonies. Moving the triad shapes to different strings adds a layer of complexity and depth to the music, making it more interesting and engaging for both the listener and the performer.

Inspiration can come from many sources, and for me, one of the most powerful sources of inspiration is the Bible. The verse from Matthew 11:28–30, "Come to me, all you who are weary and burdened, and I will give you rest," reminds me to turn to faith and find strength in times of struggle. Music has the power to uplift the spirit and provide comfort during difficult times. By incorporating spiritual themes and messages into my music, I can connect with listeners on a deeper level and inspire them to find hope and peace in their own lives.

Without a doubt, challenging myself to push the boundaries of my guitar playing is a rewarding and fulfilling experience. The journey of recovery after a stroke is not easy, but through music, I am able to find joy, purpose, and healing. Strumming the guitar is not just physical exercise, but a mental and emotional one as well. It requires focus, determination, and perseverance to continue to improve and grow as a musician.

In conclusion, music has the power to heal, inspire, and uplift the human spirit. By challenging myself to explore new techniques and ideas on the guitar, I am able to push past my limitations and create something beautiful and meaningful. Through the combination of scales, triads, and chord progressions, I am able to express myself in a way that words alone cannot. The journey of recovery is a long and difficult one, but with faith, commitment, and a love for music, I know I will continue to strum for life.

RECOVERY WEEK 162
Exploring Major Pentatonic Scales and Pushing Musical Boundaries

In the world you will have tribulation. But take heart; I have overcome the world.

—John 16:33

https://youtu.be/SIm1HhehacM

What a challenging week it has been. This week, I really pushed myself to the limit in my guitar practice. I tackled some major pentatonic scales and added a few extra guitar notes to create a unique sound. It was challenging, but oh so rewarding. I challenged myself to explore new melodies and solos across a wide range of musical genres, including rock, blues, pop, and country.

One of the highlights of this week was learning the major pentatonic scale. This versatile set of notes has a bright, cheerful character that can add a unique quality to your playing. With just five notes, you can create melodies and solos that will elevate your playing to a whole new level. The major pentatonic scale is a great foundation for developing your musical creativity and improvisation skills.

As I navigated through the major pentatonic scales, I realized the importance of consistent practice. It takes time and dedication to master new techniques and scales, but the rewards are well worth it. Each day, I made a commitment to practice diligently and push myself out of my comfort zone. The results were truly amazing, and I could feel myself growing as a stroke recovery musician with each passing day.

To all my fellow Stroke Warriors out there, remember to keep strumming for life. Music has the power to heal, inspire, and uplift us in ways we never thought possible. As we continue on this journey of recovery and musical exploration, let us lean on each other for support and encouragement. Let us remember the words of Lamentations 3:22–23, "The steadfast love of the Lord never ceases; his mercies never come to an end; they are new every morning; great is your faithfulness."

Week 162 of my recovery practice has been an incredibly rewarding experience. I challenged myself, explored new techniques, and pushed myself to new heights in my musical journey. As I continue to grow and evolve as a musician, I am filled with gratitude for the healing power of music and the support of my fellow Stroke Warriors. Here's to another week of strumming, learning, and growing together. Keep on rocking!

RECOVERY WEEK 163
Pushing Past Disabilities

*So do not fear, for I am with you; do not be dismayed, for
I am your God. I will strengthen you and help you; I will
uphold you with my righteous right hand.*

—Isaiah 41:10

https://youtu.be/SdJAx3NBsKY

My goal has been to push past all my physical and mental disabilities, to never stop trying, to never surrender, never quit. This week's focus is on improvising a soulful blues lead using the major and minor pentatonic scales, along with mixing in a few arpeggios.

This week, I challenged myself to improvise a soulful blues lead on the guitar. I focused on using the major and minor pentatonic scales, as well as incorporating arpeggios into my playing. It was a challenging but rewarding experience, as I felt myself growing stronger and more confident with each practice session.

For part A of my improvisation, I used the following guitar chords of Bb major, E dim7, C minor, and F7. This progression provided a solid foundation for the soulful blues lead I was aiming to create. In part B, I introduced a variety of chords, including C minor, F7, Bb major, F major, Eb, Bb, D7, G minor, Bb7, Eb, E dim7, Bb, G minor, C minor, and finally Eb minor. Each chord added a unique flavor to the improvisation, making it a joy to play over.

My overall goal throughout this journey of recovery and relearning has been to keep strumming for life. Playing the guitar has been a source of joy and inspiration for me, and I am determined to never let go of that passion. As 1 John 4:7–8 says, "Dear friends, let us love one another, for love comes from God. Everyone who loves has been born of God and knows God. Whoever does not love does not know God, because God is love." Love and passion are what drive me to continue pushing past my limitations and striving for greatness.

By challenging myself to improvise a soulful blues lead and experimenting with various guitar chord progressions, I have grown both as a musician and as a person. I am grateful for the progress I have made so far, and I look forward to what the future holds for me and my guitar playing. Thank you for joining me on this incredible journey.

Recovery Week 164
Finding Inspiration in "Stroke Buddies"

*Do not be anxious about anything, but in every situation,
by prayer and petition, with thanksgiving, present your
requests to God. And the peace of God, which transcends all
understanding, will guard your hearts and your minds in
Christ Jesus.*

—Philippians 4:6–7

https://youtu.be/kg2u0M1fxvA

Have you ever met someone with an unbreakable spirit, someone who refuses to let their circumstances define them? Well, that person is my friend Ismael. Despite facing a challenging recovery journey from a stroke, he maintains a positive attitude and an unwavering determination to "shred on guitar again." Ismael's resilience serves as a constant source of inspiration for me and many others who are on a similar path toward regaining their strength and abilities.

Throughout my own guitar stroke recovery journey, I have been fortunate enough to cross paths with incredible individuals who share Ismael's drive and passion for life. We often refer to ourselves as "stroke buddies," a community of like-minded individuals who support and uplift each other in our respective recoveries. The camaraderie and encouragement found within this group serve as a driving force, motivating us to keep pushing forward and striving for progress.

I decided to switch things up and challenge myself in a new way. Instead of focusing solely on technical proficiency, I made a conscious effort to explore the concept of leaving space between guitar notes while soloing. This deliberate decision allowed me to simplify my playing and give the notes room to breathe, ultimately creating a more dynamic and engaging musical experience.

One of the key aspects of my challenge this week was mastering the art of letting the notes breathe on the correct beats. By homing in on my timing and technique, I was able to create a more nuanced and expressive sound, drawing inspiration from a variety of guitar chords and scales. From the modified F major and F7th minor chords to the utilization of major and minor pentatonic scales and the Mixolydian mode, each musical element played a crucial role in shaping the overall tone and feel of the composition.

In the midst of my guitar stroke recovery journey, I have come to realize the profound impact that music can have on our physical, emotional, and spiritual well-being. It serves as a powerful tool for self-expression, healing, and connection, transcending language and cultural barriers to unite us in a shared experience. As I continue to navigate the ups and downs of recovery, I am reminded of the words found in Psalm 27:14, urging us to persevere and remain steadfast in our faith and determination.

Week 164 has been a testament to the resilience, creativity, and perseverance of individuals facing challenging circumstances. Through the power of music and community, we are able to find strength, inspiration, and joy in the midst of adversity. So let us keep strumming for life, embracing each new challenge with courage and grace.

Recovery Week 165
Reflective Stroke Journey

*I sought the LORD, and He answered me and delivered me
from all my fears. Those who look to Him are radiant, and
their faces shall never be ashamed. Oh, taste and see that the
LORD is good! Blessed is the man who takes refuge in Him!*

—Psalm 34:4–5, 8

https://youtu.be/NUj6Ccujoqk

I am reminded of the blessings in my life, particularly the support of my
dear friends Roger Alves, John Bentley, and Dr. David Hartranft. Their
unwavering friendship and encouragement have been a source of strength
and inspiration as I navigate the challenges of regaining my guitar-playing
abilities.

One verse that has been particularly meaningful to me during this time is
Isaiah 40:31, which speaks to the renewal of strength through hope in the
Lord. This powerful message resonates with me as I strive to push past the
limitations imposed by my disability and rekindle my passion for music.
The imagery of soaring on wings like eagles and running without growing

weary serves as a reminder of the boundless energy and endurance that faith can provide.

In my latest guitar stroke recovery video, I embarked on the task of integrating Dorian mode guitar scales with minor pentatonic scales. This proved to be a challenging endeavor, but one that I embraced wholeheartedly in my quest to expand my musical repertoire. Through the exploration of Dorian licks and other mode ideas, I am continuously pushing myself to break free from the constraints of my stroke and embrace new musical possibilities.

I would be remiss if I did not express my heartfelt thanks to my friend Brian from ActiveMelody.com for his unwavering support and musical inspiration. His talents have been a guiding light in my journey toward recovery, and I am truly grateful for his presence in my life. Together, we are continuing to strive for musical excellence and the joy of strumming for life.

With the support of dear friends and the strength of faith, I am confident I will continue to progress toward reclaiming my musical abilities. As I look toward the future, I am filled with hope and determination, knowing that with each strum of the guitar, I am moving closer to my ultimate goal of playing with the same skill and passion as before.

Recovery Week 166
Drawing Strength from the Bible

And we know that for those who love God all things work together for good, for those who are called according to His purpose.

—Romans 8:28

https://youtu.be/oe5np5TtRLo

Are you feeling disconnected from real face-to-face communication in this digital age? It seems like we are more comfortable sending texts or emails than having genuine conversations with people. As social creatures, have we lost the art of direct interaction? In this week's guitar recovery session, I reflected on the importance of real communication and made a conscious effort to engage more directly with others.

In a world dominated by technology, it's easy to forget the value of in-person conversations. There is something unique and special about being able to see someone's facial expressions, hear the tone of their voice, and feel their presence in the same physical space. This week, I made a commitment to seek out more opportunities for face-to-face interactions, both in my personal life and at work.

During my guitar practice session, I focused on creating a slow and melodic lead using simple chord progressions in the key of G major. By targeting chord tones and playing out of these shapes, I aimed to produce more meaningful and soulful solos. Special thanks to Brian Sherrill from ActiveMelody.com for inspiring me with this creative approach to playing the guitar.

In times of difficulty and challenges, turning to the Bible for guidance and strength can be a source of great comfort. Psalm 73:26 reminds us that even when our flesh and heart may fail, God is the strength of our hearts forever. These words offer encouragement and fortification for our souls during times of weakness and exhaustion.

As we navigate through the complexities of modern life, let's not forget the power of real communication and connection with others. Whether through music, conversations, or spiritual guidance, let's strive to cultivate meaningful relationships and nourish our souls with the richness of human interaction. And remember, it's never too late to pick up the phone, schedule a coffee date, or simply sit down and engage in a heartfelt conversation with someone you care about. Let's cherish these moments of real connection and make the most of every opportunity to truly engage with one another.

In a world where virtual communication often takes precedence, we must not forget the value of real face-to-face interactions. Through music, conversations, and spiritual guidance, we can find strength and solace in connecting with others on a personal level. Let's make a conscious effort to prioritize direct communication and foster deeper relationships in our lives.

Recovery Week 167
Have We Lost the True Art of Conversation?

Have I not commanded you? Be strong and courageous. Do not be frightened, and do not be dismayed, for the LORD your God is with you wherever you go.

—Joshua 1:9

https://www.youtube.com/watch?v=r_Bem71bboA

Are we so plugged into our devices that we have forgotten how to have meaningful conversations with one another? This week, as I ventured back into the office for a day, I made a conscious effort to engage in real conversations with my colleagues. The experience was eye-opening, and it made me realize just how important it is to connect with others on a human level.

As I listened to my coworkers speak, I paid attention not only to their words but also to their nonverbal cues. I found myself responding with more empathy and understanding, truly trying to see the world from their perspective. By actively listening and engaging in thoughtful dialogue, I was able to have more meaningful interactions and build stronger connections with those around me.

In a world dominated by text messages and emails, face-to-face conversations seem to be becoming a lost art. However, there is something special about being able to see someone's expressions, hear the intonation in their voice, and share a genuine connection. Let's make a conscious effort to put down our phones and engage in real, meaningful conversations with those around us.

This week's guitar stroke practice was all about experimenting with notes and chord shapes to create an enigmatic and mysterious sound. I focused on using a clear minor sound over major guitar chords, specifically B minor and G major. By adding space in the music with the motifs I played, I believe I was able to create a unique and captivating melodic pattern. This week's practice was an excellent challenge for my stroke-affected right hand and wrist movement; I am always pushing myself forward.

As I continue to recover from my stroke, I am constantly pushing myself to improve and challenge myself with relearning to play guitar. The verse from Joshua 1:9, "Be strong and courageous, do not be afraid; do not be discouraged, for the Lord your God will be with you wherever you go." serves as a reminder that I am not alone in facing obstacles. With faith and determination, I know that I can overcome any challenge that comes my way.

In conclusion, let's not forget the importance of genuine conversations and human connections in this digital age. Take the time to engage with others, listen with empathy, and share your thoughts and experiences. And remember, as you face challenges, have faith and courage—you are never alone in your journey.

Recovery Week 168
Human strength and Faith in God!

May the God of hope fill you with all joy and peace as you trust in Him, so that you may overflow with hope by the power of the Holy Spirit.

—Romans 15:13

https://www.youtube.com/watch?v=rqh0c4JtqrA

I did curious search on YouTube for guitar musicians recovering from a stroke. I have to say, it's amazing what these warriors are doing to relearn to play guitar. God, please bless them every day. Their stunning determination was so evident, which was uplifting and inspirational. Please, if you ever get a chance, do the same YouTube search as me. You will be amazed at the real human strength and their faith in God. You can start with my YouTube site: https://www.youtube.com/@cwebber402. I hope you subscribe, it's absolutely free.

In this week's guitar project I was circling back to the basics. However, this week's practice was so challenging for my stroke-affected strumming and picking right hand. Nevertheless, I accepted the task and pushed forward. So off I went, diving into the key of G major and dissecting those sweet, sweet chords that make music magic happen. What's cooking in G town, you may ask? A 16-bar blues in G, because let's be real, blues is the heart and soul of music. So, Stroke Warriors, grab your guitars, embrace those chords, and let's groove through the key of G like never before. It's all about having fun and letting that music flow, my friends, and strumming for life!

The Bible presents numerous challenges and trials faced by individuals and communities, emphasizing the importance of faith, perseverance, and reliance on God's strength during difficult times. The Bible acknowledges the struggles and weaknesses of individuals, offering guidance and encouragement to overcome them through faith and prayer. God is a source of strength and comfort in times of trouble, promising to be with His people through their trials and tribulations. Challenges are viewed as opportunities for growth and learning, helping individuals develop their faith and character. Stroke warriors, keep strumming for life. Amen!

Despite the challenges faced during the recovery process, the determination, faith, and perseverance of Stroke Warriors shine through. Through music and faith, they find strength and inspiration to overcome obstacles and continue their journey toward healing. Let us all take a moment to appreciate their resilience and courage and may we all find the same determination in our own endeavors. So, grab your guitar, strum those strings, and let the music guide you toward a brighter tomorrow. Stroke Warriors, keep strumming for life.

Epilogue

Thank you for taking this journey with me. Having a stroke was an unwanted event, but I have come to realize the gift I can take from it. This unexpected detour has given me a whole new perspective on music. I have a deeper connection with my guitar. I also have a greater appreciation when I watch others play their instruments, and I now know how truly transcendent music can be. It heals my body; it heals my soul.

This experience has also furthered my relationship with God. At my darkest moments, I felt the power of faith carry me through. I have an unbreakable bond with my Savior and now I know I am never alone. Just as a guitar is an instrument for me, I hope to be an instrument for God for you.

As you embark on the next chapter beyond this book, I genuinely encourage you to stay connected with me on my YouTube channel "Charlie's Guitar Stroke Recovery," found at:

https://www.youtube.com/@cwebber402/videos.

Your presence and support mean the world to me on this journey of recovery and growth.

Please remember that you are not alone in this journey. Together, we can navigate through the challenges and triumphs, finding strength and solace in the exchange of our experiences. Your contribution to sharing your story and engaging with this community will significantly enhance our collective journey toward healing and understanding.

FINAL CLOSING THOUGHTS

I appreciate you taking the time to read my book, *Strumming for Life*. It was beyond my expectations to author a book, yet here I am, presenting my journey of recovery through faith and prayer, the transformative power of music, and unwavering determination.

I am truly grateful to God for giving me the strength and hope to recover from my stroke. Since I was a young child, I have always been captivated by the sound of the guitar. It was a dream of mine to learn how to play this beautiful instrument and create music that speaks to the soul. Playing the guitar has always been a refuge for me, a place where I can express my emotions and thoughts without saying a word. Just like an artist paints a picture or a writer pens a story, music has been my way of connecting with the world around me. My guitar is more than just an instrument; it is a faithful companion that brings me joy and comfort in times of need, a sanctuary.

One moment, life was normal, and in the blink of an eye, everything changed. However, I made a declaration to myself that I would not let this stroke define me or take away my passion for playing the guitar.

Through my weekly vlog and now this book, I hope to inspire others who may be facing similar challenges. A stroke or any other setback should not deter us from pursuing our passions. It may require finding new ways to achieve our goals, but with determination and perseverance, anything is possible.

I want my journey to serve as a beacon of hope for fellow stroke survivors and anyone facing difficulties in life. Remember, God is always by our side, guiding us through the darkest moments and celebrating our victories.

To all my fellow stroke warriors and anyone on a journey of recovery, I urge you to keep pushing forward. Don't let doubt or negativity hold you back. You have the power within you to overcome any obstacle and achieve your dreams.

In closing, I want to express my deepest gratitude to all those who have supported me on this journey. Thank you for reading my book, and may you find inspiration and strength in my story. Strum on, my friends, and never give up on your passion for life and music.

Remember, keep strumming for life. Thank you, and God bless.

ABOUT THE AUTHOR
The Song of Resilience

Charles Webber's tale delves deep into the fabric of his life, woven with threads of challenges, triumphs, and the unwavering power of resilience.

He led a seemingly ordinary life until one fateful Sunday afternoon when a stroke abruptly altered the course of his existence. In mere moments, his world spun a full 180 degrees as the right side of his body succumbed to paralysis.

Born in Portland, ME, his roots traced back to Arcadian French and Portuguese ancestry. Despite humble beginnings, his family exuded boundless love, shaping his upbringing alongside three siblings in Rhode Island. Their family lineage bore witness to a historical mishap, transforming their surname from O'Bard to Webber during the migration of their ancestors from New Brunswick, Canada to Maine.

When college seemed a distant dream, inaccessible due to financial constraints, his path veered toward the skies and a pivotal decision to join the US Air Force in the early 1980s, a choice that would sculpt the trajectory of his future.

Over three decades, he ascended the ranks to Chief Master Sergeant E9, thriving in roles spanning logistics and professional military instruction. A defining chapter unfurled when he embraced his passion for the guitar, partaking in the Air Force Tops in Blue traveling show that serenaded military bases worldwide, infusing melody into the hearts of servicemen from diverse nations.

Transitioning into a civilian role post-retirement, he found solace in crafting curricula for the US Army, sculpting minds, and fostering leadership through professional courses. Yet, amidst the symphony of achievements and transitions, a singular passion remained intertwined with the chords of his being—the guitar.

Reflecting on a poignant childhood memory, the resonance of Bob Gardner's guitar melodies on neighborhood porches kindled a fiery desire within to master the craft. Enrolling at the Berklee School of Music further instilled a profound love for the strings, transcending the realms of fame and fortune, embodying an unyielding dedication to music's soul-stirring essence.

His stroke in 2021 sought to mute the harmonious bond between him and his guitar. In the throes of uncertainty, buoyed by faith and fortitude, he reclaimed his musical companion, defying the odds one note at a time. Through the darkest alleys of recovery, his family—pillars of strength he was thankful to be able to lean on—illuminated the path to resilience, each step a testament to unwavering support and unwavering love.

A humble storyteller, a guardian of melodies, a survivor of storms, it is the author's hope that this book echoes the refrain of courage, resilience, and above all, the enduring power of the human spirit.

"Strum on, dear souls, for within the chords of adversity lies the melody of triumph."

—Charles Webber

www.ingramcontent.com/pod-product-compliance
Lightning Source LLC
Chambersburg PA
CBHW030906120626
46554CB00001B/29